SHADOW
OF THE
SWORD

B A L L A N T I N E   B O O K S   ⬟   N E W   Y O R K
PRESIDIO
PRESS

SHADOW
OF THE
SWORD

A Marine's Journey of
War, Heroism, and
Redemption

JEREMIAH WORKMAN

WITH JOHN R. BRUNING

Published in the United States by Presidio Press,
an imprint of The Random House Publishing Group,
a division of Random House, Inc., New York.

PRESIDIO PRESS and colophon are trademarks of Random House, Inc.

Grateful acknowledgment is made to the following for permission
to reprint previously published material:

Hal Leonard Corporation for excerpts from "Angel," Words and Music by Steven Tyler and
Desmond Child. © 1987 EMI April Music Inc., Demon of Screamin' Music Publishing and
Universal-Polygram International Publishing, Inc. All rights for Demon of Screamin' Music
Publishing Controlled and Administered by EMI April Music Inc. All Rights Reserved.
International Copyright Secured. Used by Permission.

Edward B. Marks Music Company for excerpts from "The Ballad of Ira Hayes,"
written by Peter LaFarge, used by permission of Edward B. Marks Music Company.

ISBN 978-0-345-51212-3

Printed in the United States of America on acid-free paper

www.presidiopress.com

2 4 6 8 9 7 5 3 1

First Edition

Book design by Jo Anne Metsch

Devon, Jessica, Raleigh, James, and Eric—

this book is for you

CONTENTS

Contents

PART III

PART IV

STAIRWELL TO NOWHERE

I'M BEING CHASED. I can hear their footsteps below me, echoing up from the depths of the dimly lit stairwell. The brown concrete walls play acoustical tricks, casting echo upon echo and making each footfall sound like a gunshot. The noises boil and swell around me, growing first loud, then soft, then loud. I know only one thing: I have to get away.

My breathing is ragged. I feel heavy and slow, like I've been running for hours without respite.

"Allah Akbar!" shouts a voice below me.

I turn up the next flight of stairs, reach the next landing, turn and climb again. Soon I've put two more landings between me and them. Ear cocked under my grimy Kevlar, I pause to listen. Have they given up?

More sounds. Pant legs swishing together. Footsteps bark a pursuit. I am the hunted. And I have no way out but up.

I swing up another flight of stairs. They're not far behind now. Not far at all. I'm on the edge of my endurance. Part of me just wants to sink to the stairs and wait for my fate to catch me.

The marine in me says keep moving. Never give up. Never. In our line of work, you fight; you die. You do not turn pussy.

Up another flight of stairs, no pause at the landing. I spin and hit the next flight in full stride, bounding upward, taking three steps at a time. If I had my M16, I'd lay in ambush and kill them all as they came for me. But I've lost my rifle. I have no grenades. I can't even feel the normal comfort of my K-Bar knife tucked away on my hip. I've got nothing left but my fists.

"Allah Akbar!"

If they catch me, I will die. It won't be painless, and it won't be quick.

The stairs seem steeper now. I climb them two at a time, and when I look up, they seem to go on forever, like those long sets of stairs running to the top of those ancient Mayan temples in Mexico. Each new flight seems ever steeper, ever more of a challenge to my fading strength and endurance.

"ALLAH AKBAR!" They're right behind me.

Move, Marine! Move! I will my legs to carry me forward. I grip the handrail and pull myself to the next flight. Just as I hit the stairs, a metallic rattle echoes behind me.

A spasm of light seizes the stairwell. Thunder reverberates off the walls, demolishing my hearing just as smoke billows up around me.

They're throwing grenades.

Again.

The blast knocks me off my feet. I get up and unleash the last reservoir of strength within me. It propels me upward, feet chugging. There are no doors, no avenue of escape. I can only climb and keep climbing. But the stairwell never ends.

Another grenade detonates on the landing below. Shrapnel whips and scythes around me, pockmarking the walls. Everything below me is shrouded in smoke.

I'm losing the race. Fight or flight. It is the last option of every mammal. Terror sends me up the next flight of stairs. I reach another landing, my right hand scrabbling for purchase on the railing. I slip and fall facedown. Below me, I hear them coming.

A coil of smoke spins away from the landing below. It reveals a figure. Wraithlike, it slides back into the shadows.

Please God. Please. They're too close. I'm done.

Fight, Marine. Fight.

I run on legs of rubber. I smack off the wall, lose my balance and fall. Get up. Keep going.

Knees are almost shot. I test them with every step. One more stair. One more. The landing is just out of reach.

My legs are finished. They're but deadweight now. It's over.

Another metallic clatter as a grenade lands a step below me. I kick it away. It ricochets off the wall and explodes. The concussion pins me flat on the landing. A dull, hammerlike blow deadens every sense. The world goes gray.

How am I alive? I feel no pain. I crawl forward, pulling myself to the next flight with only my arms. My legs trail behind me, as useless as a paraplegic's.

Footsteps. I turn to see a cloud of gray-black smoke roiling and twisting up the stairwell at me.

There is movement in the smoke.

"Allah Akbar!"

The first coils reach me. I try to hold my breath as a tendril snakes along my body and across my face. The smoke probes me, searching for entrance. I can't hold my breath long, and in a spasm I suck in corrupted air. The world goes dark. The last thing I see is a dirty boot on the landing.

This won't be pretty.

Please. Please. Jessica.

No. I will not plead. I will be a Marine to the end.

The smoke engulfs me. I have lost.

PART
I

REFLECTION OF THE DAMNED

Spring 2006
Parris Island, S.C.

THE DREAM WAS bad, the worst in weeks. The ceiling comes into focus. I blink the sleep out of my eyes. My heart races, sweat stains my sheets. I'm burning up. Every morning, it is always the same.

I remember everything. Every move, every unearthly sensation and disorienting noise. It is the most vivid dream I've ever had, and I have it night after night after night.

A year ago, when the nightmare first invaded my sleep, I drowned it in liquor. At the time my unit, 3rd Battalion, 5th Marines, or 3/5, was stationed at Camp Pendleton in Southern California. One night, I wandered into a tavern called The Harp in Newport Beach. On one wall rested a plaque commemorating the achievements of 3/5. Right then, I knew I had my watering hole. In the first month after I got back from leave, I ran up a three-thousand-dollar tab at The Harp.

I discovered that Jack Daniel's did what nothing else could. I'd drink until I passed out, and in that darkness the nightmares and memories could not find me. Every morning, I'd peel my eyes open, unsure of who I was or where I'd ended up. Self-awareness only gradually penetrated the crushing hangover. I didn't mind that; it gave me time to slip into myself and prepare for the shock of who I'd become. By noon, I'd be up and about, focused only on that night's binge, longing for its numb sanctuary.

Not anymore, not for the last five months. That's when I started drill instructor school and had to devote everything I had left to graduate. Ever since I was a raw recruit, I'd wanted to be a drill instructor. A year removed from my tour in Iraq, I fulfilled that dream and graduated tenth in a class of sixty. Be careful what you wish for. That cliché has become the story of my life.

I've always been an achiever. Varsity football, baseball, and wrestling back home in Ohio taught me to compete without reservation. I came of age in a tiny town of about twenty-five hundred people called Richwood, where Tractor Days was the year's biggest event.

My friends and neighbors all hailed from hardworking, blue-collar stock; the kind of Americans who have quietly held this country together generation after generation. They aren't revered as they should be anymore, and the blue-blood Eastern city folk look down their noses at us Red-Staters, but the fact is, the heart of America beats in towns like Richwood, whether the elites want to admit it or not.

We lived a sort of *Varsity Blues* existence in our little town. Football games dominated the fall weekends, baseball dominated the spring. In between, there were school dances, Saturday-night dates, and cruising after we got our driver's licenses.

I had come to Richwood after living in Marion, Ohio, until seventh grade. When I was six, my parents divorced. Dad moved to Richwood, Mom stayed in Marion and remarried a man I came to despise. When I could, I escaped to live with my dad, who worked in a local steel mill.

I was the new kid in a town of less than a thousand surrounded by corn and wheat fields. Everyone knew everyone's business. I dropped in from what folks considered a big city—Marion's population is about 40,000—and was instantly put on probation by my peers. Where would I fit in? Would I be an outcast?

I threw myself into sports, and my football and baseball skills gained me acceptance. Soon everyone knew my name, and I could walk downtown after a Friday-night game and receive backslaps and attaboys from people who months before were total strangers.

I'd never been accepted before, so the attention just fueled my desire to excel, do better, grow faster and stronger. I didn't mind the hard work that that required. I didn't mind pushing myself to exceed, and I always had the drive to achieve my goals.

That's why I became a Marine. The Corps harnessed that drive in me and let me explore it in ways college never could have. I finished boot camp, endured Iraq, and came home to graduate from DI school and from Swim School a few weeks later. The latter is the second toughest school Marines can attend. For me, it was the aquatic equivalent of the Bataan Death March.

It started with three weeks of conditioning. I thought after drill instructor's school that I was in the best shape of my life. I've always been lean and muscular. In high school I was an all-conference running back until I broke a collarbone and suffered a knee injury. Swim School knocked all the arrogance out of me. We started with a seven-hundred-meter swim. That's almost a kilometer. It nearly killed me, and I thought I was a good swimmer.

They made us tread water while holding bricks. We dragged them across the pool again and again, the instructors pushing us like nobody had ever done. From four to midnight every day we tortured our bodies in the huge pool at Parris Island. By week four, I could hardly bring myself to continue. Instead, I'd sit in my pickup truck in front of my apartment and will myself to go through with another night of agony.

In slow motion, I'd see my hand turning the key. Twenty minutes later, I'd be in the pool wondering if they'd let me drown as all the gear kept pulling me under. Every night for six weeks, I'd flail my way to the side and puke in the scum gutter that skirted the pool.

It was the toughest thing I've ever endured. Well, next to Fallujah.

That's why I love the Corps—there is always a new challenge awaiting those with the desire to push a little harder.

I slide out of my rack. When I hit the floor, I feel clammy and off. I haven't felt right in months. Now that the booze remains in the bottle, the memories and nightmares plague me every night. What little rest I get is always interrupted.

Beside the bed, I stretch and yawn. A typical morning routine, but the engine's not firing. Something's missing.

Hope. Faith.

Oh yeah. The realization wipes out the last of my sleepy grogginess.

I shamble over to the bathroom sink and find my razor. Water running, I start to lather up.

My eyes focus on the sink. I know I'll have to look into the mirror, but I avoid it as long as I can. I dread this time. I cannot hide from myself. In my reflection, there is no escape.

My eyes flick up. I stare at a gaunt and haggard face that could once have been mine. It looks sunken, like my cheekbones are about to cave in.

I've lost so much weight my ribs are visible.

Were you a prisoner of war?

No. I am a veteran of close-quarters combat. I fought. I survived. At Fallujah.

Guilty as charged: I survived.

I make eye contact with my reflection. Eyes are a window to the soul, right? I see nothing. It scares me. I want to avert my gaze, but I'm frozen in place.

Why are you still alive?

I can't answer my reflection. It is the shell of what I once was. The jawline is still the same, my hair color hasn't changed. The remnants are there, visible to those who really knew it. My mother. My wife Jessica. Her folks. They once looked upon my face with love and endearment. So did the people in my small town. I was the star running back for our high school football team. I was somebody once.

This new face is different. What I have left only inspires fear. Those vestiges of the past I see in the mirror serve now as a cruel reminder of all I've lost.

You should be dead, Jeremiah.

I want to pick up the razor and shave. I want to get through this morning ritual of hate.

You should be dead.

My reflection is right. I should be. I *wanted* death. I yearned for it.

Why are you still here?

I can only say, "I have every right to be here."

Three dead Marines. That's what I see every time I dare to look into my eyes.

I wanted to be with them. That house in Sector 19 should have been my tomb. Now I live on in limbo, cheated of my destiny. I did not leave the fight willingly. They dragged me out of it screaming. There was killing left undone, vengeance unsecured. I yearn for a reckoning that will never be made.

You didn't deserve to live.

My reflection pulls no punches. I drop my eyes. I can't bear to look at myself any longer.

I take a long breath. The air is stale and I smell my own sweat. Another breath. Exhale. Breathe. Calm down.

I am here. At least, what's left of me is here. The best of me was burned away inside that house, lost forever on December 23rd, the last firefight American forces would fight in that shattered city during the Second Battle of Fallujah.

The memories flicker by like reels on a slot machine. Nothing makes sense.

Then I see Phillip Levine, bloody and shocked, shouting for a pistol. For a moment it seems so real that I want to reach out for him. I've never seen a man do what he did that day.

I open my eyes as gunfire echoes around me. A moment later, the vision of my best friend passes and my bathroom is salved with silence. I'm left staring at little icebergs of shaving cream afloat in an overflowing sink.

What made you worth saving?

My reflection taunts me.

"I don't know," I manage as I look up into the mirror.

I stare into the eyes of three dead Marines.

"I'm so sorry," I say.

There is no forgiveness in their eyes.

Chapter Two

THE MAN WITHOUT A FACE

Spring 2006
Parris Island, S.C.

I FINISH PUTTING ON my uniform. I brush away a few balls of lint, adjust my collar until it is crisp and straight. Presentable now, I flee the mirror and forage in the kitchen for a bite to eat. All I find is a half gallon of expired milk and a bag of Oreo cookies. I get a glass of water and take a handful of Oreos with me into my apartment's tiny living room.

Around me, the stillness and the silence make me edgy and suspicious, like I'm awaiting the first signs of an ambush. Those are my Iraq instincts. I have yet to figure out how to shut them off.

I peer out a window. The parking lot of my complex is empty. There's no all-night SoCal party scene here like there is around Pendleton. People here work for a living and go to bed at reasonable hours. I wish I could be one of them. My workday starts at three-thirty and ends long after the majority of my neighbors have turned in for the night.

Beyond the parking lot, the street is deserted. The darkness is broken only by a few street lamps shining in isolation. Their pools of light seem to barely hold back the night. It is lonely duty amid the bleakness of the hour.

Each day, my own pool of light grows a little weaker. The darkness encroaches further into my sphere until it seems there will be no way I can resist its pressure.

The things that are happening to me I do not understand.

For the last three weeks, I've been the "Kill Hat" for a platoon of recruits at Parris Island. Tell a former Marine that you're a Kill Hat, and just watch their eyes narrow. We are feared and loathed. That is our job.

There are three levels of drill instructors. The Senior is the father figure to his platoon of recruits. They come and complain to him; he encourages and mentors them in return. The Heavy is the workhorse and backbone of the Corps' training system. He teaches and educates, gives them real skills. The Kill Hat, also sometimes called the Third Hat, is the drill instructor with the least seniority. Standing on the bottom rung of a strict hierarchy, we do the dirty work. Our job is to scream, yell, demean, and break the will of these civilians who strive to become Marines. The Kill Hat is the drill instructor of countless movies, the one whom recruits remember most vividly decades after they've gone through the mill here at Parris Island.

For three weeks I've run, shouted, berated, and emasculated the ninety men in our recruit platoon. I return home after eighteen-to twenty-hour days with my voice so raspy and raw that my wife can't understand me when I call her on my cell phone. My legs ache from all the running I've done. Part of my job requires sprinting around the recruits while they're marching or standing in formation, looking for mistakes or attitudes that need adjusting. When I see a recruit screwing up, I pull him out of the ranks and smoke him with a series of brutal calisthenics. Wherever they go, I have to run faster and farther, circling the platoon formation at full speed for hours on end. It is the most exhausting work I've ever done. It makes me wish I was back in Iraq.

When I first arrived at Parris Island fresh from DI school, I went to meet the recruits while they were out on the rifle range. On the way there, I encountered Staff Sergeant Shelby, one of my superiors in the company. He's a barrel-chested staff NCO who stands about six foot three. He reminds me of the old WWF wrestler, Sergeant Slaughter.

"Sergeant Workman," Shelby said to me after he introduced himself, "you've got a good Senior. You've got a good Heavy. Rely on them. Here at the rifle range is where you'll earn your money. You've got two weeks to prove yourself. By then, you should have gotten at least two of these bitches to hurt themselves."

The litmus test for my new job, he was telling me, was the number of recruits I could push to attempt suicide. I didn't even know how to respond to that.

I went to work. That evening, I smoked a screwup in front of the entire platoon. I worked him over so hard that he snapped and lunged at me. When he went for my throat, it was as if a tumbler clicked into place and a safe door popped open deep inside me. Cold fury spewed forth. I parried his thrust, then snatched him by the throat. I lifted him off his feet and then body-slammed him to the squad bay's deck. He lay helpless on his back, his eyes full of terror. But the safe door was open, and I was not finished. I jumped atop him and went for his throat again. Finally, my Senior, Staff Sergeant Edds, and my Heavy, Sergeant Allen, pulled me off the cowering recruit. They led me back to the DI's office at the far end of the barracks. I thought I was finished. Day one, and I already went too far. Ashamed of my violent response, I was expecting the worst from my leadership. When the door closed, Staff Sergeant Edds smacked me on the back and said, "Right on, Workman! That's exactly what we're looking for."

The next morning, I found that recruit cowering in the head; a poor, broken soul, slashing at his wrists with a Gillette Mach 3. One down. One to go.

In Iraq, I took care of my men. That was my sole job. I loved them like brothers; they became my family. Now, I am asked to destroy men who want to be Marines. I am the crucible they must endure to make it in the Corps. The role does not suit me, but I must perform my duty. I have three years of this left, but every day has been increasingly difficult to get through.

I can't help but hate myself for what I have to do.

I leave my apartment and walk to my Toyota Tacoma pickup parked nearby. Outside, there is no hint of sunrise yet on the eastern horizon. The morning is stillborn quiet. I feel like a trespasser. A few minutes later, I've wound the Tacoma up to sixty on the causeway linking Parris Island and the rest of the South Carolina coast. For every recruit living east of the Mississippi River, Parris Island is their first destination after they sign their enlistment papers. That's the way it has been for generations. "The Island" is where new Marines are minted. The civilians who enter this place emerge tough and tempered and ready to kill. In World War II alone, we trained 200,000 Marines here.

In decades past, they went on to thrash the Germans at Belleau Wood, storm the beaches of Tarawa Atoll and Saipan. They fought their way across Guam and Tinian and Kwajalein, hoisted the flag on Iwo

Jima. Another generation fought the Chinese and the freezing weather around the Chosin Reservoir in 1950. Parris Island's baby boomers beat back the Tet Offensive in '68. Now, my own generation has our own war, and our own hallowed ground thousands of miles from this birthplace of Marines.

Parris Island is our tradition and our heritage. It is a proud place that sets the heartbeat for the entire Corps. The men we mold into Marines need to be *hard*, motivated, and determined. What I want to do, but can't, is to treat them like men and teach them how to *survive*. No screaming, no belittling. I want to tell them how we lived through our ordeal in Fallujah. But that's not the way things work, not for more than a hundred years. I wish I could be proud to be a part of this heritage and tradition, but my self-hatred gets in the way. I wouldn't treat a dog the way I'm expected to treat my recruits.

For these past three weeks, I've stumbled along and shed a little more of my humanity each day. I torment the recruits and push them beyond their limits. They despise and fear me; I have only respect for them and their ability to absorb every new torture I throw at them. But I can't show it. They take it and move on, clinging to the goal of one day standing before friends and family and earning the right to be called a Marine.

They are better than what I do to them.

I notice the causeway's guardrail whirring past on my right. I'm so weary that it takes several seconds to register the danger. I'm too close. Somehow, I've wandered into the break-down lane.

I try to focus on the road. In my enervation, this proves extraordinarily tough. I feel so heavy and slow, yet at the same time I have this ethereal sensation, as if I'm simply riding a pocket of air and floating along above the road. The sensation frightens me.

I see the guardrail again. It gives me an idea. I could just floor the accelerator, and give the steering wheel a little flick to the right. Would I break through and plummet into the black waters beyond?

I have a vision of myself as the cab fills with water. The Tacoma sinks faster and faster. There seems to be no bottom. I stay at the wheel and feel the chilly water numb my body. As the water reaches my neck and submerges my mouth and nose, I feel my brain go slack.

Would anyone really care? Jess would feel guilty of course.

Good. She should.

What about my mother? She would be devastated. That gives me pause, but only for a moment.

In my vision, I see the water crest the top of my head. I'm totally immersed now. It numbs everything, like a body-shot of Novocain. The wretched memories of Iraq flow away as I let the water into my lungs. I drift. No more emotional self-mutilation. No more nightmares. The guilt floats away.

I could do it and nobody would know that it was not an accident. Everyone would say I simply fell asleep at the wheel. I could erase myself and still retain my dignity, my honor.

I peer beyond the window. Curls of fog drift across the water. It is a damp morning, not rainy, but dew-laden. The road is slick.

An accident. There's nobody out here to judge.

My foot hits the gas. The Tacoma rushes forward. One swift move, that's all it'll take to finish the work the insurgents failed to do in the house. Since December 23, 2004, I've lived on stolen time, cheated of the end that fate had arranged for me. It would have been an honorable death. Instead, I robbed the dead to be back here, and I've lived in the shadows of their memory ever since. And in those shadows are things I can't handle seeing anymore.

The speedometer needle kisses a hundred and moves on. I'm close to the edge. It is time.

Make your move.

The guardrail is mere feet away. My hands are rigid on the wheel, poised and cocked to execute.

I wanted to die in battle. That is where I belong, up front with my men, leading them into the thick of a fight. Someday, I will get back to the war and fate and I will have our rendezvous. At least that gives me a fragment of hope. I ease off the gas. The coward's way is no way for a Marine to die.

At 0325, I park the Tacoma in front of the barracks. I stay in the cab and watch the digital clock tick off the minutes until I have to make the transformation. Out here, I am Jeremiah Workman, marine combat veteran, lover and husband to Jessica, former high school athlete and small-town American. My kind has been celebrated in movies and John Mellencamp songs all my life.

Inside the barracks, I am Remarque's petty and violent Corporal Himmelstoss, the drill instructor who tormented Paul Bäumer and his

schoolmates throughout boot camp in *All Quiet on the Western Front.*
I just want to be Kat, the veteran who holds them all together.

The clock reads 3:30. I put my campaign cover on and walk toward
the squad bay.

At the front hatch, I haze the fire watch until the recruit there looks
ready to wet himself. I move on and raise hell with the rover. I check
the head. No feet appear under the stalls this time, no Gillette Mach 3.
That's a relief.

At 0400, Sergeant Allen appears and the recruits begin their day. I
try to run through the squad bay doing my thing, but I feel sluggish,
like I'm running in a dream and getting nowhere. I see a recruit lag-
ging behind the others and I get in his face.

"Bitch! Run . . . run . . . run . . . run!"

There's nothing behind my words. I feel gutted.

Sergeant Allen approaches me. "Sergeant Workman, let's get the
recruits to chow."

"Roger that."

Allen shouts, "Get out!"

The platoon replies as one, "Get out, aye, sir!" The men race outside. I find a recruit struggling with his cartridge belt. I wade into him
without mercy. He quails as I belittle him. Finally, he gets his gear
sorted out and he flies out the door.

I drag myself after them. Outside, the recruits have formed up. Sergeant Allen is counting down from a hundred. Anyone not in the formation at the end of the count will feel my wrath.

Sergeant Allen takes up position in the middle and to one side of the
formation. He barks a new command. "Right face! Forward march!"

The recruits move as one, their boots clicking across the concrete
walkway in unison. It sounds as rhythmic as a metronome. Or gunshots.

"Ah left . . . left . . . left right . . . huh!" Allen calls a cadence. This is
my time. I'm supposed to sprint around the platoon and correct any
flaws I see. I start to run, but it feels like I'm five hundred pounds. I
move with a strange and awkward gait. I'm too worn out to wonder why.

Regulations require the men to march with their arms swinging exactly six inches forward and three inches to the rear. This sort of pre-
cision is what makes a Marine marching formation look so impressive.
I see a recruit whose arms are swinging too far forward.

"Six and three! Six and three! Arm swing! Arm swing! Arm swing!"

The kid corrects himself. The others around him stare straight ahead, but as I make my high-tempo circuit I can feel their hate hot on the back of my neck. When I come along the other side, I see a recruit bouncing in his step. Marines march like ballroom dancers. We don't bounce. We don't bob. We glide, graceful and deadly.

"Bobblehead! Bobblehead!" I call to the recruit. He doesn't get what I want at first so I lay into him. "Stop bouncing, bitch!" That did it. His boots stop trampling the concrete and start skimming across it.

Fifty yards from the chow hall now. In order to get there, Sergeant Allen will need to order a left turn.

"Left! Right! Left! Hup!"

The platoon is a well-oiled machine. The best I can do is nitpick.

Sergeant Allen gives the order for the left turn. The ranks pivot sharply. My job is to look for anyone who does not pivot smartly.

I'm struggling to make the circuit. I feel myself slowing down. My voice has a weary quality.

"Pivot foot. Pivot foot . . ."

I get a few sidelong glances from the recruits. They've noticed something's off with me today.

The platoon completes the turn. I come around to the left side. We're marching alongside a row of trees covered in Spanish moss. It is still pitch dark, but through the moss, one of the base safety lamps shines like a searchlight.

The light.

A hitch in my stride slows me further.

The light.

Spear points break through the Spanish moss in a crazy quilt pattern. The bright rays of light flash and turn as I move along the tree line.

The world narrows. The darkness washes away. All I can see is light.

Lights in the smoke. My Marines have their SureFire flashlights turned on. The house is full of gray-black smoke.

I'm standing in a foyer at the top of a flight of stairs. Alone. I hear the chatter of their gunfire, converging into a bedroom. Then I see him. Across the foyer from me there's a Marine lying behind a desk. Is he dead? Is he wounded? Who is it?

We've got to get to him, but the volume of return fire is too great. Bullets smack into the corner of the wall next to me. Others gouge the wall behind me. If I take another step, I'll die.

Within the smoke, a muzzle flash erupts. That's no AK. I hear a long string of automatic weapons fire. Bullets chew up the floor in the foyer in front of me. The gunner has shot low. Bits of carpet and masonry careen around me.

My M16's at my shoulder. I pull the trigger as fast as I can. My magazine runs dry. I drop it out and recharge my weapon. Another thirty rounds and I'm out again. As I reload this time, Corporal Steve Snell comes up the stairs behind me. He's carrying an AK-47. He pulls alongside me and levels the weapon. The barrel is inches from my head. When he pulls the trigger, a sheet of flame shoots out beyond the flash suppressor. He rocks and rolls in full auto, tearing off a long burst that empties his magazine in seconds. How many are we up against? I can't tell, but it sounds like dozens of rifles are firing, including at least one RPK or PKC crew served machine gun. I realize I've been struck nearly deaf by the tornado of noise.

Behind me, my fellow Marines are stacked up in the stairwell. Their SureFire lights pierce the smoke, and as the men jostle the crazy patterns of light on the shrapnel-scarred walls make me dizzy. I turn back to the enemy and fire until my M16 runs dry.

Something yellow flies out of the bedroom. With dawning horror, I realize that it is a grenade. It rolls straight for me, then spins in a little circle. Before I can even move, my world turns to fire.

Light and flames.

Light.

I'm not running anymore. I hear bootsteps on concrete, but they sound like echoes of a memory, unreal and vague. I can't see anything. I can't feel anything. Have I gone blind?

A presence on my right. My head turns in slow motion, as if I'm under water. My peripheral vision is gone. I'm looking at the world through a soda straw. Everything is distant and unreal. The presence is a recruit. I see his eyes as he runs past.

I know where you're going.

I want to shout it, but I can't. My jaw is frozen solid.

You're going to Iraq. I want to be your brother, not your tormentor.

My head swivels forward, and the light hits me with its fullest intensity, like the desert sun.

I'm taken back to December 23rd, staggering toward one of our Humvees under fire. Sergeant Allen's voice pierces the scene. He sounds like he's talking through a tin can.

"Sergeant Workman? What the hell are you doing?"

From the back of the Humvee, I hear myself answer, "I don't know."

The sun beats down on me and my pupils constrict. I see nothing for those brief seconds, though I can hear the firefight raging up the street.

"I need some help here!"

Did I really just say that?

I look away from the sun. The scene refocuses. Through the soda straw I can see that I'm standing at the chow hall door.

Sergeant Allen orders, "Platoon halt! Stack weapons!"

"Stack weapons, aye, sir!"

I see Allen turn to me. His movements are so slow it almost looks as if he's floating.

This is my time. I'm supposed to kick over rifles, scream and bellow and rant. I move to the recruits automatically. But I take a few steps and come up short. A recruit is staring at me with wide blue eyes.

Eyes.

I look in his eyes. The distance between us seems more than spatial. It is temporal.

From the back of the truck, I call for help again. "Doc! Doc! Get over here, now!"

Our corpsman stands only a few feet away. "Don't worry about it, Workman."

"Doc, we've got wounded men back here! They need help, god-damnit!"

"Workman, they're okay."

I look down.

Through the soda straw the recruit stares at me with saucer eyes full of terror. I suppose he's never seen a drill instructor coming apart at the seams in front of him.

I see my friend Raleigh Smith lying on his back next to somebody else. He's got his arm up shielding his eyes from the early afternoon sun. His lips are curled into a frown of pain. He needs help.

Raleigh's the kind of guy who never asks for anything. He's overly generous, willing to give the shirt off his back to a fellow Marine. He's a small town kid, just like me, only from Montana.

Why won't Doc get his ass over here?

"Raleigh? You okay, bro?"

No answer.

When he first joined the 81's platoon, he seemed kind of mousy and shy. That didn't last. He was just watching us, seeing what we were all about. When he felt comfortable, he unleashed a wacky and completely un-PC side we never expected in him. He came so far out of left field with his craziness that we nicknamed him Section Eight.

I move his arm. It sloughs off his face and falls away.

His eyes are closed. I slap his ashen face lightly.

He doesn't move.

Before he left for the Marines, he was at a party in Montana. He punched a guy right in the face. "What'd you do that for?" the guy asked. " 'Cause I like ya!" came Raleigh's rollicking reply. His sense of fun always makes us forgive his antics. Hell, we love them.

"Doc! For God's sake get over here now! Raleigh needs you."

"He's okay, Workman." Doc's voice is strained and odd.

I don't understand this. I smack Raleigh's cheek again. He doesn't flinch. He must be unconscious.

"DOC!"

"Workman, he's fucking dead!"

Edges of darkness curl away the light. The recruit still eyes me warily. He is Raleigh.

My hands shake. My knees go weak. He's lying next to somebody else, left arm canted slightly where I let it drop. His eyes are closed and his face is a grimace of pain.

Sergeant Allen's voice thunders across time and space. "Drop gear!"

"Drop gear, aye, sir!" the platoon sings out. Their voices sound so removed, so utterly without form and substance I could be hearing the dead.

Or the doomed.

Through the straw I see the recruit's face disappear as he dumps his cartridge belt and gets ready to line up at the chow hall door.

On the back of the Humvee, Raleigh is at my feet, unmoving. There is no blood. He looks like he's asleep.

There's someone lying next to Raleigh. Who is it?

Don't go there, Jeremiah.

Sergeant Allen barks another order, "Form for chow!" His words echo across six thousand miles.

"Form for chow, aye, sir!"

They're ready to get inside the chow hall. I do not move. I cannot move. How can I? I'm not even there.

Back in Fallujah, my head turns away from Raleigh.

Next to him, I see blood on cammies. A hand. Limp. Whose is it? I must look.

Don't do this.

There is no face to see. Just a bullet wound in the temple and all the damage it caused.

"Ready! Move!" shouts Sergeant Allen above the din of battle.

I look hard, wondering who this is, but still I cannot see his face. I see bone and blood, but blackness obscures his features. Something's keeping me from seeing the full, terrible truth.

His chest tape reveals his name.

Hillenburg. This is all that's left of my brother Lance Corporal Eric Hillenburg. Hoosier. Marine. Friend. He was supposed to get out next summer and was going to go to college. He had the quirkiest sense of humor of any man I knew. Even in the worst moments, he always had an off-beat joke, a ribald comment that would leave me shaking my head and laughing from the belly. We called him Ernie.

He also had the darkest eyes. Black like coal, but bright and shining as the desert sun.

It's like a transformer in my brain has blown. I leap off the Humvee and charge up the street. I am a running back again, this time I have no pads, just a flak vest and an M16. I run past Kraft and Snell and Levine, who is still trying to cage a pistol off anyone who will listen to him.

I do not see them. All I see is the man without a face. And the only way to drive that vision from my mind is to drive headlong into the enemy.

I could kill a thousand insurgents and never lose a minute of sleep. The sight of the two dead Marines tears my heart out.

I could not save them. I know that I will never be whole again.

I don't deserve to live.

I run for the house, swallowed by fury and a lust for revenge.

Sergeant Allen's voice arrives like a distant whisper. "Workman?"

Pain propels me forward. Through the soda straw, I see recruits dodge out of my way. I plant my shoulder into one of them and send him spinning away like an undersized linebacker. Another goes down. I plow through them and storm through the door.

I'm inside the chow hall. Other platoons are already eating. The recruits eye me curiously.

As the aperture of my vision opens wide, I can see them. I've come to a stop, finally, beside a Coke machine. Come to a stop. I'm breathing again.

I'm on Parris Island. My brain feels numb from the sensory overload. I've blown its neural pathways like an engineer blowing bridges in a desperate retreat. Now I feel nothing.

Dimly, I'm aware of Sergeant Allen next to me. "Workman, what's the matter with you?"

The answer tumbles out from the wreckage of my brain. I hear my words before I'm aware I've spoken them.

"I don't give a fuck about you, and I don't give a fuck about these recruits."

I've cared too much. Now I have nothing left.

Allen pulls me farther from the recruits into a corner by the Coke machine. "Listen, Dog, I can't afford to have you around with an attitude like that. Why don't you go home."

"You don't have to tell me twice."

I turn and flee my failure, to where I don't know or care. I am supposed to be a maker of Marines, part of the system that takes American boys and forges them into fierce warriors. Now, I don't even feel like a Marine myself.

Under the eyes of a hundred aspiring Marines, I run through the chow hall door, my humiliation complete.

Chapter Three

MOP-UP CREW

December 23, 2004 0900
Fallujah, Anbar Province, Iraq

THE SUN RISES on a skeletalized city, ravaged and picked over like a desert corpse. The early morning shadows are fractured and Picasso-like. They paint a black picture of destruction across the ruined streets. Smoke plumes tower overhead to mark burning arms caches and ammo dumps. They are Fallujah's funeral pyre.

The stench of death lingers in the air. It is oily, and pungent, and it permeates our clothing so we carry the reek of rotting flesh with us wherever we go. We are used to this and our stomachs are long since immune to its effects.

This morning starts our third week inside the city. Through November, our heavy weapon's company remained north of town, using a railroad embankment as cover while we supported the Marine units fighting their way south to Highway Ten, the main east-west road through Fallujah. Day after day, we pounded insurgent positions with our 81mm mortars. My crew loaded and fired as fast as we could to rain destruction down on the Jihadists resisting our brothers in the line companies. My men refused to slow down, even when our enemy plotted our position and launched a counterbattery attack against us with 122mm rockets. Instead of dashing to our dugouts, we stayed at our tubes and dished it back at the Muj.

Now we've traded our mortar tubes for M16's.

In the Corps, we are riflemen first. We train to carry an M16 and kill the enemy. It doesn't matter if you're a supply clerk or a Jump-Jet pilot; we all possess basic rifleman skills. It is a tradition that predates World War II, and there is a good reason for it. During the Pacific War, there were desperate moments on long-forgotten islands where commanders threw their last reserves into the battle. Cooks dropped their ladles and picked up M1 carbines. Buglers abandoned their instruments to man antitank guns. There are some key moments in the Corps where such scratch-built forces performed with heroic devotion. On Wake Island, for instance, a fighter pilot named Hank Elrod died throwing grenades at Japanese landing craft as they ground ashore around him. On Peleliu, a Japanese counterattack was stopped cold by typists and orderlies and other rear area troops.

We are all infantry in the Corps. It is tradition. At times it is also a necessity. And here in Fallujah in 2004, in the waning days of the battle for this city, my mortar platoon reverted to our foot-slogging roots. The Coalition needed manpower to search through every room in every building for weapons, ammunition, booby traps, and bombs. This has to be done before the town's civilians can be allowed to return.

Simultaneously, the need for indirect fire ended when the main resistance collapsed in mid-November. So they gave us rifles, Humvees, and trucks, and told us to go empty Fallujah of its remaining weapons of war.

Imagine going into Kansas City to search for every gun and every bullet hidden there with less than a division of men to do the job. That's what we face. We are Fallujah's mop-up crew. Since early December, we've wandered among the destruction in search of secret caches. There's no glory in it; the national media declared the battle over in November. The press has gone home. The nation's lost interest, and the military historians are already busy writing the story of the battle. If we're lucky, our sweating, thankless efforts will merit perhaps a footnote in the campaign history.

The work is hard and dangerous. Every room we enter is a potential trap. Insurgents have left trip-wire detonated mines and IED's all over the place. One shove on the wrong door, and letters will be sent to our loved ones back home.

Clearing hundreds of buildings and thousands of rooms every day requires a methodical and detailed approach. But we are only human. As the days wear on and we grow exhausted from our repetitious task, our security posture slips lower and lower. At times, we're reminded

of the danger that die-hard insurgent holdouts present to us. Last
week, I entered one house that was pitch-black inside. We flicked on
our SureFire flashlights to begin our search and discovered two de-
composing corpses in the kitchen. I stepped over them and moved
down a hall toward a closed door. When I reached it and pushed
it open, I found myself inside an Iraqi's bedroom. The place was in
disarray—sheets torn and strewn on the floor, clothing heaped here
and there with pieces of broken furniture topping the mess.

Something moved in the darkness. I brought my M16 to my shoulder. Just as I did, a shape charged out of a closet straight at me. Startled, I fired wildly—and killed a goat. Lesson learned: Next time, it
might just be a Muj. Don't ever let your guard down.

This morning, we are extra alert. Yesterday, one of our patrols
reached Sector 19 in the northeast corner of the city and encountered
stiff resistance. A long, ragged firefight broke out between die-hards
and our Marines. When the patrol returned to our apartment complex
base at the edge of town, the men looked drained and hollowed-out.
Thank God nobody had been killed.

We spent the night cleaning our rifles and ammunition to ensure
we would not suffer any jams should we get in a firefight as well. I
think we all sensed that come dawn, we would face the enemy.

We rolled out of our base at 0600. For three hours, we picked
through a neighborhood on the cusp of Zone 19. All we found were
corpses and an occasional AK-47. It was a dry hole, so battalion
moved us into the heart of Zone 19.

The place is as quiet as a morgue. We find ourselves in the middle
of a residential district. Here, rich Baathists who had curried Sad-
dam's favor came to retire. The beige cement houses are drab but
stoutly constructed. They're flanked by ten-foot high walls, which
make each house a mini-medieval fortress. As I gaze up the street, I
can't help but wonder if a military engineer didn't design this neighborhood. No wonder the locals call it the Soldier's District.

"On me," I tell my men as I dismount from my Humvee. We've
split the platoon section into two squads. Sergeant Jarrett Kraft takes
one squad; I take the other one. Between us, we have nineteen mortar men doing their best to channel their infantry roots.

My men gather next to me. We are walking firepower. Each one of
us carries an M16A4 rifle and at least sixteen magazines. That's almost

500 rounds of ammunition. Most of us also have slung an AK-47 over our backs and five or six magazines for them stuffed into our pouches. We don't fully trust our M16's. We've heard too many stories of insurgents getting shot with that 5.56mm round who refuse to die. The AK at least has stopping power with its bigger 7.62mm bullet. Also, in a pinch we can fire them fully automatic, something we can't do with our own M16's.

A few of us carry 9mm pistols, holstered at our waists. Grenades and bayonets dangle from our flak vests. Every man carries at least two M67 frag grenades and a flash bang. To this mix I've added a concussion bomb. I saw one go off once, and its devastating pressure wave blew the eyeballs clean out of a stray Iraqi dog. In a fight, I want that kind of power.

Kraft calls over to me, "Hey, Workman! I'll take the left side, you take the right."

"Roger." Our first street we must clear runs north to south. We'll leave the Humvees at the start of this block as we work through each house.

"You guys ready?" I look at my men. They give me the thumbs-up.

"At least we're not hiding behind our tubes anymore," Levine says in his Bronx accent. For weeks now, I've listened to him complain about not getting into the fight. Getting rocketed wasn't enough for him. He wants to kill his enemy face-to-face. For him, it is vengeance. He lost family in 9-11.

"Let's go," I order, and we start walking up the block to the first house. We don't get far before we see our first corpse. I barely notice it, but Levine does a double take. "What the hell?" he asks while staring at it.

The corpse is moving. We stop and study it. Headless, missing parts of both legs and arms, its chest has been blown open by a 25mm cannon shell, the kind of weapon mounted on an army Bradley Fighting Vehicle.

The corpse twitches. I recoil at the sight. It twitches again. A tail emerges from the chest cavity like an orange-striped periscope.

"Oh my God," says Smokes, one of our two African-American platoonmates. We've nicknamed him Token, after the black kid in *South Park*.

"Here kitty, kitty, kitty!" somebody calls.

"Hey, now there's a Christmas present for your wife's little sister, Workman!" Levine says to me. "Bring her home a man-eating Fallujah kitten."

"Shut up. That's just wrong."

The orange cat tugs away at something inside the corpse, causing it to twitch yet again. It is eating the insurgent from the inside out.

"This is the filthiest place on earth," somebody else spits in disgust.

We move on. Over these past few weeks, we've seen a lot of animals feeding on the dead. The worst are the dogs. They're feral and bloated and we've watched them eagerly attack even the most blackened corpse. On one of our first patrols, we encountered one dog chewing at a legless insurgent's stump. We killed it with a 9mm pistol. No matter what we think of our enemy, even they do not deserve that fate. The feeding dogs absorb much of the ammunition we expend each day.

As we reach the first house, I hear a pistol crack behind us. I barely notice. We have a difficult tactical situation here, and I'm focused on solving it. The only entry point is through a gated driveway. It is a funnel, and if an insurgent die-hard happens to be over watching it, we could be in real trouble.

"Okay, we go through the gate fast. Got it?" I tell my men. I assign them fields of fire to cover, then remind them to get to the front door as quickly as possible. Everyone's ready. I nod to Levine. He pulls it open and we flow inside the front yard. Everything's quiet. We reach the door without incident and stack up again, one behind the other. My M16 has a broomstick handle attached to the bottom rail under the barrel. I've taped my SureFire's pressure switch to it. All I need to do is squeeze and the brightest flashlight in the world will illuminate whatever's in front of me.

My left hand squeezes, triggering the SureFire. The front door is open, and I shine the light inside. Nothing of interest comes into view.

On a silent command, we all surge into the house. We break up into teams and check each room. Levine and I go upstairs. I've heard stories of insurgents hiding in closets and under beds, and given what happened yesterday, I'm not in the mood to take any chances. When we swing into the first bedroom, I double tap the armoire and put several rounds into the bed. Nothing moves. White smoke spins out of my M16's barrel.

The house yields no weapons. We move on to the second one. It's big and has a long second story with balconies overlooking the walled-in yard. It takes us several minutes to clear. We come up empty again.

Back out on the street, I see Kraft has kept pace with us. He's about to start on his third house, too. Though we've been at it for less than a half hour, we're already covered in sweat. The night's chill has been driven off by the morning sun. It will be a scorcher today—well over a hundred, as usual. None of us carry canteens or camelbacks. Marines use canteens as urinals and spittoons, so no matter how many times they've been turned in and cleaned, the water inevitably tastes disgusting. Instead, we loaded crates of bottled water in our Humvees and try to take periodic breaks to rehydrate ourselves.

"Okay, stack up," I order. Smokes gets behind me first, Snell follows, and Levine ends up third this time.

We push open the gate and storm the house. Once inside, I head to the right and into a living room. Smokes and Levine turn left into the kitchen while Snell stays with me. The rest of the squad spreads out down a hallway. My SureFire sweeps the darkness, uncovering only a few sleeping mats and an odd blanket or two.

"Clear!" comes the word from the rest of the squad. The first floor is secure.

I'm about to move on when I hear a commotion coming from the kitchen. "What's going on?" I yell.

No answer. Snell and I pivot and run for the kitchen.

We find Smokes battling a pissed-off chicken.

"What the hell?"

"Damn bird!" He shouts and swings a frying pan he's found at it. The chicken squawks and dodges the blow. As he winds up for another swing, the bird pecks his leg, then ducks under the sink.

Snell and I can't help but laugh. Before this deployment, Smokes had guarded Camp David, the Presidential retreat. Oh, how the mighty have fallen.

"Smokes!" I try to stop him, but he gets down on his knees and whacks away at the chicken.

Levine's laughing as hard as I am.

Vigilance. Maintain security.

We've done this so much now with nothing but animals and corpses to be found inside these houses, it is impossible to keep our alert level pegged for long. But today, we've already slid. I need to get everyone back to a hundred percent.

"Okay, come on, we've got a job to do." Smokes takes one more whack at the chicken and gives up. The fowl squawks angrily from under the sink. Obviously, we're in its territory.

"Will a chicken eat a corpse?" Levine wonders out loud.

"Dude, you have been in Fallujah far too long if you're thinking shit like that," Snell replies.

"I'm just sayin'. I mean, the thing looks pretty fat. What's he been eating?"

"I swear it tried to eat me!" Smokes exclaims.

I shake my head and stifle another laugh. "Upstairs, let's go. Smokes, White, Mullins, Doc, and Snell, follow me. The rest of you pull security."

"On what?"

"The chicken."

I take my team upstairs. At the end of a short hallway, we find a closed door. Despite the humor of the moment, I'm in no mood to take chances. What if somebody's been feeding the chicken? He could be up here.

I shoulder my rifle and trigger off a half-dozen rounds through the door. As soon as I finish, I kick it open and we swing inside to discover an empty bedroom. Snell shoots into the bed while I pepper the closet.

Nothing moves.

"Hey, what's that?" Smokes calls out. His head is cocked, as if he's listening. Then I hear it, too: gunshots from across the street.

"AK's," I say. Kraft is probably shooting his way through his house, just like we are.

Suddenly, a ragged full-auto volley echoes through the house. A few M16's bark and crack. Somebody tears off a long burst from what sounds like another AK.

"They're under fire!" I shout. "Come on!"

We flee the bedroom and fly downstairs. My radio chatters, but I can't understand what's being said over the growing battle coming from across the street.

Eliminate the threat. Charge to the sound of gunfire.

My squad's assembled by the front door now. Levine looks eager. So does Snell. Smokes watches the street from the doorway. He's gone absolutely silent. He was out yesterday with the other patrol that got hit. The reality of the moment strikes him harder than the rest of us.

"Kraft may need us," I tell the men. "We're going over there."

I step out into the front yard and lead the squad to the gate. It is made of sheet metal, just like every other one on this block, so it won't stop an AK round, but it does offer a little concealment.

I peer around the corner, trying to reveal as little of myself as possible. Across the street, gray and white smoke pours from the windows on the second floor of Kraft's house. The volume of fire has spiked even higher. Now long automatic bursts from multiple AK's overlap each other into one sustained cacophony. I can't tell how many there are, but it has to be at least a half dozen, maybe more.

A bullet skips off the roadbed a few feet in front of me. Another one smacks into the wall and gouges out a little pit from the concrete.

I duck back behind the gate.

"Let's go! Let's go!" Levine shouts.

Snell's all about it, too. "Come on! What's the hold up?"

Don't let them push you into doing something rash. We have to get across the street, and we've got to do it right, or somebody will die.

"Shut the hell up! Look, we're going to get across the street and stop at the wall on the far side, okay?" I pause. Everyone nods. "Good. Look, we're going to be under fire, so I want everyone shooting at the windows on the second floor, okay?"

"How many are there?" someone asks.

"Two. One on the left, one on the right. In between, there's a doorway leading to a balcony, but I didn't see anyone on it. Focus on the windows."

"Roger that."

"Follow me."

I ease out to the end of the gate. The squad stacks up behind me. I feel Smokes's chest against my back. I decide to take one more look before we risk this kill zone. Usually, the best way to deal with open space is to skirt it. Avoid it. Find another way. But the street cannot be avoided. In this case, we'll have to just suck it up and get across as fast as our feet will carry us.

I hold my M16 away from the end of the gate so I don't reveal what

I'm about to do by accidentally popping its barrel into the open. That's a classic tell in situations like these. Instead, just part of my Kevlar helmet, nose, and one eye appear around the corner.

Somebody's sweeping the street with fire. Bullets ricochet in every direction. One spins off the asphalt and whines overhead.

"Jesus Christ! Let's go."

My stomach turns to liquid fire. It melts my legs and pins me in place. I feel like a giant's just clutched me with one calloused hand and is slowly squeezing the life out of me.

Move! Come on Jeremiah! Kraft needs you.

I can't breathe. More and more AK's open up. The insurgents aren't conserving ammo. The tide of sounds becomes a tsunami until I'm convinced at least a dozen or more AK's are firing.

Jessica. My wife is back home. What will she say if the contact team arrives on her doorstep?

We regret to inform you that your husband was killed in Fallujah . . .

What will she think about the moment it sinks in? Will she remember our first date back in Richwood? She and her friends were cruising our little town after school. I rolled up in a fifteen-year-old Honda Accord and convinced her to come with me. She jumped in, and we just drove around for hours. We finally ended up at her parents' house, where her folks greeted me like I was already their son-in-law.

Would she think about that day? Or would she think about the bad times first?

A fleeting thought skitters into my mind. I've always wanted children. So does she. I cross that street, I risk that. If I die here, I will leave no legacy.

You must cross. Go to your brothers.

I still can't move. Behind me, my guys are getting edgy. Levine pipes up, "Come on, what's the hold up? Let's do it!"

"Workman, let's go!"

Well, here's your Vietnam. Do you have the stones for this?

I swing around the gate and bring my rifle up. A step forward, then another. I don't bother with the ACOG four-power scope sitting on my weapon's top rail. Instead, I simply point my weapon at the window on the left and pull the trigger.

Two more steps and I'm almost halfway across the street. I sense the rest of the squad is right behind me, blazing away at the windows. Whoever's inside the house flays the street with bullets. They kick up little puffs of dirt and asphalt. Others skip off the wall to our front.

Keep moving! Keep moving!

Every instinct in me wants to flee. Instead, I find myself sprinting toward the AK barrels pointed our way.

Another wave of bullets sweeps over us.

I reach the safety of the far wall and press myself tight against it. I'm in the lee of the storm now, out of reach from the weapons in the windows. A second later, the rest of the squad joins me.

"Everyone okay?"

"Yeah! We're all here," Levine replies.

"Good."

What next?

Chances are any second Kraft's guys will snuff out the last bad guy and drag all of their corpses out of the house. At least, that's what I hope will happen.

The firing never slows. In fact, as we hug the wall, it increases again. Behind all the gunshots, I can hear men screaming. Whatever's happened is bad. We're going to need to get inside.

What if this is a trap?

I glance down the street. It is possible. Maybe they want us to get sucked into a fight here, then they'll hit us with a counterattack. Or maybe there's a sniper on a nearby rooftop waiting to engage us when our guard is down. Either way, we need to be prepared.

Toward the back of my stack, I see Lance Corporal Jason Flannery. He's a skinny but muscular guy from small-town Missouri who always rides a fine line between confidence and cocky. He's also a veteran of the 2003 invasion.

"Hey Flannery! Take three or four guys and go down the street and post security."

Flannery doesn't even blink. "Fuck that, Workman. I'm going with you."

"What?"

"I'm going to get some!"

No time to argue. "Okay, fine. Stay close to me though."

I creep along the wall until I come to the open gate. Like the one across the street, it is made of sheet metal. Already it has bullet holes in it. My feet feel like they're encased in concrete blocks. I force myself forward until I can see around the corner.

The house sits in the middle of an oasis. A beautiful green lawn inset with several concrete walkways stretches across the front yard. A few small trees and saplings provide a little bit of shade. A garden lies beyond the trees along the side yard. I don't see any of Kraft's men anywhere.

We'll have to run at least forty feet across open ground to reach the front door. The twin second-story windows are like eyes watching me. How am I going to do this?

Be their leader. Show them by example.

I want to, but I've never felt such crippling fear before. Every neuron is sending "flee" messages to my brain. Any sane man would run from this chaos.

"Sounds like a platoon plus in there," Smokes says in a flat voice.

Kraft and his men need you.

That does it. Thinking of them suddenly makes me resolute. For the moment, the fear seems to fade into the background. I clench my jaw.

"Workman! Let's go! Let's go!" shouts Levine.

Corporal Steve Snell echoes him. "Hurry! Come on! Let's get into the damned house!"

I step around the gate, and sprint flat-out for the house. I'm giving it all I have, but it feels like time has slowed down. The doorway yawns before me, like a mouth about to swallow me whole. Yet the harder I run, the more unreachable the doorway appears. Gunfire echoes around me, intermingled with screams in both Arabic and English. Someone wails in agony. I can't tell where it is coming from; all I can do is keep driving for the door.

Suddenly, time speeds up. I launch myself through the door and come to a crashing halt in a hallway about two yards from a stairwell that leads to the second story. Behind me, the rest of the squad squeezes through the door. I turn and order them to clear the first floor. The men fan out, rifles leveled.

Overhead, the gunfight grows even more intense. Over the constant *rap-rap-rap* of many AK's, I hear a steady ripping sound. It reminds me of our M240 Golf machine guns, only deeper and with a slightly slower rate of fire.

It dawns on me. There is a crew-served weapon upstairs.

I look over at the stairwell again. Kraft is there, pinned against a wall. He's shouting something at me, but I can't hear him. His words are smothered by the gunfire.

"Kraft! What the hell is going on?"

He shouts something to me again and throws a radio at me. I can't make heads or tails of what he said, and I have no use for the radio, so I toss it into the front yard. Then I see Sergeant Sam Gardiola next to him. He half-crouches on a landing about fifteen steps up the stairwell. Just above his head is a ragged line of bullet holes.

Thunder erupts overhead. The right stairwell wall dissolves into bits of flying concrete and dust. Gardiola ducks just as bullets chew into a strip of inlaid marble on either side of his head.

Another fusillade rips through the stairwell. Kraft and Gardiola both dive for the first-floor hallway. Behind me, my squad consolidates. I hear Smokes and Flannery shout, "First floor's clear."

Kraft pulls my arm and leads me back outside. We're in the kill zone again, running for the street. I don't know what he wants, but we all follow him. Bullets tear up the precisely manicured lawn as we go.

Somehow, we all stream through the gate and get back against the wall. For the moment, we're safe and unhurt.

"Hey! Do we have Marines in there?" I hear someone yell. I look up the street and see Lieutenant Putnam running up to us. The sight of him puzzles me. I'm not sure why he's here, as he's not part of our company. When he reaches Kraft, he asks again, "Do we have Marines in there?"

Kraft nods. "Yes, sir."

"How many?"

"I don't know. Raleigh and Phillips for sure. They're trapped on the second floor."

The LT swears furiously, then says, "Okay, we gotta go get 'em out. Clear?"

"Yes, sir."

"You men!"—he points to several of my squadmates—"Set up a support by fire position across the street. Get some fire into the second floor!" As they dash off to execute that order, the LT turns to the rest of us. "Everyone else follow me!" The LT charges through the gate like a halfback going through the defensive line. I jackrabbit after him. Again, I'm in the kill zone, out in the open. My breathing is fast and shallow, and my eyes are cockades, wide and pregnant with fear. I'm running into the fight again, but this time, I know we'll be going upstairs.

At least the lieutenant will lead the way this time. I'll have a human shield in front of me.

It is time to earn my pay.

I follow the LT right across the lawn. He makes no effort to zigzag or throw the gunners off in the windows above our heads. This time, we face no incoming fire, at least none that I can detect. We make it through the front door unscathed. As we do, the LT spins around and covers down on the front yard. I'm alone for several heartbeats, staring at the bullet-scarred stairwell.

Then it dawns on me. I'm in front again.

Another stab of fear drives into my heart. For a second, it is so intense I feel like the wind's been knocked out of me. I try to breathe but hitch and stall. My face flushes. My hands shake. I don't know if I can do this.

Too late. You're screwed. You're not leaving this house alive.

I see myself on the landing, M16 in hand, blood pouring from multiple wounds. That is my fate. This is the day I am to die.

The realization comes like a slap in the face. It clears my head and drives the fear from me. My hands stop shaking. I can breathe again.

I am going to die here, and the thought is a comfort, not a curse. I won't disgrace myself. I won't die screaming. I will go out hard, fighting to the end.

I drop my M16's magazine out and replace it with a fresh one. Thirty rounds. I'm ready to go.

Behind me, the rest of my squad, Kraft, and the LT have arrived. I move toward the first step. I see it is marble, and the stairs themselves are built from wrought iron. There's dead space under the stairwell, and I shine my SureFire in there to clear it. The light casts a fishbone-like shadow of the stairs against the far wall. Nothing's there. We're good to go.

"Grenade!" somebody shouts. I see a frag careen off a wood railing near the landing. Then it comes bouncing down the stairs straight for me, as inexorably as a Slinky.

"Grenade! Get down!" I scream. The squad scatters. I have nowhere to run and no time to do it. I take three strides forward and leap under the stairs. I slide into the corner and turn my head just as the grenade explodes less than ten feet from me. A whoosh of shrapnel rushes overhead. My ears go numb. A persistent ringing is all I hear. I check myself over and am surprised to find no wounds.

What the hell? Who pulled that stunt?

Somebody whispers something to me. Through the smoke in the hallway I see Kraft and Levine. Their mouths are moving in exaggerated ways. Then I realize they're shouting. I'm so deafened by the grenade that I barely hear their voices.

A long burst from an AK punctures my silence, but it sounds distant and muffled. The fighting on the second floor continues.

I get to my feet and dash back to the squad. Levine grabs my shoulders and yells in my ear, "You okay?" He sounds like he's shouting at me through a fish tank.

I give him a thumbs-up. "Good to go."

The LT reappears. "Sorry about that."

Before I can call him any one of the many names that come to mind, he tells the squad, "Okay, on three we go upstairs, got it?"

Everyone nods. The men stack up. Behind *me*. The LT disappears toward the rear.

"One!"

You've got to do this. The men upstairs need us.

"Two!"

There's no finer way to die than leading men in battle. Cling to that. Let it be your guiding thought, if not your last one.

"Three!"

I close my eyes, grip my rifle, and run.

Chapter Four

DIAGNOSIS

Spring 2006
Parris Island, S.C.

AT OUR MAINSIDE BARRACKS, in the drill instructor's hut, I stand before Staff Sergeant Shelby. He's pissed. I've just come from our company's First Sergeant's office, where he ordered me to go home on leave.

"What do you want, Workman?" Shelby spits. He has heard about what happened.

"Staff Sergeant Shelby, the first sergeant told me to tell you that I'm going on leave."

His jaw sags and his eyes bulge. "What? Oh hell no! You just got here. You're not going anywhere."

"Yes I am."

Shelby shakes his head. "You been over sucking the first sergeant's dick, eh?"

"No." I manage to keep the anger out of my voice.

"Go back to the first sergeant and tell him you're not going home."

I turn and leave. I walk through the squad bay for the front hatch. The recruits are assembled here, and I feel their eyes on me as I walk past. They're curious and hostile and pitiless all at the same time.

I try not to care.

A few minutes later, I enter the first sergeant's office again.

"Workman, what are you doing back here?"

"Staff Sergeant Shelby sent me back to tell you that I'm not going on leave."

"What? Why? What did he say?"

Now there's a loaded question. I consider my response and decide to just lay it out. "Well, First Sergeant, he said I must have been up here sucking your dick to get leave so soon."

"Goddamnit!" the first sergeant roars. "Look, go back and tell Staff Sergeant Edds that you're leaving. Then get your shit and go home."

I'm playing political ping-pong, and I'm the ball.

I return to the barracks, unsure of how Staff Sergeant Edds will receive me. Of all the DI's, he and Allen have been the best to me since I got here. They've mentored me along, kept me pushing the envelope even when I thought I went too far.

But Shelby has always been a jerk. The first day I met him we sparked a negative flow between us. When he told me my job was to push at least two recruits into suicide attempts during my first couple of weeks, I thought he was kidding at first. Then one look in his eyes stifled any thought of laughter. He was dead serious, and it made me revile him.

Later, after I found the kid slashing his wrists and took him to the base hospital, Staff Sergeant Shelby approached me and offered warm congratulations. I'd just destroyed that kid. He had failed because of me, and that humiliation was so complete he was willing to end his life. I didn't think the moment merited praise. In fact, if anything, I thought I'd become a pretty despicable human being for pushing him that far. Shelby didn't think so. He patted me on the shoulder and told me, "I hear you're really tearing things up. Damn fine job, Workman. Keep it up!"

I reach the front hatch again. Recruit eyes follow me to the DI hut. Inside, I find Staff Sergeant Edds. He greets me warily.

"Workman, how are you feeling?"

"I don't really know. The first sergeant has told me to take leave."

Before Edds can answer, Shelby appears. "Staff Sergeant Edds, please leave. I need to talk to Workman alone."

As Edds departs, Shelby spins to face me. He stands six three with close-cropped brown hair. His face is meaty and ovoid. Again, he reminds me of the WWF wrestler Sergeant Slaughter—a caricature of a real drill instructor.

"Workman! Give me your belt and cover."

The order surprises me. At Parris Island, only a first sergeant or a company commander can take a DI's belt and cover.

He sees me hesitate. "Give me your FUCKING belt and campaign cover. NOW!"

I take them off and hand them over. He throws them onto a chair.

"I don't have another cover, Staff Sergeant," I say. Every Marine on base must wear something on his head. Right now, I'm probably the only Marine uncovered.

Shelby offers a sick little demi-grin. Anger flares inside me when I see his expression.

"Beautiful. Just beautiful," he says with a full grin now, his voice almost guttural. The man is toying with me.

He steps to the doorway and whistles a recruit over. The young kid practically sprints to him. Shelby tears his eight-point cover off his head then dismisses him.

Holding the recruit's cover, Shelby turns to me and gets right up into my face. "Here's your fucking cover, Workman. That's what you're worth!" He slams it down over my head and jams the bill low across my nose. The sudden assault catches me totally by surprise. The cap is greasy with the recruit's sweat. It stinks.

My fists clench. I burn with sudden rage. I try to lock my eyes with his, but he averts my gaze. Instead, he turns his back to me and steps away.

I stand there at parade rest in complete humiliation. The cap on my head a stigma worse than a scarlet letter.

Back in World War I, some British flying units would identify their cowards and then sew yellow fabric to their uniform tunic in front of a full formation. Everyone would see the coward's humiliation, and he would be sent back to England that way. I wonder how many committed suicide rather than enduring that terrible indignity.

Shelby's done the same thing to me with the cap. The recruits outside can't help but know what's going on. They can hear. They can see.

I've never been degraded by anyone. Not once in my life. Back home, I was venerated as a gridiron hero. People I didn't know wanted to shake my hand.

Have I fallen that far?

"Workman, I don't know who you think you are." Shelby's shouting right into my face now. His jowls are swaying with every word. I want to break his face.

"You come here, and you pull a zero. You failed us."

My fist. I see my fist slamming into his nose. I want to feel the gristle as it splinters from my blow. I want to hear it crack, and I want to see him double over in pain. Then I'll hit him again and again until he's nothing but a bleeding supplicant, pleading for mercy. I won't give him any.

I start glancing around the room for something to wield as a weapon, something I can use to break his face.

"You're screwing over Staff Sergeant Edds and Sergeant Allen! They're working their asses off. They're the best DI's in the company. And you've let them down."

Shelby pauses for a reaction. I don't give him the satisfaction.

"You know the Third Hat you replaced? He let them down, too. He flaked out. Now you pull this shit? How dare you!"

Flaked out? The man I replaced had to have hernia surgery.

"You're just going to walk away?" Shelby demands. He's so close to me now that I can smell his sour breath.

"I don't want to go on leave," I say. Every word is an effort of self-control.

He stares at me. My eyes go to his uniform. He has four stateside ribbons on his chest. Four. I'm getting chewed out by a candy-ass Marine who has avoided fleet duty his entire career. I never used to pay attention to how many ribbons a man wore back in my pre-Iraq days. Now I know they're the measure of a Marine. Are you a POG (Person Other than Grunt) who hides stateside in wartime, or are you a warrior?

"You don't think we've got issues? We all have issues, asshole! Do you think that gives us some pussy excuse to not do our jobs? Our duty?"

I say nothing. I want to do my duty, I tried my best. I have no answers for what happened.

"Look at Sergeant Allen! He's been here almost three years. He never sees his wife. Never."

Jessica. She's still in Ohio. I haven't seen my wife in six months. We all pay that price here.

"These men have worked their tails off. And you've been here for three weeks. Three lousy weeks. And *you* want time off?"

"I told you I don't want time off. I am being told by the first sergeant to go home."

Shelby ignores this and changes gear. "Let me ask you something, Workman."

I say nothing.

"Would you pull this shit in Iraq?"

What do you know about Iraq? You fought the battle of Beaufort in the bars downtown while I was in Fallujah. I want to throw that in his face.

Discipline holds me in check. I say nothing.

"Would you let your Marines down in Iraq?"

Words form. My lips start to move. I crush them with one last effort of self-control.

Shelby gets right in my face again. Nose to nose, his eyes are bare inches from mine. "I know the real reason why you're fucked up, Workman."

He waits, studies my eyes.

"Oh yes, don't think I don't know. You dropped your gun, didn't you?"

I want to seize his neck, crush his windpipe, and savor the moment of his fall. Instead, I'm a statue at parade rest, arms behind my back, fists clenched tight.

"You dropped your gun and Marines died. And that's why you can't man up and do your duty here."

Five years into a global war, Staff Sergeant Shelby has yet to even deploy. And he has the right to say I got my Marines killed? Bilious hatred boils in me. I want to spit in his face.

He cocks his head, inspecting my eyes. I try to hide my hate.

"Well, what if we were in combat here, Workman? Would you let all of us down again?"

That shatters my self-control. I hear myself bellow, "FUCK YOU! If we were in combat I'd kill you myself!"

Shelby reels backward, surprised by the vehemence of my retort. He senses how close to the edge of violence he's pushed me, and I glimpse fear in his eyes.

"Workman, get the fuck out of here now! Plant your ass on the bench outside my office and wait for further orders."

I leave, still wearing the recruit's cover as a hallmark of my degradation. A few minutes later, I find the bench outside Shelby's office. It is painted red. I sit down and check my watch. Eight-thirty. All of this has happened before normal civilian work hours.

I sit and wait. And wait. My watch ticks past nine. Then nine-thirty. Shelby has left me here as punishment. I'm swollen with anger and resentment, twisted by humiliation.

My watch hits ten o'clock. I've sat for an hour and a half on this bench. People coming and going past Shelby's office have eyed me in puzzlement. Why's Workman sitting there with a recruit's cover on his head?

Finally, at eleven-thirty, I pull out my cell phone. Jessica. I need to talk to Jess. I dial the number and she answers right away. "Hello?"

"Goddamn, Jess. I hate this fucking place. I hate these people." I'm shaking so hard now that holding the phone becomes an effort.

"I . . . Jess. Something's happening to me. . . ." I don't know what to say. How do you explain to your wife a day like this one?

"Jeremiah, what's the matter?" The concern in her voice is some-how reassuring. Despite everything we've done to hurt each other since Iraq, she still cares. There's still that connection between us that carried us through high school and into adulthood together.

The office door next to me swings open. Shelby sticks his head out, looks down at me and barks, "Get off your phone, Workman. You've got an hour for lunch. Then get your ass back here and ride that bench."

"Jess, I've got to go."

"Wait, Jeremiah? Talk to me!"

I hang up. Instead of going to chow, I return to the first sergeant's office.

"Workman?" he says, "Why are you still here?"

As I explain, the first sergeant grows furious. "Where's your belt and campaign cover?"

I explain that, too. He reaches for his phone. A call later, and my belt and cover are returned to me. I tear off the recruit's cover and put my own back on.

"Okay, go see the battalion sergeant major," the first sergeant tells me. "I'll give him a call and explain things."

Will this never end? All I want to do now is leave. I want to put this place behind me and seal the memories of it in a vault that's buried deep in the recesses of my mind.

But I can't do that. I walk to the sergeant major's office. He's waiting for me with a scowl on his chiseled face. It is hard not to be intim-
idated by him. He's a stern-looking man with a horseshoe haircut, a
square jaw, and a look that says he doesn't brook bullshit. I wonder
what he'll do with me, a malfunctioning Marine who's made a scene
on his watch.

"Come on, Workman," he says with compassion in his voice. "I'll
take you down to the clinic."

As we walk, he says, "You know, a lot of the Marines I served with
have been wounded in Iraq."

"I didn't know that, Sergeant Major." The sergeant major's an old-
school Marine. Going on twenty years in the Corps, he served in an
elite recon battalion before coming to Parris Island.

"I just want you to know that you have nothing to be ashamed of,
Sergeant Workman. Nothing. Unless you've been in it, there's no way
to understand what combat does to a man."

He doesn't say anything else, but that's all I need to hear. He understands.

We reach the clinic, and the sergeant major says goodbye to me. He
turns and leaves and I find myself alone again until an orderly ushers
me into a small room.

A big blue recliner dominates the space. A small desk sits opposite.
The walls are lined with books. I'm in a shrink's office.

The realization crumbles the last remnants of my self-worth. The
sergeant major must think I've gone crazy.

What's worse, he may be right. Am I a lost cause, one of the walking dead from Fallujah?

"Welcome, Sergeant Workman." I look up from my misery to see a
navy doctor smiling warmly at me. "I'm Doctor Goldberg."

"Hi Doc," is all I can say.

He slides past me and takes a seat behind his desk. He opens a file
and produces a pen. "Tell me what's on your mind today?"

What are my options here? I can hide everything and lie. I can tell
him what happened at the chow hall. Or, I can tell him everything and
see what he makes of it all.

I'm too tired and too depressed for games. I uncork everything
that's been bottled up inside me these past months. The words flow

like pus from a suppurating wound. I can't even look at him as I speak, but I can tell he's listening because I hear his pen scratching notes in the file he's opened.

I focus my eyes on a book resting on the shelf nearest me. The spine reads *DSM IV.* It is a mental illness handbook. I bet when I leave, he'll crack that sucker open and conclude I'm a nutcase.

A dam has burst. Even if I wanted to stop the words, I don't have enough left to do so. They tumble out. Fallujah, my brothers-in-arms. Jessica. The house. I talk for over an hour straight, never looking at Doc Goldberg.

Finally, the flow ebbs. I hold my head in my hands and say, "That's about it."

Silence captures the room. At last, I gather the strength and look at the doc.

He's rigid behind his desk. Jaw open. Pen on the desk where he'd dropped it who knows how long ago.

"That good?" I offer weakly.

"Sergeant Workman," Goldberg says slowly. "You have no business being a drill instructor."

"To tell you the truth, Doc, I don't really want to be a Marine either."

Did I just say that? It fell out of me without warning. Is it true? What would I do if I wasn't a Marine?

"We can talk about that later. But for now, I'm going to start the paperwork to get you reassigned."

"Thank you."

"We're also going to get you on some medication, but that'll need to be done through the Beaufort Naval Hospital. I'll make sure you get an appointment over there right away."

"What's the matter with me, Doc?"

He looks surprised at the question. "Sergeant Workman, you've got post-traumatic stress disorder."

"PTSD? You're kidding me."

My mind jumps back two years, when I was still with 3rd Battalion, 5th Marines. I was just about to deploy to Iraq, and one of the units we were replacing had just returned from its tour. One morning, I saw these men gathered together, smoking quietly in exclusive huddles.

Four here. Five there. As I walked past them, I studied their faces. They looked hollowed out. Gaunt. Off.

I remember thinking that I'd never end up that way. I was better than that. Better than they were. All that PTSD nonsense was for pussies who couldn't hack a warrior's life. The very acronym was a stigma.

But who do you see when you look in the mirror now, Jeremiah? Who do you see?

I see a gaunt and broken man who wears the same visage as those veterans I scorned back before I endured what they endured.

I have become one of them.

I have always been tough. If it hurts, you man up and drive on. That's what got me through sports in high school. That's what got me through life with my mom and an abusive stepfather. That toughness carried me to the Marines. It forms the basis of my pride and self-esteem. Up until this moment, I thought I could take anything.

Have I lived with a false identity all these years?

I wrestle with these questions as Doc Goldberg fills out some paperwork. When he finishes, he hands it to me and says, "We'll talk about your future as a Marine in a few weeks, okay?"

"Aye, sir. Thank you."

"For now, I want you to go home and get some rest."

I leave the clinic. Marines are not supposed to be frail—mentally or physically. And only the frail suffer from PTSD, right?

Right?

Walking to my Tacoma, I pull out my cell phone and dial Jess.

"Jeremiah? Are you okay?" she asks the moment she answers the phone.

"Honey, I have to tell you something."

"What? You sounded so strange earlier."

I suck air and wait. How do you tell the one person you love most in the world that your brain is messed up? How do you make that confession?

"Jessica, I just saw a doctor."

"Are you hurt?"

"Well, yeah. In a way."

Another long breath. I search for the right words.

"Go on," she urges. "What's the matter? Jeremiah, talk to me."

"Jess, the doc diagnosed me with PTSD this afternoon."

A long pause. Oh shit. This is going to end it. She doesn't need a damaged man for a husband.

Her response catches me totally by surprise. "What's PTSD?"

Chapter Five

A MIND AT WAR

Spring 2006

IN THE DAYS after my initial diagnosis, I learned more than I wanted to know about PTSD and how it affects the brain. Of course, it all starts with trauma and the interaction the traumatic incident has with the human brain. Everyone has psychological barriers, protective walls that are supposed to defend us from harm should we see or experience something truly horrible like a car wreck; the loss of a mother, or father, husband or wife—or worst of all, of a child.

Everyone's walls are different. Some of us have low ones, frail and patched together after a childhood of too much pain. Others have walls so thick it seems like nothing will ever get through to harm the fragile psyche bunkered down behind them.

In the end, though, our walls are never thick enough. Profound trauma can always penetrate them; it is the terrible silver bullet too many have been felled by once home from combat. Violence, death, imminent harm—these are the stressors that can trigger a total collapse of our psychological walls with devastating results.

Once a brain receives an overdose of trauma, it sustains physical damage. Its neurochemistry actually changes. New neural pathways are forged, and old ones wither from disuse. These changes alter the landscape of the victim's character and personality, often with tragic and deadly painful results.

Worst of all, the trauma doesn't go away. The brain absorbs it, but can't process it. Once it pierces the defensive walls, it rattles around inside, ricocheting from corner to corner, inflicting even more damage.

Think of the human mind as a record. Put the needle down, and the record plays its tune. But what happens when something gouges that record? The scratch becomes the needle's nemesis. The tune cannot continue, the scratch makes the needle repeat over and over, and it will never escape the damaged part of the record on its own.

That's exactly what happens with PTSD. The brain gets stuck in mid-process. It can't continue the process of healing as the silver bullet scythes back and forth through the victim's psyche. And so, the trauma becomes the damaged brain's obsessive fixture. The needle skips and skips and can never move past the scratch. The brain replays the traumatic event in the same way. Over and over, conscious or not, the victim never stops experiencing the worst moments of his or her life. It becomes a permanent part of every waking moment, and every dream that invades the victim's restless sleep.

Exactly how PTSD affects a person varies widely depending on the victim's psychological makeup and the level of the trauma, but there are some common elements among victims. First, the trauma never lessens, never ebbs away. Time heals all wounds, right? Not with PTSD. The trauma remains as painful, as powerful, and as horrifying as the first time its victim experienced it. If anything, it gets worse. The pain sends the victim into a spiral of depression. Self-medication with alcohol or drugs often follows. Nightmares, flashbacks, sudden bouts of terror, and rage develop. There is no way to purge these emotions; the damaged brain has no positive outlet. The result is poison to the soul.

Victims of PTSD sometimes turn violent. Others overreact to ordinary life stresses. The rage and despair form a self-destructive cocktail that sometimes leads to suicide, other times to murder. Those are the extremes, of course, but on the path downward, the middle ground is filled with anger that only those suffering from PTSD truly understand. A misplaced toy, a casual remark, a wayward glance, or a traffic jam is all it takes to trigger the overreaction. It can easily spiral out of control.

Pride and prejudice come into play about this time, and both these things wage a war without any hope of recovery. In the military, weakness is not allowed. A Marine does not flinch at physical wounds. Nor does he admit to frailties of the mind. The proud soldier, the stellar

Marine, hides his agony and pretends that nothing is wrong for fear of destroying his military career. Worse, he holds it inside for as long as he can, and conceals it from his platoonmates and peers for fear of losing their respect and trust.

This wall traps PTSD inside the victim's mind. The damage worsens; the spiral deepens. Yet too many never reach out for help.

All of this takes a toll on the victim's family. Divorce rates skyrocket. Relationships break down under the weight of all the negative emotions, self-medication, and despair. As PTSD drives the victim's closest loved ones away, the pain and trauma of these failed relationships feed right back into the original traumatic event. Each replay becomes even more vivid and emotional. The reactions become hyperfueled, the outbursts increasingly worse. It is a vicious cycle, and once in the spiral the victim may never get out.

It isn't an isolated problem either, nor is it one that started with our war. In 1914–1918, it was called "Shell Shock"; in World War II, it was called "Battle Fatigue," and in the British Royal Air Force, "LMF— Lack of Moral Fibre." Only during the Vietnam War's final stages was there a major effort undertaken to understand the effect of combat on the human mind. Ironically, it originally came out of the anti-war movement.

In 1980, the American Psychiatric Association officially acknowledged the symptoms of PTSD, and the condition was integrated into the Diagnostic and Statistical Manual of Mental Disorders. At the time, the feminist movement played a significant role in getting official recognition for PTSD, as the same symptoms are often prevalent in rape victims. Since then, considerable research has been devoted to understanding and trying to mitigate the effects of PTSD.

During World War II, the National Center for Post-Traumatic Stress Disorder estimates that one in twenty American veterans suffered PTSD symptoms in their lifetimes. That doesn't sound like much until one realizes that there were about eight million Americans in uniform during the war years. That five percent figure totals several hundred thousand veterans.

During the Second World War, for every man in combat, there were between ten and two hundred men and women providing logistical support who saw no danger outside of operational accidents.

When that is factored into the NCPTSD estimate, a frightening percentage of combat veterans came home and suffered from PTSD—and received little to no treatment for decades.

In 2004, the VA reported that 25,000 World War II veterans still received treatment for PTSD in its clinics and hospitals. Sixty years after D-day, minds traumatized by battling the Third Reich and Japan were still struggling to process the experience.

The Vietnam-era veterans suffered worse than their WWII counterparts. Between 1986 and 1988, the National Vietnam Veterans Readjustment Survey concluded that 479,000 men and 610 women who served in Vietnam continued to suffer from PTSD. That represented a 15.2 percent rate among the 3,140,000 men and 8,100 women who served in Vietnam.

But, recent surveys paint an even grimmer picture. Of the Vietnam vets who served in combat, 30 percent were afflicted with PTSD. More than thirty years after the last helicopter launched from the embassy roof in Saigon, over 160,000 Vietnam veterans still receive disability payments for PTSD. Since the War on Terror began, however, there has been a resurgence of Vietnam veterans seeking treatment for combat trauma. The images on television, combined with the fact that in many cases these vets have sons or daughters in harm's way, reopened old wounds and caused major problems within their lives again. Since 2003, the number of Vietnam vets seeking help for trauma has increased 36 percent.

Time does not heal all wounds.

In fact, with PTSD, time can make it worse. With Gulf War veterans, the number of reported PTSD cases doubled between the end of the war and two years after it.

Korean vets seem to have had it the worst—up until now. Thirty percent of those who remain from that war continue to suffer from PTSD.

For a shocking number of our veterans, the wars they fought never ended. Never.

When preparing for the invasion of Iraq, the VA and the Pentagon estimated that there would be 8,000 cases of PTSD stemming from combat in the Middle East. In December 2007, the RAND Corporation issued a report that stated that about 300,000 veterans of Iraq and

Afghanistan either suffer from major depression or PTSD. Another 320,000 have received traumatic brain injuries, mainly from roadside bombs, that frequently cause PTSD-like symptoms.

A 2007 editorial in the *Journal of General Internal Medicine* remarked, "Iraq has become a more effective incubator for PTSD . . . than any mad scientist could conceivably design."

Exactly what percentage of Iraq and Afghanistan veterans have PTSD is unclear. It also varies from service to service. Some early-war estimates put the figure at 12 percent. More recently, further studies revealed that almost half the National Guardsmen who've been deployed suffer from PTSD, while 38 percent of Marines have some form of it. In some studies, the figure of 20 percent has been used. If that is the case, when the last soldier, airman, and Marine returns home at the end of the War on Terror, there will be at least another 360,000 cases of PTSD or PTSD-like conditions for the VA system to handle.

They planned for 8,000. Instead, there will be almost 700,000 of us by war's end. By 2004, the VA and the military's ability to handle the influx of PTSD cases was simply overwhelmed. In some cases, soldiers and Marines slipped through bureaucratic cracks, and at one point, the overburdened VA system had some 600,000 claims backlogged and waiting to be processed. For some, the wait proved to be too much.

We combat veterans tend to make this situation worse, since we see PTSD as stigmatizing. Between 23 and 40 percent of us have sought treatment. The vast majority of us continue to suffer in silence. According to internal VA memos and emails, eighteen veterans of Iraq or Afghanistan kill themselves every day. Of those, only four to five are actively seeking help from the VA.

As a result, the PTSD rates in my generation are almost certainly significantly higher than any other war. Part of the explanation for this lies with the nature of the fighting—frequently up close in urban settings against enemies who wear no uniforms. Part of it also rests with the fact that there are no safe rear areas as there were in most of America's other wars. One study discovered that 86 percent of all Iraq veterans had experienced a firefight or a roadside bomb incident. When the front lines become blurred, and there are no safe havens, the chance for trauma increases.

The statistics don't offer much hope for us—not if the Greatest Generation or the Baby Boomers are any indication. Chances are, those of us who suffer from chronic PTSD will still be suffering from it when we're eligible for Social Security.

Right there is the key. After learning about what had happened to me, I needed a healthy path to take to avoid that fate. But how do you pull out of the spiral? Who is there to help along the way?

Unfortunately, understanding PTSD and overcoming it are two very different things.

Chapter Six

BEAUFORT

Spring 2006

SEATED IN A CIRCLE, we stare away from one another. Nobody makes eye contact. Words are stillborn; silence golden. Even without introduction, I can tell every Marine in the room is a combat veteran. They share the same expression of semi-repressed anguish. Below their daily façades, a war rages. I know the look because I have it, too.

"Guys, don't leave me hanging." The counselor is a graying army veteran of Vietnam. "Group is about knowing your brothers understand your pain. We've all been there. I've been there. Who wants to start?"

The counselor's words drape awkwardly around us. I steal a glance at my silent brethren. We're seated on cheap plastic chairs at a rectangular conference table. One Marine sits with his arms crossed defensively. A huge scarlet scar laces his throat. Another clutches a cane across his chest. He sits hunched over, staring into his lap.

I didn't know there were so many veterans at Parris Island. They must have come from the weapon's training range. I had heard something about those instructors having some time overseas. One thing for sure, there's not a faker in the bunch. These men are hurting, there's no denying that.

The counselor regards us. We avoid eye contact with him. "Guys, you're killing me here. We are all combat veterans. At least eighteen percent of returning Iraq veterans suffer from PTSD. At least that's what the Defense Department thinks. Personally, I think the number is a lot higher."

The Marine with the throat wound shifts uncomfortably in his seat. The movement catches the counselor's eye. "What's your name, son?"

"James." He answers in a raspy, damaged voice. His eyes look dead.

"Want to tell us about yourself?"

"Not really, no."

"Okay, how about you?" The counselor points at me.

I nearly swallow my tongue. He wants me to share with these guys? What can I say that they haven't already endured?

"Jeremiah. I served with three-five."

"Want to tell us about it?"

"No." Hell no, actually.

The counselor looks dismayed. "I've been there. I've had the nightmares. I've felt the rage. I've suffered the uncontrolled outbursts. I've wanted to hurt the people I love the most. I've been numb. I've been so full of hate that only the thought of killing offered relief. You do not have to hide from me."

Not a sound follows. The Marine with the cane closes his eyes. Like me he's clearly not here voluntarily. Last week, when I was sent here to the Beaufort Naval Hospital to see a psychiatrist, she told me that I needed to go to group therapy at least once.

"Give it a try," she encouraged. "Who knows? You may get a lot out of it." Then she prescribed some medication for me.

And so, here I am, enduring this misery-fest. There are a dozen men around me. All of them have had their lives turned to shit since they came home. That fact is stamped on every face I dare to inspect.

"Would you like to say anything?" the counselor asks another Marine. He looks like he just got caught passing notes in algebra class. "Uh, no sir. I'm just here because I got a DUI."

That resonates. Back in Southern California, I had a crotch rocket, a Honda CBR 600. Every night, after drinking at The Harp, I would tear ass home as fast as I dared. The more risk, the more danger, the happier and more normal I felt.

In Iraq, we lived on the edge. Our bodies grew accustomed to the daily adrenaline infusion combat gave us. I became a junkie, and when I returned to the safety of the States, I went into withdrawal.

I went in search of a replacement. Nothing on earth compares to the high that riding the bleeding edge between life and death offers. It makes living more lush and vivid. It magnifies every emotion, every experience. When you don't know if you're going to still be breathing from moment to moment, every breath becomes significant.

Coming home, the opposite happened. Without the threat of death, life lost its luster. The lushness dulled like a faded photograph.

The crotch rocket offered a poor substitute to combat, but a substitute nonetheless. I drove hard and recklessly, hitting speeds that would make my mother cringe. But the high that produced proved short-lasting, and I had to find other ways to venture close to the edge again.

I started driving drunk. It was crazy and wrong, but I didn't care. I craved the rush, and trying to stay upright at a hundred miles an hour with a blood alcohol level somewhere north of .15 provided the thrill I needed. At least, until I pushed it too far.

One night, somewhere in Oceanside, I was so blurry that I missed a turn and skidded up a driveway doing at least fifty miles an hour. I hit the brakes just before I struck a wrought iron fence. The front wheel wedged between two bars and stopped the Honda cold. I held on for dear life and somehow didn't get catapulted forward, which probably would have killed me.

I don't really know how I survived that crash, and I think part of me regretted that I did.

After that, I gave up my career as a poster child for a MADD campaign. Of course, that sent me searching for new ways to kick-start my adrenal gland, which led to even worse trouble.

The counselor's voice calls me back to the present. "Okay, let's go, ahead and take a test."

A test? The faces around the table grow even longer.

"This will determine the level of stress in your lives and give us a good baseline to start out with for future sessions."

If I have to sit through another one of these meetings, I'm going to smoke myself.

The counselor hands out the test, along with pencils. "Answer honestly. It will help us."

I open up the test and start reading through the questions. I find myself checking most of the boxes. When I'm done, I total up the points I've scored. I'm over 300.

I turn to the Marine next to me. "What do you think my score means?"

"Means you're Jeffrey Dahmer. I am, too." He shows me his score. Three twenty-five.

"Funny, I don't feel like eating anybody. Just killing them."

He laughs. "Yeah, me, too."

The counselor comes over and reads my test answers. "This suggests you are depressed, Jeremiah."

Duh. Both Doc Goldberg and the shrink here at Beaufort already figured that out.

"Yeah, well, what's there not to be depressed about?"

I see a head or two nod. The others know what I mean.

The counselor looks over everyone else's tests. We're all depressed. We all have Dahmer-level stress scores. No surprises.

"Okay, let's change gears. How many of you are easily angered at work?"

Nobody responds, but I can see we're all listening.

"How about at home? Do little things just send you off the handle?"

He has our complete attention.

"Nightmares. Do you have the same dream over and over? Or do you have different ones of a similar theme?"

The room remains quiet. I've been to funerals with a better atmosphere. The other Marines stare at the floor, or the table, or their laps—anywhere but at the counselor or one another. The one with the cane clutches it hard against him, as if it were a talisman that could ward off the reality he's facing.

"Have any of you had trouble at work? With coworkers, or doing the job?"

He's describing my life. And I can't help but hate him for that.

"Do you drink to sleep? I know when I came home, that's the only way I could get through the nights."

A quick glance up and I see admissions on every face. We've all been doing this.

"Have any of you had flashbacks to Iraq or Afghanistan?"

The question triggers a memory. When I first got back from Fallujah, I was given thirty days of leave and flew home to Ohio. My little town gave me a hero's welcome complete with a mini-parade, banners, and music. I was totally humbled by it. Hundreds of people came out to greet me and offer their support. I spent the day cradled in my past, and for once I felt safe and at ease.

That night, at my mother's house, Jessica came over and we ate dinner together as a family for the first time in over two years. We laughed and talked and reminisced. I felt almost normal.

It was a perfect evening. But then things went terribly awry. Just after Jessica left, I grabbed my duffel bag off the living room sofa and started for my room up on the second floor.

When I reached the stairs, the smell of gunpowder assailed me. I froze. For a second, my mother's house disappeared and I was back in the Soldier's District, stuck on the stairwell as bullets smacked the concrete wall above my head.

I tried to take a step. My legs refused to move. My mother wandered into the living room and saw me. "Jeremiah? Are you okay?"

My face squeezed in anguish, my heart thudded in my chest so heavily I thought I'd explode.

"Jeremiah?" My mother's voice became shaky.

My eyes went wide with fear. I couldn't take another step. My legs melted and I fell facedown. I remember the smell of carpet intermingled with my memory of cordite and blood.

"Jeremiah!" my mother cried. "What's going on? What's the matter?" Tears poured down her face. I couldn't move. I couldn't answer. She ran to my side, pulled me to my feet, and led me to the couch.

I never got to my bedroom on that trip. I spent the entire time sleeping on that living room couch.

So flashbacks, yeah. Had those, too.

Are we all damned by our experience? Is our fate to be our counselor's? Those who counsel drug addicts the best are the ones who used themselves and made it through rehab. All they know is their experience with addiction. It consumes their life. Will that be our fate as well? Will this collective experience come to dominate who we are and what we've become? I don't want the rest of my life defined by PTSD.

The questions send me spiraling downward. I don't know if it is even worth staying around to find out.

The meeting ends with hardly another word. The counselor tells us he hopes we'll come back, but I doubt any of us will. Our private hell is just that. Sharing it will only make it worse and reinforce the magnitude of what we've all lost.

Normalcy. That's what we've lost. And that's all we want to return to, but sitting here today convinces me that probably will never happen. I understand now why those who fought the Great War came to be known as the Lost Generation.

The Marine with the cane struggles to his feet. He looks like an old man as he hobbles for the door. He can't be more than twenty. The Marine with the wounded throat holds the door open for him. He offers a quick thanks, but they don't exchange eye contact. We are all ashamed.

The wreckage of my generation. I am part of this aftermath. We're caught in the clutches of something we don't understand and have no idea how to fix.

The Marine with the cane limps out of sight, dragging one leg as he goes. I want to cry.

I flee the meeting room for my psychiatrist's office. I'm ushered inside, and the doc, who is a navy lieutenant commander, sees the anxiety level on my face.

"How'd group go?" she asks.

"Miserable. I feel worse now than before I went."

She smiles at me, but I am not reassured. "Well, I guess you won't be going back."

"Yeah. Guess so, Doc."

She reaches for her prescription pad and starts to scribble. "These will help. Take them only as directed, okay? Nothing more, nothing less. And don't skip or stop taking them."

"Roger that."

She hands the prescription to me. I look down. I've already been put on Zoloft and Saraquil. This one's for something called Clonopin.

"Take it at night. It'll help you sleep. Be sure not to drink any alcohol. Come see me in two weeks. In the meantime, I've recommended you for limited duty."

"Thank you, Doc."

That night, I take the Clonopin. I've never done any drugs before, not even pot. The hardest I get is Wild Turkey neat. But within minutes of taking the Clonopin my life suddenly has no edges. Everything becomes soft and muted. I stop caring. As I reach my bachelor's bed in my near-empty apartment, I feel the omnipresent sense of anxiety release its grip on me. The misery vanishes, replaced by a neutral sense of nothingness. The Clonopin neuters every emotion. I find blessed balance in its artificial peace. As I fall asleep, boots still on my feet, I have one final cognizant thought.

Oh yeah. I can get used to this.

Chapter Seven

DRUG TRIP

Spring 2006

CONSCIOUSNESS RETURNS SLOWLY. No nightmares. No lingering memories of Jessica and our good times to wake up to this morning. The last fourteen hours have been a drug-induced nothingness. I peel one crusty eyelid open. The other seems glued shut. My bedroom is just a blur, like an out-of-focus photo shot by a drunk.

My head throbs. As I try to sit up, a wave of nausea overtakes me. I struggle not to puke in my sheets.

Welcome to the aftermath of a Clonopin ride, Jeremiah. It is the morning-after price of the chemical-born peace it delivers.

I force open my other eye. The world's edges start to return. Focus is overrated. Still, I've got to get moving. I risk getting to my feet. Bad move. I sway backward and nearly fall onto the bed. A few staggered steps later, I make it to the shower, where my death grip on the faucet handle is about the only thing keeping me on my feet.

The hot water streams across my face and kick-starts my heart. I start to return to the land of the living.

More like the land of the lost.

Twenty minutes later, I'm shaved and dressed and as ready for the day as I'll ever be. Ready except for one new ritual. In the kitchen, I find a glass of water. First I take a Saraquil tablet. Next I take the Zoloft. By the time I reach the Tacoma, my legs feel as if they are encased in lead.

Get the door open. Climb inside. Now I've got to reach over and close the door, but this leaves me fatigued. Since going on the medication, my life has become a series of mini-mountains to overcome. Things that everyone else takes for granted and does without thought take conscious effort and energy. For me, the game is radically different now.

I pull the door closed as my chin hits my collarbone. I drift, eyes closed, mind floating gently. I don't care. I feel no emotion. Nothing. I could watch my mother die right now and just shrug it off.

Something startles me awake. I look around, shaking, unsure of where I am. Then cognizance flushes back into my brain. But it is muted and dull, as if my thoughts are swimming through deep water. My mind shouts at me, I have places to be, obligations to fulfill. I couldn't give a shit. The voice I hear resembles the teacher's from the old *Peanuts* cartoon: Dissonant, vaguely disturbing, but not intelligible.

It dawns on me that I've got to put the Tacoma in gear. My hand fumbles on the shifter, and I start rolling. Today, I have to return to Parris Island again. My ten-day leave ended three days ago. Now, I must arrive every morning to the glowering looks of my fellow NCO's. I live in the shadow of my shame every day. If I could feel, it would be unbearable. But thanks to the cocktail the shrink at Beaufort has cooked up for me, all I feel is a distant discomfort.

"Workman? Hey, Workman?"

My eyes fly open and I see Staff Sergeant Edds peering through the driver's-side window at me. How'd he get to my apartment complex? How'd he even know where I lived?

Then I realize I'm at Parris Island. The Tacoma's parked across two spots in the lot near the Mainside Barracks.

"What?"

"Hey, you okay?"

God, how I hate that question. I don't even remember getting here.

"I'm fine. Just tired."

Edds opens the truck's door. "Yeah, you were snoozing away when I saw you."

I unbuckle my seat belt and slide out of the truck. Edds closes the door then grasps my shoulder.

"Come on, we'll go over to company headquarters together."

Since returning from leave, Edds and Allen have been just about the only two Marines who have even talked to me. Everyone else avoids me like the Ebola virus. At the chow hall every day, I sit alone, a circle of empty spaces around me to underscore my outcast status. Nobody wants to sit next to the crazy guy.

We check in at company, where I get my assignment for the day. Apparently, last night a recruit broke his hand when a spring-loaded window in the barracks snapped shut on him. My job is to check every window to make sure they're functioning properly. Each squad bay has sixty windows. Each company has six squad bays. I've got to open and close three hundred and sixty windows today.

Eighteen months ago, the Corps entrusted me with a mortar crew. I rained death down on my country's enemies in Fallujah. Now all I'm fit for is janitorial work.

Whatever. The drug cocktail numbing my mind prevents me from caring about this latest indignity. I shamble off to the barracks and get started.

Halfway through the first bay, Captain Ricardo Hope, our company commander, comes looking for me. "Sergeant Workman, the battalion commander wants to see you."

Uh-oh.

"Aye, sir."

"He's in my office. Let's go."

I follow Captain Hope in silence. When we reach his office, the battalion commander rises from a couch.

Now I'm in for it. Whenever an E5 NCO like me gets on a lieutenant colonel's radar, it is never good. I knew there would be repercussions from the chow hall incident. Here it comes.

I go to parade rest.

"Sergeant Workman," the battalion commander says with stiff formality.

They're going to charge me with something. Dereliction of duty? The Zoloft-Saraquil cocktail tramples down the panic I start to feel. I stand expressionless, awaiting my fate.

"Yes, sir?"

His hand reaches out to my shoulder. "Sergeant Workman, we have just learned that you have been awarded the Navy Cross."

The news leaves me utterly speechless. I blink and stare dumbly at my lieutenant colonel.

"Sergeant Workman?"

"Sir?" My head is swimming. The news has cut across my medicated fog. I'm reeling.

Why me? What about Raleigh and Hillenburg? What about Kraft?

"You should know that your company commander in Iraq put your name in for the Medal of Honor."

"He did?" The Medal of Honor is the highest award for bravery the United States bestows on its warriors. There has not been a living recipient of it since 1971. The Navy Cross is the second highest valor award. Less than sixteen have been approved since 9/11.

"We will schedule a ceremony within the next few weeks. You'll want to have your family come out for this."

When I first joined 3/5, we went down to Twenty-Nine Palms for some pre-deployment training. While there, we stood in formation and watched as Captain Brian Chontosh received his Navy Cross. The moment inspired awe in me. Here was a man—no, a legend—who had killed twenty Iraqi soldiers in close combat fighting inside a trench network outside of Baghdad during the 2003 invasion. To those of us in the formation, he was the ultimate rock star of the Marine Corps, a warrior who showed us all the way with the example he set under fire.

After the ceremony, I joined the reception line to congratulate him. When I shook his hand and locked eyes with him, I felt humble and small, like I'd just met Michael Jordan. His accomplishments made mine look pale.

I am not worthy of this medal. There were others that day who deserved this accolade.

The battalion commander offers a wide, genuine smile. "Sergeant Workman, we could not be more proud of you. Congratulations."

We shake hands. Captain Ricardo Hope takes his turn. "This is a great honor for our company."

As I shake his hand, a memory intrudes on the moment. I'm on the back of the truck on that street in Fallujah, staring down at my three unmoving friends. Raleigh's arm sloughs away from his face and slops against the truck bed. Why isn't anyone helping my brothers?

"Doc!!"

"Sergeant Workman! He's fucking dead." Our corpsman's words echo from the past.

Three dead Marines. And I'm the one they've made a hero.

Chapter Eight

THE LAST MEDAL

May 12, 2006
Parris Island, Peatross Parade Deck

A BIBLE SITS ON my mother's nightstand. She's had it there for as long as I can remember. It isn't anything special—not one of those leather-bound volumes that dates back a hundred years and has all the family births and deaths written into it. No, nothing like that. It is a simple Bible with a purple soft cover. She reads it almost every night, but the pages contain something more to her than God's words.

After my grandmother died in December 2003, I came home for the funeral. One evening, after all the guests had left our house, I turned off the lights in the living room and went to say goodnight to my mother. I found her in her bedroom, staring at the Bible on her nightstand. She opened it to reveal two ribbons and medals.

"These were your grandfather's," she told me as she lifted the first one up. It was a Purple Heart.

"Where'd you find that?" I asked, incredulous. My grandmother had told me he'd served in the Army, but I had no idea that he'd been wounded.

"In your grandmother's things."

She handed the Purple Heart to me. I held it like it was an ancient treasure with the ribbon draped over my index finger. Its gold edges gleamed in the bedroom's light.

"He was wounded during World War II."

"How?"

"Nobody knows. He never talked about it. We just know he was infantry and fought in Europe."

"My grandfather was a hero?" Why hadn't I heard about this? My grandfather always seemed such a sore subject, almost taboo. We never spoke of him. All I knew is that he died long before I was born.

My mother looked away. She said nothing for a long moment, and I wondered if I had somehow said something wrong.

Slowly, she withdrew another medal from the Bible. As she handed it to me, she said softly, "He was a brave man. Once."

I regarded the second medal. It was a Bronze Star for Valor, awarded for courage under fire.

"What did he get this for?"

"I don't know."

"Did Grandpa die in the war?"

"No. He just didn't talk about it."

Whatever my grandfather did during the war, he was a hero. At least he was to those who fought with him and led him into battle.

When I came home to Ohio after my Iraq deployment, I gave my mother my Purple Heart. She clutched it to her chest as tears streamed freely. She put it in the Bible with my grandfather's medals. They're close to her heart there.

As I sit in the VIP section of the reviewing stands at Parris Island, dressed in my service charlies and still looking like a drill instructor, I see that Bible in my mind: Simple, unadorned, and unpretentious, just like my mom and the life she's lived. Tonight, she'll have another medal to tuck away. I hope it'll be the last to find a home in that Bible. There's a premium paid for each one of these awards, and I pray that her future grandkids won't have to pay it as we did. Two generations. We never met, but today I feel Grandfather's presence.

The afternoon is beautiful. The sun shines, but it lacks the intensity of summer. A cool breeze blows and it feels crisp in my lungs. I turn my face skyward and close my eyes. There are precious few days as perfect as this one here at Parris Island. They always seem to be too cold, too humid, or too hot. Today, though, we've been blessed by the weather gods.

The parade deck stretches out in front of the reviewing stands. Alpha Company from our battalion graduates today, and the men parade before us, ready to move forward and become Marines. They'll soon feed the machine in the Middle East.

A band plays. These freshly minted Marines march with pride and perhaps a little bit of a swagger. Jessica sits next to me, the wind playing with her shoulder-length strawberry blond hair. She's wearing a new black sundress for the occasion. Beside her sit her folks. My mom's a row behind me. My dad hasn't spoken to me since I left for Iraq. I don't even know where he is anymore.

The recruit company comes to a halt. They turn and face the review stands. The band plays a new song. That's my cue. I rise from my seat and march out of the bleachers and onto the asphalt parade deck. I try hard to forget the thousands of eyes that are on me now. The spotlight does not suit me. I'd much rather be closeted away from the world, hidden from view. Today, I'm on display.

I will be gracious. I will be a gentleman. But how can I not feel like a fraud when I came home and Raleigh and Hillenburg and Phillips did not? This is their Navy Cross, not mine.

I stand at attention. The graduating recruits form up behind me.

The event narrator comes over the PA system to introduce me. A round of applause follows. It sounds like machine-gun fire, crackling in the distance.

"Attention to orders!" the narrator continues. Our depot sergeant major and Brigadier General Richard Tryon march out in front of me. I stare straight ahead. The narrator begins to read my citation.

"The President of the United States takes pleasure in presenting the Navy Cross to Jeremiah W. Workman for services set forth in the following."

Why are they doing this? Don't they know that I'm anything but a hero?

"For extraordinary heroism while serving as a squad leader . . ."

The words fade and echo away. I can hear my own breathing. My vision starts to narrow.

Oh God. Not again. Not here.

". . . Corporal Workman fearlessly exposed himself and laid down a base of fire that allowed the isolated Marines . . ."

Gunfire erupts around me. Instinctively, I want to duck, but through my tunnel vision I see General Tryon smiling at me. It's okay. I'm at Parris Island. There's no shooting.

Cordite. I smell cordite. Then I hear the *tink-tink-tink* of spent casings bouncing off concrete. The sound causes me to start sweating.

Hold it together, Jeremiah. You've got to get through this. I take a deep breath. The world goes out of focus.

". . . Corporal Workman's heroic actions contributed to the elimination of twenty-four insurgents . . ."

General Tryon is gone. In his place, I see three faces staring accusingly at me. Raleigh Smith, Eric Hillenburg, and James Phillips regard me in cold silence. Hillenburg's temple is shattered by a bullet wound. Blood leaches from it and trickles down his cheek. His eyes are black as coal.

I want to reach for them and scream I'm sorry. I'm sorry I could not save you. I'm sorry I have stolen your valor.

". . . By his bold leadership, wise judgment, and complete dedication to duty, Corporal Workman reflected great credit upon himself and upheld the highest traditions of the Marine Corps and the United States Naval Service."

Raleigh steps forward. His face is devoid of color, his eyes lack definition. I want to embrace him. I want to flee. Instead, all I can do is stay rooted in place.

A roar of gunfire assails my ears. It grows like thunder until it overwhelms every other sound. My eyes jerk left and right, searching for the source until I realize it is only applause. Thousands of hands clap for me. People whistle. The crowd rises as one and cheers wildly.

Raleigh's gone. General Tryon has stepped close to me. He pins the Navy Cross to my uniform and shakes my hand.

The applause grows even louder. Whistles like incoming artillery shells cut across the parade deck. My legs quiver. Will I make another public spectacle of myself?

The sergeant major shakes my hand and offers his congratulations. I smile as best I can, but it is a phony effort. I have never felt such utter despair as I do now.

The three of us march off the parade deck and back to the VIP section of the stands. I don't look down at the stairs as we climb back to my family.

"Jeremiah! Jeremiah!" my mother calls to me. The general leans forward and gives her a hug. She turns and wraps her arms around me, suffusing me for a few fleeting seconds with a childhood sense of safety. But then I hear the *tink-tink-tink* of shell casings on concrete, welling up from the past again, and the moment is lost, replaced by an awkward sense of complete vulnerability.

Hillenburg stands beside me. I see him from the corner of my eye. He's flanked by Raleigh Smith and James Phillips. I didn't know James that well, but every time I saw him it seemed he was either talking about his girl, Kitty, back in Plant City, Florida, or his hot rod Mustang. I had an '03 for a while. We shared a love of pony cars.

I cannot bear to look at them now. Not while I'm surrounded by family and a thousand cheering fans. But they know what I did. They know what happened. And they are never going to let me forget. I failed them, and they paid the price.

General Tryon introduces himself to Jessica and gives her a quick hug. Her eyes are glassy and moist. I see pride on her face. Behind that pride something else tries to hide. It takes me only a moment to recognize it: Deep, abiding, guilt.

Part of me wants to console her and take her in my arms. I'd tell her all the things I've needed to say for all these months we've lived in marital limbo. We'd figure out a way to return to how it was before we thrashed each other and destroyed what was once between us. Perhaps the only redemption for either of us lies in our effort to stay together.

My mother's arms are still around me. She sobs against my chest.

The general interrupts. "After the pass and review, there are some reporters who want to talk with you."

That is going to take supreme effort to endure. "Yes, sir," I tell him. I'll let Captain Chontosh's example be my guide. At Twenty-Nine Palms, he was mobbed by people wanting a piece of him. He stood and took it with a graciousness that impressed everyone that day, especially me. I will have to do the same. Then I'll lock myself away somewhere far from humanity and not emerge for a week. If ever.

Jessica slips into my arms. She clutches me hard, and I give her a kiss on the cheek. It is salty from her tears.

As we pull apart, we make eye contact. It feels like a stab in the heart. Her guilt and my shame connect for that split second, and both of us verge on breaking down. She hugs me again, if only to break the spell. I hear her whisper in my ear, "Jeremiah, I had no idea what you went through."

No, you didn't.

I don't know what to say.

"I wish I had been there for you," she says through a barely controlled sob.

I wish that, too.

We break our embrace, and I sit down next to her. The applause ripples and fades, like distant gunfire in a dying city. My face turns to the sun, eyes closed as I absorb its mild spring warmth.

When I open my eyes, I see only a smoke-shrouded stairwell.

Chapter Nine

TEN-STEP KILL ZONE

December 23, 2004
Fallujah

Jeremiah?

What?

Open your eyes, Jeremiah.

Now why the fuck would I want to do that?

Screaming, shouting, bullets flying. I've reverted to a three-year-old's mind-set: It can't hurt me if I can't see it.

My feet are moving. I feel my boots drumming across a carpeted floor.

Get your eyes open, Marine!

My right boot hits concrete and I know I've reached the stairs. Automatically, I lift my left foot. It scrapes the lip of the second step, throwing me off balance. For an instant, my blind charge almost devolves into a belly flop.

I open one eye. I'm looking down at my legs. Keep going. Don't stop, or the guys behind you will get hung up in a kill zone and die. Suddenly, I'm a running back again, dodging and weaving through linemen and linebackers, only this time the roar of the crowd has been replaced by the sound of assault rifles barking for my demise.

Two yards. That's all I need to gain. I feel myself sliding, balance shot, the tackle imminent. I've broken free before, and on the gridiron I learned how to throw myself those extra yards in defiance of equilibrium and gravity.

Right boot slaps another step. I'm upright again, balance restored. Left boot. A bullet smacks the wall to my right. I felt that one, hot on the back of my neck. A burst of automatic fire sends chips of concrete and dust spinning into my path. Shards careen off my eye protection while others cut my face.

Two more steps. The gunfire swells. The stairwell echoes with whining ricochets. Dust and smoke curls spin in the turbulence created by my wake.

Somehow, I am not hit as I reach the tenth and final step.

I reach the landing in a dead sprint that carries me straight into the wall. I slam into it just as I pivot to the left, ready to make the last dash to the top of the stairs. Above me, smoke shrouds most everything from sight. Muzzle flashes flare like lightning in a thunderhead. Are they shooting at me? Are they friend or foe? I have no idea.

A bullet cracks past me, gouges the wall just above my head and whistles away. I duck slightly while bringing the M16 to my shoulder. Who's shooting at me? I don't see a soul upstairs.

"You see anyone?" I shout to the men stacked behind me. No response—at least none that my grenade-damaged ears picked up. I shout again. Nothing. I flick my eyes right.

I'm alone on the landing.

What the hell? Did everyone else get killed coming up the first flight of stairs?

I turn and duck lower, searching for the rest of my squad.

"Workman!" A voice cuts through the din of battle.

In the gloom below, I see the entire stack, still standing in the hallway. The lieutenant shouts something unintelligible at me.

"Get up here!" I yell back. Everyone shakes their head. Kraft and Smokes motion frantically for me to come back.

"Fuck that! Get your ass down to us!"

Back through the kill zone? No thank you.

What the hell? Why did they abandon me? Why do they want me to come to them?

Because there's a river of bullets between us, that's why.

I didn't come this far for nothing. The landing offers some cover, and I inch along the wall, past a dirty yellow-and-green curtain that covers a small window. Whoever is shooting at me can't see this part of the stairwell, yet they spray and pray. The wall flanking the first set of stairs erupts once again as bullets tear into it.

I reach the second flight. Ten more steps upward and I'll be in some sort of a foyer. I glance back down at the rest of the stack. Kraft waves frantically at me. The lieutenant's lips are moving, but I can't hear what he's saying. Smokes looks like he's playing a game of charades.

Ignore them. Find those Marines.

From my new position, I can see part of the second floor's layout. Two rooms open off the foyer on the right. Another opens off the left. A door to an outside porch stands open across the foyer, casting a rectangular beam of light through the smoke and dust.

I take these steps two at a time. Four shy of the foyer, I pause and hug the wall on my right. If I go any farther, the Muj in the far room will be able to see me.

What about the left side? Rifle up, I peer over my sight into that room. From what little I can see, it appears to be a bedroom. Nothing moves in it. For the moment, it doesn't seem to be a threat. I inch upward, and lean out to the left to try and get a look around.

Muzzle flashes wink from the far right room. An instant later, bullets snap past me. The wall flanking the first flight of stairs takes the brunt of the fusillade again. The barrage spooks me badly, and all I can do in return is fire a few unaimed shots back into the smoke. It doesn't affect the Muj, who continue to hammer away with a machine gun.

This was a prepared fighting position with clear fields of fire. They've drawn us into a fight on their terms on unfamiliar ground for us, inside a well-built house that mitigates our firepower advantage. We can't call a tank to help us out. We can't call in an airstrike. They've got us in a point-blank embrace, and all we can do is slug it out with the weapons we hold.

"Workman! Get down here!" somebody yells at me.

Movement in the smoke catches my attention. Somebody's in the foyer. I hold fire and scan for this new target. I can't kill what I can't see.

A tumbleweed of smoke pinwheels past the top of the stairs, peeling back the shroud that obscured my view. Forms take shape, and I realize I'm looking at a heavy oak desk positioned just to the right of the open door to the porch.

There's somebody underneath it.

"Raleigh? Is that you?" I realize that I've spoken in an almost conversational tone. The words are swamped by the din of battle.

Another tendril of smoke drifts clear of my view. I'm right. Raleigh Smith, our platoon's one-man comedic act, lies huddled under the desk. Back to the outside wall, he's holding his M16 and looking toward the far right room.

"Raleigh! Raleigh!" I call to him, but my voice cannot carry over the gunfire. He remains fixated on the room, his moon-shaped face in profile to me. He's a redheaded kid from Montana with a dusting of freckles and a perpetual grin. He specializes in the most outrageous, nasty, and politically incorrect humor I've ever been around, all of which always leaves the rest of us in stitches. For all that craziness, somebody started calling him Section Eight. It caught on, and he loved it; I think it encouraged him to play the part.

He's not smiling now. His face is covered with dark gray dust and grime. Sweat has dripped from his brow and created little tiger stripes of clean white skin. His lips are tight and bent into a sort of slack frown. I've never seen a man with such an expression. What's the matter with him?

"RALEIGH! FOR GOD'S SAKE! RALEIGH!"

His brown eyes shift toward me. I take this as a good sign until I see them, dark, saucer-wide and gutted, like he's a dead man waiting for his body to acknowledge this fate.

"RALEIGH! ARE YOU HURT? ARE YOU HIT?"

Nothing. No sign of comprehension, no sign he's heard me. He continues that empty stare into the room to our right.

A few days before, our platoon took a break during another long and boring patrol through Fallujah. We'd found piles of Soviet-bloc weapons, everything from your basic AK-47 to Moison-Nagant bolt-action rifles. In one house, I tumbled across a stash of 7.62mm ammo stamped with the Nazi swastika that dated from 1939. Grenades, mortar shells, plastic explosives, mines, rockets, and RPG launchers rounded out our haul for the day.

There, in the middle of this devastated city, my boys were like kids in a candy shop. All the weapons proved irresistible to their sense of mischief, and soon they were blasting away at the ruined buildings with some of the more exotic goodies in the day's catch.

I stayed in one of our Humvees, watching the display of foreign fire-power, afraid that Major D. would tumble onto what we were doing and give us all a serious ass-chewing. We love Major D.; he's the most hard-core officer we have, but he can be hell in a uniform if he gets pissed off.

Raleigh walked by the Humvee, a huge, toothy grin on his face. In his hands, he held a Soviet grenade.

"Raleigh, don't even think about it!"

He turned his moon face to me. All freckles and fun, his mirth-filled eyes and silly smile broke my resistance, and before he even said anything I started to laugh.

"Raleigh, come on man."

"Sorry, Jeremiah. I gotta." He gave a little nod toward a nearby well.

"Don't do it!" I offered weakly.

Raleigh bounced over to the well, primed the grenade, and with great flourish, dropped it. A second later, we heard it splash down. Raleigh backed off, grinning like a Cheshire cat.

When the grenade went off, it triggered a veritable volcanic erup-tion of brackish shit water. It spewed out of the well and poured down around Raleigh, who fled from its wretched stench. I laughed so hard, I nearly fell out of the Humvee. When the eruption ended, Raleigh gave me the thumbs-up and went off in search of more devilry.

Bullets splinter the oak desk, but Raleigh doesn't even flinch. He is eerily still and silent. I call to him again and again, but he cannot hear me.

Move to him, Jeremiah.

If I climb the remaining four steps, I will die for nothing.

It doesn't matter, go to him, he's not just pinned down. He's got to be hurt.

I can't see any blood, just dirt and filth on him.

Keeping low, I inch up to the next step. Another few inches, and I'll lose the protection of the stairwell wall. To test the waters, I lean out to the left and peer around the corner.

The Muj shift targets. The oak desk stops shuddering and the air around me fills with raging wasps. I pull my head back. No good.

I've got to get to Raleigh. He's only ten feet away from me, but the gulf between us may as well be the Atlantic Ocean.

"Come on, Raleigh!"

With supernatural slowness, his head turns slightly. His eyes are un-focused. He looks my way, but recognition eludes him. All I see in them is endless darkness.

I'm alone. The realization strikes a hammer blow, and suddenly I feel like the last man on earth, peering over a precipice that yawns down into blackness. I reel backward, cold terror seizing me in its grip.

I tumble down the stairs to the safety of the landing. The din of battle is even louder here, as the gunfire echoes around the confines of these concrete walls.

Below me, ten steps and a kill zone away, the rest of the squad stands in the first-floor hallway. They're still calling to me, trying to get me off the landing.

There's no way I can do this alone. We need to overwhelm the Muj in the far right room with every bit of firepower we have. Then we'll be able to cross the foyer and get to Raleigh.

"Get up here!" I scream at my men.

"Get down here!" the lieutenant shouts back.

Fuck all. Will I really have to do this again?

The wall flanking the first flight of stairs dissolves into flying concrete again. The Muj have me pinned down. I don't want to cross that river of bullets, and the rest of the squad doesn't want to charge up through it.

Raleigh doesn't have time for this impasse.

No, he doesn't.

Go get your men, Jeremiah.

Time for a goal-line, up-the-gut plunge. In high school, I was very good at those dramatic leaps. I'd sail over the defensive line to crash down in the end zone, ball in hand, victory in our grasp. Can I do it now? I don't know. With my flak jacket, I'm wearing about sixty pounds of gear and carrying two rifles. All that weight will work against me.

Raleigh needs us. Do it.

I fling myself down the stairs, headfirst. The Muj are ready for me, and the raging hornets return. A bullet skims right past my forehead as I arch and plummet for the first-floor hallway. Another one nearly strikes the back of my neck. Another one skips off a concrete step, bounces into the wall, and spins back upward and past me.

I don't make it. Instead, I belly flop four steps short of the goal line. As I come down, my chin slams into one of the steps so hard I wonder if I haven't shattered my teeth. My neck snaps back, my back wrenches in a spastic reaction. I slide forward, dragging my chin down one more step and leaving a smear of blood and scuffed skin behind.

I'm still in the kill zone. The Muj pour it on. Their machine gun tears off a long, unfocused burst. Bullets saw back and forth over my head. They're aiming too high, and that's the only thing that saves me.

Hands reach out and grab my arms. They pull me off the stairs and back to the safety of the first-floor hallway. I'm pulled to my feet, and I find myself next to Smokes and Kraft. They ran forward and risked the fusillade to save me.

"You okay?" Kraft yells in my ear. His lips are only about five inches from my head, yet it sounds like he's on the other side of town.

I try to answer, but no words come out. My legs feel unsteady, and I lean against the wall as I try to clear my head. No good. The belly flop and chin blow have concussed me worse than any helmet-to-helmet hit I ever took. My mind swims. Coherent thought eludes me.

"Hey, Workman! What's going on up there?" Smokes says, getting right in my face.

"Yeah, what'd you see?" Kraft echoes.

I can't answer. Everything seems surreal. The walls spin slowly. I can't get my balance.

Kraft grips my shoulder, and I flinch in pain. "Workman? How many Muj are up there?"

"Did you see 'em? Did you see our guys?" Smokes demands.

My head clears enough to answer with another question. "What the hell happened? Why the fuck didn't you guys come up with me?"

Smokes and Kraft exchange an angry glance. Neither speak for a moment. I press them, "What's going on?"

"The lieutenant hesitated," Kraft tells me.

"He stopped. We couldn't move. Then you got on the stairs and all hell broke loose," Smokes adds.

I'm seized by raw fury. That LT had no business being with us, and then he screwed things up by freezing? Fucker.

I look around for him, but he's made himself scarce.

"What are we going to do?" Smokes asks.

The world pitches and rolls as if I were lost at sea amid storm-tossed swells. I start to stagger, but Kraft catches me.

Slowly, as if caught in a dream, I look back to the stairwell. The wall looks like grated cheese. The steps are covered with chips of concrete. Dust hangs in the air. Shadows zigzag across the scene, driven by the open outside door on the second floor. Just looking at it brings a new bolt of terror.

I can't go through that again.

You've got to get to Raleigh.

The world pitches, and for a minute it seems I'm thrown almost horizontal. The sensation generates a seasickness-like nausea. I press my back hard against the wall and pin myself in place until the moment passes.

Man, my bell's rung big-time.

Enough. Get to it.

Kraft and I make eye contact. We've known each other for over a year now. We've been in combat together. We both know what we're thinking, so not a word passes between us.

Smokes gets it, too. He nods at us and shouts to the men behind us. I turn and grip my M16 so hard my palms start to ache. I'm in front again.

Will they follow me this time?

Trust these men. They're good Marines.

I know I can trust Kraft. He's been the quiet strength of the platoon since we arrived here. He's one of the few NCO's who has been through infantry squad leader's course, so all of us, including our platoon sergeant, come to him for advice and help. Not only is he knowledgeable, there's no question about his courage. I've seen him do things no other man would risk, all in the name of protecting his men.

Bravery is a genetic trait in his family. His sister's a Marine based at Camp Fallujah. His grandfather is a full-blooded Navajo who served as a Marine code-talker during World War II. When he came home, he joined the FBI and was recently inducted into the Bureau's Hall of Fame.

Kraft won't leave me hanging. It's time to do this thing.

"Ready?" I call over my shoulder.

The men form up into a solid line, our bodies touching. When the last man is ready, he sends a shove forward. The next man in the stack does the same thing. It works its way to me, and this time Kraft has my back. He knees me in the butt, the signal to go.

I charge the shattered stairwell. I'm still riding on an angry sea, but somehow I keep my balance and reach the first step. The Muj react immediately. A cascade of bullets assault the wall. Again they've fired high. Before they can adjust, I ascend the stairs in a dead sprint. Behind me, I hear shouting. Somebody curses.

As I run, I swing my M16 over my shoulder and fire blindly up into the right side of the foyer. It's the best I can do at the moment to suppress the enemy.

At the landing, I pivot. The floor tips and I careen off the back wall and slide to the second flight of stairs. I'm out of the line of fire, but that's only the beginning. The real challenge lies ten more steps ahead.

I tackle the second set of stairs and close on the foyer entrance. Five steps from the top, I slow down and shield myself from the Muj by hugging the stairwell wall. As I start to stretch forward to catch a glimpse into the foyer, Kraft bumps into me. When I look back, I see the rest of the squad stacked down to the landing. The sight clears my head. The queasiness evaporates. They've followed this time, and their presence emboldens me.

I move to the top of the stairs. I'm exposed, but I don't care. If I go down, Kraft will lead the men to Raleigh. Right now, I've got to suppress the Muj and give the rest of the squad a chance to get their guns on line.

At the last step, I kneel down and get my barrel pointed into the far room's doorway, hugging the edge of the wall for cover. Pregnant clouds of smoke hang in the air, but through the doorway, I can make out an orange couch lying on its side. The Muj are probably using that for concealment.

I've got a target, and I light it up. My finger flutters on the trigger with hummingbird speed. In seconds, I've drained the magazine. I drop it out and slam another one home. I don't bother with my ACOG four-power scope, the action's just too close for it to be of any use. Instead, I keep both eyes open and try to watch where my bullets hit. My first mag goes high. The second, I aim a little lower, which sends bits of the couch careening around as the bullets tear into its stuffing.

I pause to reload one more time. As I do, I glance over to the desk. There's no sign of Raleigh.

Where the hell did he go? A quick check reveals the back bedroom on the left is still empty. He's not in there. Maybe he crawled through the outside door and is on the balcony. Good, this gives us a little extra freedom to use the firepower we're carrying.

Behind me, Kraft pushes out to the left until he's got a shot into the far room as well. He starts laying down suppressing fire as well. Snell moves up alongside me, staying as low as he can. He trains his AK-47 right next to my shoulder, flips the safety down one notch, and pulls the trigger. The assault rifle's barrel ejects a solid sheet of flame inches past my head. He lays on the trigger, spraying and praying with a full auto burst that empties the magazine in seconds. He drops it out and slips a fresh one in.

"Snell! You're breaking my goddamn eardrums!" I shout as I fumble for a fresh mag of my own. He either ignores me, or doesn't hear my comment. His barrel was so close to my left ear that I wonder if I'm permanently deaf now. All I hear is a steady ringing, like chimes in church.

I finish reloading and settle back down into a crouch. The volume of return fire hasn't diminished. We're still getting peppered by that automatic weapon. What is it? An RPK? PPK? RPD? Does it matter? It's lighting us up. We've got to knock that gun out if we're going to have any chance of assaulting forward.

I inch forward until just my rifle, head, and left hand are exposed past the corner of the wall. Thick smoke boils from our target room, masking the couch now. I make my best guess, and start pulling the trigger. Before I can get off three shots, a bullet blasts a thumb-sized chunk out of the corner right above my head. Something pings off my Kevlar helmet. I duck back and nearly lose my balance. Just then, Snell unleashes another skull-splitting full auto volley right next to my head.

For a good ten seconds I don't hear a thing. The action unfolds like a colorized silent movie. I see Kraft's lips moving as he tries to shout orders to the guys behind us. Snell's reloading again. At the landing, my closest friend, Levine, has edged out into the ten-step kill zone to get eyes on a target. He's blazing away with his M16. Next to him, our corpsman fires his 9mm pistol. Both are horribly exposed to the machine gun in the far room. Their bravery sends a sudden high voltage current of emotion through me.

What are you doing? Don't let these men down. Get back in the fight.

Okay. I'm better positioned than they are to take these Muj mother-fuckers out. I fold down in a shooter's crouch and grab the corner. I feel my M16 buck with every trigger pull. I can't see into the second room now—there's just too much smoke—but I lay it on anyway.

Magazine's empty. Reload. Slap the new mag home. Keep firing. Keep firing.

I lose track of time. Everything seems to slow down. The din grows so loud my already damaged ears simply can't process it all. By my third mag, I can't hear anything but a crazy bass drum beat.

I reload again. Streams of bullets hack furrows out of the foyer's gray-marble floor. The Muj gunner has shot low this time. The barrage causes a shower of marble shrapnel to spray across the three of us at the top of the stairs. We return fire as fast as we can load and reload.

At some point, I reach into my mag pouch and realize I'm down to two full mags. I grab one, ram it home, and start emptying it into the bedroom. We're giving it our best shot, but the Muj seem totally un-affected. They return fire furiously, and their bullets demolish whole sections of the wall and marble floor.

This isn't working. We've got to try something else, or we're never going to get up there.

Another fierce storm of bullets engulfs us, forcing me to slip behind the wall until it passes. When I swing back out to finish off this maga-zine, something flies out of the room. Bright yellow and shaped like a softball, it sails out into the foyer and lands heavily right in front of me. It spins to a halt less than five feet away.

"Oh my God! Grenade! GRENADE!"

Kraft and Snell have no time to react. I manage to turn my face to the wall and tuck my knee against my chin.

The world turns to flame.

Chapter Ten

BREAK CONTACT

December 23, 2004
Fallujah

B LOWTORCH ON MY neck. Blackness sheathed in flames. Charred flesh. Charred hair. The stench of both mingles with cordite and blood.

Falling now. Head spinning. Dizzy, dazed, and smoked.

Where am I?

Cathedral bells toll. Body shaking. I'm the clapper, slamming against the giant bell's copper side. Each impact sends shock waves through my system. One toll. Two. Then two more.

I cannot move.

Silence. Heat. Something's burning.

Baseball bat against flesh. Somebody's beating my leg. Each pulse of my heart sends pain to my brain.

I open my eyes to—darkness.

Am I dead? Is this hell?

Echoes in long hallways, distant and dim, rise from somewhere I cannot see. The echoes grow, swallowing the silence whole, until it's rushing at me like a runaway train. Eyes wide, yet unseeing, the sound waves collide with my ears. It roars to a crescendo, like the mother of all "1812 Overture" performances, but with the treble turned to ten on the stereo. I writhe in pain. Eardrums splitting, head bursting, resistance fading, I cannot stand against this tide. My shattered nerves slacken. I feel myself go limp.

I try to breathe, but I find no air. My chest seems compressed. The wind's been knocked out of me. I struggle and gasp. Finally, my lungs break the grip, but instead of oxygen, I inhale only smoke.

Throat burning, lungs aching, I cough and spasm until I throw up.

"Workman!" A distended voice calls to me in the darkness. It is ethereal, disconnected, and remote. I try to speak, but I've got no air for words.

"Workman!" The voice is louder now, but still muted and bass heavy.

Eyes open again, the blackness clings to me. Have I gone blind?

"Can't see!" I choke.

"Workman! You okay?"

Stirrings in the darkness. A form appears and begins to take shape. Kraft. I'm looking at Kraft. He's filtered through gray lenses, making him appear grainy and incomplete, like a washed-out bit of film found in some long-forgotten vault.

"Hey! Where you hit?"

I realize that I'm lying on my back halfway down the second flight of stairs. Consciousness seeps back into me. Kraft's face swims out of the grayness and resolves in vivid color. Smoke-stained skin, eyebrows burnt, his blackened lips stand in stark contrast to his pearl-white teeth.

Kraft. Thank God. I want to say something. Anything. His face, damaged, filthy or clean, is reassuring. Hell, I bet under his Kevlar and all that grime on his face, his hair is still pristine. Even in Fallujah, he tried to wash and gel it three or four times a day. Comes with being a California kid, I guess.

The edge of the wall at the top of the stairs dissolves into a flurry of fragments. They rain down on Kraft and me. The Muj are still shooting.

"Workman, goddamn, man! Are you hurt?"

I shake my head weakly.

"Good. Then get the fuck up!"

For a moment I see him back in the States, one night two weeks before we deployed. Nine hundred Marines turned out on the beach at Pendleton for one last bash before we went to war. Kraft and I were two of the new guys in the company, and we'd not fully escaped the awkwardness of being former Security Force Marines in a unit full of combat veterans from the initial invasion of Iraq. We stuck together, talked and drank ourselves stupid. That night, he became my first real friend in 3/5.

He pulls me up to a sitting position, and I realize the darkness was caused by a thick sheet of black smoke. It hangs around us, tasting like oil and smelling of kerosene. The grenade must have been some sort of homemade incendiary device.

On the landing, I see our corpsman has stopped firing. He's working on Levine, our fire-eating, Bronx-born New Yorker.

I look at Kraft. His pant leg is slick with blood. He's been hit. So have I. My leg aches, and blood leaches through my torn cammies and smears crimson on the stairs.

Just about everyone's been struck by shrapnel. Levine seems the worst off. A sliver of metal somehow got under his Wiley X glasses. Now his eye has filled with blood. He pushes away our Fijian corpsman, Doc Sunny, and I hear his Bronx-accented voice shout, "Fuck off, Doc. I'm good. I'm good."

"I'm good!" somebody else shouts.

Well, then so am I. I get to my feet. The insurgents on the second floor haven't eased up. If anything, they're burning through bullets like they've got a year's supply stockpiled up here.

Not reassuring.

I move back to the corner. Several fresh gouges greet me right at eye level, though I don't know if AK rounds or shrapnel dug these out. I've got a mag and a half left. I'll try to make them count.

One. Two. Three. I slip out around the corner and swing my weapon into firing position. A solid wall of smoke greets me. I have no targets. I can't even see the wall or the doorway on the right. Only the dimmest light from the open balcony door punctures the smoke.

Snell eases up next to me. Together we open fire. Kraft joins in. Soon, everyone with a shot returns to the action.

I pepper the smoke, hoping I'm getting at least a few shots through the right doorway. A click reveals I've emptied this mag. I drop it and grab my last one.

I sense movement behind me. I glance back and see Snell moving into firing position again. He's got an intense, almost eager expression on his face. Snell's one of those guys you can always trust to do the killing. He's quick with his weapon and has no problem pulling the trigger. He's also one of the most obnoxious human beings I've ever known.

Blond, good-looking; women seem to fall out of the sky and land on him, a fact that he loves to rub in our noses.

Right now, smoke has airbrushed his face, too. He pulls alongside me and uncorks his AK again. My ears explode and I start cursing him.

I'm halfway through my last mag when I realize Snell's gun isn't blasting in my ear anymore. I duck back against the wall and discover the squad's pulling out. Somebody gave an order that I couldn't hear.

Doc Sunny's close to Levine, pulling him toward the first flight of stairs. The others are backing up, getting ready for a rush through the ten-step kill zone. Kraft reaches up and takes my shoulder. Just as he does, the machine gun opens up again. Bits of concrete fly around us. Marble from the foyer floor is torn and shredded. I hug the wall and cringe as bullets ricochet around inside the stairwell.

When the latest volley stops, Kraft and I make eye contact. No words pass this time, but I know exactly what he expects me to do. I've got to cover the squad's withdrawal.

I'm going to be alone again. The thought sends another current of terror through me.

Levine and Doc Sunny look up at me. They're waiting to make the rush down the stairs, but they're exposed now.

A breath. Another quick one, and I spin and lean. Smoke fills the entire foyer now and I can't see more than a few feet in front of me. It doesn't matter, I've got to suppress the Muj. Rifle to my right shoulder, I lean out a bit farther. The stock feels reassuring, and I'm confident with my weapon. I just wish I had a human target.

I squeeze off a shot. An AK round wings off the edge of the wall in return. Below me, Doc Sunny and Levine make their dash down to the first floor. The machine gun snaps out a burst, but it goes high one more time. The lieutenant goes next. I pop off two more shots, then a third. My fire has no effect. The Muj suddenly bring everything they've got.

The stairwell erupts with singing, bouncing bullets. They zip from wall to wall like a bad Saturday-morning cartoon. The rest of the men tumble down the stairs as the automatic fire snaps at their heels.

Kraft reaches the landing. I put a few more rounds into the right side of the foyer, then grab the wall to await their response. When I glance down to see if Kraft has gone, I find him still on the landing, looking back up at me. Tension floods his face, but I see no fear. He's the rock. The man we'd all follow anywhere, anytime. Never a brag-gart, never loud or garish, he is a man of measured words. When he speaks, we listen. When he gives orders, he treats everyone like men. None of this, "Get the fuck over there, motherfucker!" style of lead-ership for him. He's calm, focused. Deliberate.

And right now, he's counting on me to keep him alive. I nod once, stand up, and start shooting.

Kraft makes his move. The machine gun sounds like an old Buick stripping its gears, but he makes it, too.

Five more shots, and my magazine's just about empty. I've lost count, but I've got maybe ten left, plus one in the pipe. Time to go—for now.

I back down the stairs, then edge out to the left. For a split second, the far room's door materializes out of the smoke. That's my target. I hammer it, trying to shoot low this time.

AK's bark. Their 7.62×39 rounds skip off the edge of the foyer and embed in the ceiling. More expensive marble gets chewed up. One round bounces off the wall to my left, zings behind me, and shatters the window at the back of the landing.

There's no safe place, just degrees of risk.

I back down two more steps, pause, shoot again, then move. Spent 5.56mm shell casings tumble to the steps. *Tink . . . tink . . . tink.* The AK's chant their mantra. The hornets buzz.

I reach the landing and slide into the right corner, next to the bro-ken window. The landing's covered with a film of black soot mixed with broken bits of glass, marble, and concrete. It makes for slippery footing.

The ten-step kill zone awaits. I can't see the enemy. I can't see Raleigh or any of the other Marines who were supposed to be on the second floor. We need to find them, but without any ammo, what good am I? What good are the rest of us?

Down on the first floor, Doc Sunny's working on Levine's eye. I can see the New Yorker protesting, but I can't hear his words. He's more than earned his pay today. For a long time, I wondered if he was all talk. When we were operating our mortars in the weeks before we went into the city, he complained constantly that he couldn't look the Muj we killed in the eyes. He lost people in the Twin Towers and joined the Corps to exact revenge. The mortars may have been vital to the Marines in the city, but for Levine, they denied him the opportunity to get in close and watch our enemies die.

Kraft hits the first floor and motions for me to make my run. After what happened the first time I came down, there's no way I'm going to do this upright. I drop to my belly, staying low as a snake, and scrabble across the landing to the first flight of stairs.

Time to go. I heave myself off the landing and do my best impression of a fleeing anaconda.

Somehow, through the smoke and chaos, the Muj detect me. Multiple guns erupt, and bullets start bouncing off the walls and steps, but once again, the enemy shoots high. Thank God. I crawl for my life until I reach the last two steps. Hands yank me forward into the first-floor hallway. Other than the blood seeping from the shrapnel wound in my leg, I appear to be unscathed.

"How you doin'?" Kraft asks me.

I give him a weak smile and a thumbs-up. "Livin' the dream."

Above us, the gunfire suddenly blossoms into a full-fledged symphony of destruction. AK's intermix with the machine gun. For a moment, I think I hear a SAW, then several M16's.

We need to get back into this fight as soon as we get Levine out and get more ammo. There's plenty of that waiting back at our trucks. But first, we'll have to run the gauntlet in the front yard.

PART II

Chapter Eleven

LINK BY LINK

June 2006
Richwood, Ohio

I OPEN MY EYES to the summer sun. Today we're blessed with shorts-and-shirtsleeve weather, and the cloudless sky gleams a brilliant blue. It is more than enough to lift my sagging spirits.

I'm home. For the first time since Iraq, I feel normal. Away from Parris Island, away from the Corps, things are coming back into focus for me at last. I can't help but smile.

"What's with the grin?" my wife asks.

"I'm happy," I say with honest surprise.

"That's a switch."

I don't answer that. She's seen nothing but misery from me since I came home, so I guess I deserved it.

"Hey Mom, check this out!" Jessica's sister calls to their mother, Alma Beal.

"What?" Alma asks, looking up from her flower garden. Her yellow mums are in full bloom, which gives the backyard a splash of color.

Sarah rifles a softball across the yard right into my mitt. I didn't even have to move. For a sixth grader, the kid's got a cannon for an arm.

"Very nice," Alma says then returns to weeding her flower garden.

"Keep your feet under you, Sarah," coaches Von Beal, Sarah and Jessica's dad. He watches us from across the yard, where he's fussing over a John Deere riding mower.

The weekend squire comes out to mow his lawn. . . .

I'm having a *Pleasant Valley Sunday* sort of moment. Thank God. I've needed one for two years. It feels good. Really good.

Von's a city councilor here in Richwood and has been a civic leader since Jessica and I were in high school together. He's also been like a surrogate father to me for years.

Jessica waves at me. "Come on, Jeremiah."

I toss the ball over to her. It slaps home in her mitt—the siren sound of summer here in the Heartland.

"Thanks for coming out," I say. Jessica was an athlete in high school. But ever since, she's been reluctant to do anything like this. I can't even remember the last time we've all played catch together.

Jess throws a pop fly to Sarah who, quick as a gazelle, snatches it up in her mitt.

No doubt about it. In a few years, Sarah's going to be a force in high school. She's tall and lanky with an easy grace that belies her speed. Ever since Jessica and I started dating, I've seen Sarah as my little sis. We used to have a great relationship. Now, we're in a rebuilding phase, just like Jess and I.

The ball comes my way. I catch it and toss it to my wife.

I didn't have the best family life as a kid. My folks divorced when I was very young. Mom remarried to an abusive drunk who ran the family with controlled terror. He destroyed all dissent either with his fists or with his voice.

A small wading pool sits near the flower garden. Von's two dogs caper in the water, and I pause to watch them. They're happily splashing and snapping at each other. Water drips from their snouts. Their eyes are bright and full of excitement.

After the divorce, my best friend was our family's dog, a rottweiler named Bart. It hated my stepfather, and tried one too many times to protect my mom from his violent outbursts.

"Jeremiah, come on! I'm going gray over here!" Jessica chides me. I flip the ball her way. It lands short, but she deftly scoops it up and launches a heater over to Sarah.

One day, I came home from school and watched my stepfather put a .22 rifle to my dog's head and pull the trigger. I guess he got tired of the dog standing up to him all the time. He was the only one who did.

I cried for hours. He called me a pussy. My stepfather taught me how to hate.

My good mood dims at that recollection. When I came home from Iraq, I wanted revenge. I was well-equipped to inflict it, too. He and my mom had long since split up, but I tracked him down and stood in his front yard calling him out. Content to beat up little kids and my mom, he turned coward the moment a Marine combat veteran wanted a piece of him. He sent his eighty-year-old dad out instead. I finally gave up and left with all the misery he inflicted on my family unavenged.

That was probably a good thing. Had he come out himself, I would have killed him. Iraq blurred my ability to govern how far I take things.

Since coming home, every confrontation or conflict comes down to a simple choice: win or lose. There is no in between, no diplomacy. We were trained to crush our enemies, overcome any obstacle no matter what the cost. That's been a real problem between Jessica and me. A spat will start, and I don't want to let it linger. I'll barrage her with vile words and low blows until she surrenders.

I've got to do better than that, but I don't know how. I go for the jugular every time. It seems instinctive now.

"Jeremiah, would you like anything to drink?" Alma asks me as she rises from her mums.

"No thanks, I'm good." She smiles warmly and disappears into the house.

"You know, Jess, we haven't done this since high school," I say.

She nods and suddenly flushes with sadness. Or maybe it's nostalgia. I can't tell.

Better times. She's thinking of better times.

"Eat this!" Sarah winds up and blasts me with another fastball. I snare it, pull the ball from my mitt, and give Jess some heat. "Double play!" I exclaim as Jessica catches it.

Sarah pumps her fist and smiles.

Don't dwell, Jeremiah. You brood way too much these days.

I never used to brood. I lived in the moment and enjoyed life's little things.

My mom's in a better place now. She found the strength to leave my stepfather years ago. Now she's married to Don Johnston, who is a hell of a nice man. He takes good care of my mom.

Everyone's happy but you these days, Jeremiah.

That's not fair. I'm happy now, in this moment, with these people who are my own.

I never had to work to be happy. At least, not after I met Jess. She became my girlfriend, but it quickly became more than that. I gained a family.

Von utters a curse and stands up from the riding mower. He studies it for a moment, then turns and storms into the house, probably in search of a tool or something.

The three of us play catch in the young summer's sun.

Maybe we can go back to the way it was.

I got hurt my junior year and ended up on crutches for most of the fall semester. Even though we hadn't been going together very long, Jessica took care of me. I'd go over to her house and the family would dote on me. Jess would put my leg up on the couch and bring me goodies to eat. Her mom and sis would go the extra mile to see that I was comfortable. Von would sit down and chat with me, not adult-to-teen, but man-to-man. I respected him from the first time he did that. In the years that followed, I learned to love him as a father.

For those last two years of high school, the Beal household became home base for me. I slept at my dad's house, but the rest of the time when I wasn't working or in school, I was over with Jess's family.

I felt comfortable. Safe. They showed me what a normal family life was like. With them, I grew out of my shell and found that life didn't have to be endured, it could be lived and enjoyed.

We'll barbeque tonight, and then Jess and I will bunk down in the basement living room. When I came home on leave from the Marines, I always slept down there. It's cool in the summer and isolated. Jess and I need to get to know each other again and remember why we've loved each other for so long.

Sarah catches the ball and feeds it over to me. "Wow! Your arm's gotten a lot stronger, kid!"

"I'm just warming up!"

The sis I never had.

The wife I always wanted.

The family I once joined.

Jess and I had our reception here. We got married in one of the newer churches in town after I proposed to her in a letter while still enduring boot camp. Von and Alma rented a couple of big circus-style white tents and set them up in the backyard. Ample food, plenty of friends, my adoration for Jessica—it seemed so perfect. But, like so many other things, it went wrong. Some of my friends started drinking, and Von cut them off since they weren't quite twenty-one yet. We had words. The words turned into a fight. The fight spread and fractured the wedding party. I ended up at my dad's house, surrounded by all my buddies, drinking and having a bonfire while Jessica's side occupied the reception tents.

We spent our wedding night apart, and I remember the mixture of anger and despair that invoked. I wanted nothing more than to run back to her, sweep her into my arms, and cast my pride aside to tell her what our connection meant to me. I couldn't do it. Too damn immature, I guess. Or too much pride.

Sarah throws another fastball my way. I drop it, and she teases me. Frowning, I scoop it up and toss it over to Jess.

"What? You're looking serious all of a sudden," she says to me.

"Just thinkin'."

"Don't think, it isn't good for you."

"Yeah, tell me about it."

Apologize? It took us days to do that. We drove south on our honeymoon trip, stopping off at our new apartment in Georgia to leave our dog in the care of some friends. By the time we got to Daytona Beach, we figured out a way to say sorry to each other.

I had picked our hotel based off an ad on the Internet. What I thought was a five-star resort turned out to be a hook-up hellhole complete with garish dolphins and flowers poorly painted on the building's neon blue walls. I rented the honeymoon suite for a week. When we went inside to explore it, we found a round bed and a heart-shaped Jacuzzi tub in a room that only Mayor Quimby, or a slumming Kennedy, would love. Overdone décor, obnoxious colors, and card-table cheap furnishings completed the place.

It rained all week. We never got out on the beach, which was only a few feet from our back window. Instead, we stayed inside, floated in that Jacuzzi tub, and ate chocolate-covered strawberries. By day two, the hurt of the reception was long over.

We've always had a crazy-deep, roller-coaster sort of connection, Jessica and I. Our highs defy description. Our lows are so bad people wonder why we're together. In between, we used to have tons of fun and loved each other as hard as two kids just starting out in life knew how to do.

The weather didn't matter. We hunkered down in our suite, talked for hours, and burned away all the problems we had with the sheer passion of our love. When time came to start our life together, we packed up and returned to Georgia, where we found our dog had been violently ill while we were gone. Our first act as a young married couple was to clean dog diarrhea out of every room in our apartment.

We just never could catch a break, could we?

But now, on this trip, I am going to make sure we do. I'll do this right and figure out a way to rebuild that roller-coaster connection we loved so much. I've got forty days to enjoy here in Ohio. I won't have to return to Parris Island until mid-July. This time will be for Jess and me, and we'll do it right this time.

Truth is, I am loathe to return to the Island. After the Navy Cross ceremony, reporters mobbed me. People wanted my autograph. Others asked how many insurgents I killed.

What kind of a question is that to ask a man?

After the mess hall incident, I became a pariah. Nobody would eat with me except Staff Sergeant Edds and Sergeant Allen. The rest of the NCO's refused to even make eye contact with me. They acted like whatever I had could infect them if I so much as looked at them.

The Navy Cross ceremony changed all that. Suddenly, everyone wanted to sit with me, buy me drinks, and hear my war stories. It seemed so two-faced that I didn't want anything to do with it. I just wanted to escape.

Here I am, running from what I've become by fading into the echoes of my past.

I'll take it. But this time, I will do better. I will give Jess what she needs, and I will do my best to overcome what she did to me. To us.

"Hey Jess," I call to her just as she throws a curveball to Sarah.

"Mmm?"

"'Member when I first got back from Iraq? We stayed in that cabin?" She smiles at the memory.

God, I love her smile. I haven't seen enough of it since I got back.

"Yeah."

"We need to do that again."

Sarah sends the ball back to me, and I throw it right back at her. As it smacks home in her mitt, Jessica turns to me and I see genuine happiness in her eyes. "I'd like that."

"Oh God. You're not gonna get all mushy here. Come on, let's just play!" Sarah scowls at us. But we've had our moment. Maybe there is hope.

Dare I believe that? The cynic I've become balks at such vulnerability. Still, the shreds of who I once was want to cling to that chance.

Sarah pitches another fastball my way. This time, she misses the mark. The ball whizzes over my head and lands in the neighbor's backyard.

I turn to go fetch it. Alarmed, Sarah shouts, "Jeremiah! Don't go get it. There's a big, nasty dog back there."

The neighbor's dingy backyard is furnished in midseventies red-neck-style, complete with an old trailer up on blocks. I walk over to the chicken-wire fence separating the two yards and take a look around.

Under the trailer, a bulging black-and-white rottweiler stares malevolently at me. He's got to be at least a hundred and thirty, maybe even a hundred and fifty pounds. It's all muscle. His fur is filthy and covered in burrs. His owner's chained him up, and I can see where his movements have worn away the grass in the backyard, leaving only a circle of dirt and sand. The ball sits at the far edge of that perimeter.

"Jeremiah. Leave the ball. We'll get another one," Jessica says, concern in her voice.

I ignore her. Come on, it's only a damn dog. I've faced worse. Much worse.

"Nah, don't sweat it. I got it."

I climb over the short fence and plant both feet in the backyard. The neighbor's junkyard dog twitches with anticipation. He's a bully, and he looks like he's going to savor this.

"Fucking Cujo," I whisper at him.

I make my move. With a quick sprint, I reach the ball and scoop it up. Cujo charges. I see him coming, but I know I'm faster. I pivot and run for the safety of the fence.

I'm too slow. The rotty barks and growls as he closes the distance. I'm not going to make it. At the last second, I dive headfirst, then tuck and roll.

I stand up, thinking I'm out of Cujo's line of fire. Jessica looks angry. "Jeremiah, get back here!"

Something causes me to look down. The dog's inches away at the edge of his chain's reach, glowering at me. He's barking, but I can't hear him.

Blood spurts from my right leg. Already, a small smear of it has stained the grass.

Everything goes black, like a fuse has blown somewhere in my mind.

A smear of blood on concrete.

Cordite. I smell cordite. I start to cough.

Tink. Tink. Tink. Shell casings tumble to the stair steps.

Eliminate the threat, Jeremiah.

A pinpoint of light, like sunshine at a tunnel entrance.

I feel my body turn. Did I command it to do this? No. I'm on auto-pilot.

"Jeremiah, leave him alone! He didn't bite you!" Jessica's voice is worn and thin; it whispers to me through time and space.

Blood on concrete.

Burnt hair. Burnt skin.

More light. The tunnel mouth is closer.

An AK barks. No, it is the dog, ready to lunge again. I don't see him, can't see anything but brutal light now filling my vision.

Eliminate the threat.

The light flares. Blindness fades. Through a straw I see the dog, angry, flecks of foam fall from his mouth. He looks victorious, knowing he's just kicked my ass for coming into his yard.

The sight sends adrenaline gushing through my system.

"Motherfucker!"

I feel my body bend over. I'm reaching for the dog. His feral snarl evaporates. He expected me to run like everyone else he's ever hounded out of his yard. Instead, I've surprised him with my counter-attack. It makes him nervous, unsure of what he's facing. He looks up at me, trying to get a handle on that.

As we lock eyes, his smug look of triumph gives way to alarm. He intuits he's in trouble.

Oh, Cujo, you have no idea.

Stop Jeremiah. Don't do this.

Eliminate the threat.

I take a step. The dog recoils back, trying to scrabble for the safety of his trailer.

". . . Jeremiah . . . no!" Kraft? Jessica? There was no timber in the voice.

All I see is the dog's face, masked with trepidation now. I revel in that sight. I am going to win this contest.

Adrenaline courses through me. It makes me dizzy with such excitement that it borders on a natural high. Time crawls, like a paused film moving frame by frame, jerky, slow, and without context.

The dog backs up. He's almost to the trailer.

Oh no you don't, little friend. Too late.

His chain lies in the dirt in front of him. It drags along as he continues his withdrawal.

I seize the chain. The dog has no escape. He howls with fear. His misery thrills me. It is a sign I'm winning.

Link by link, I drag him toward me. He fights hard, his back legs pumping, his front legs locked and rigid as he tries to dig them into the soft dirt.

Another link. Another. He's four feet away, a hundred and fifty pounds of meat and teeth keening in growing terror. He knows he's met his match in me.

One more link. I feel myself lean back and give an enormous tug. His collar bulges from his neck as he fights with all his strength.

Marines don't lose. We protect. We kill anything that tries to hurt us, or our brothers. We eliminate the threat or die trying. It is our way. It is my way now. That's what autopilot is for.

I should have died trying in that house. Raleigh. I see him across a gulf of bullets and smoke, his eyes gutted. I want to reach for him. I want to leap from the stairs and race for the oak desk. I should have tried. Oh fuck, I should have tried.

Another sudden jerk and the dog's at my feet. I pull him off his paws until he dangles by his collar, legs kicking for purchase, but finding none. I smell death, the ripe meatiness of Fallujah, and it makes my blood race faster.

I hoist the chain above my head. The dog hangs at eye level. He unleashes a long, anguished howl that's cut off when my right hand flies out and grips his throat. I drop the chain. He hangs from my fingers, gagging and kicking. I squeeze. Harder. Harder. He whines. His tongue lolls and his eyes roll back.

Eliminate the threat.

I will eliminate the threat.

Screaming now, from somewhere far away. Is that Raleigh?

"Doc! Get over here!"

I'm looking down at three dead Marines. My heart ruptures and poison bursts forth out of the seam. It is sheer hate. Pure rage. All I feel is lust for revenge. I want blood, *need* blood, like an addict craves a hit.

More screams. This one I will win.

The Marines vanish. I stare at a dog's face, slack and empty. My hand's around its neck. It kicks weakly at me, in a last ditch of self-defense. I feel his vertebrae within my grasp. His windpipe's crushed. I cannot lose. I redouble my grip.

Smoke obscures his face now. Down the stairs my men call to me. I won't leave this time. Not again. I'll see it through and win, no matter what the cost. It is a Marine's way.

I'm backing up, firing the last of my ammunition into the smoke.

The creature in front of me goes limp. Have I killed a Muj with my bare hands?

I hope so. They deserve no mercy, and I will not deliver justice. Only death.

The dog hangs motionless in my grip. I throw him to the ground. The chain coils over his chest and stomach. Splatters of my blood stain the dirt.

"Jeremiah! For God's sake! Stop! Stop! Stop!"

Jessica?

What's she doing here?

A light switch flicks on. The obsidian darkness vanishes. I find myself standing in the neighbor's backyard again, the dog unmoving at my feet.

Somebody's sobbing. I turn from the dog and find the entire Beal family gaping at me. Alma looks shocked. Von's face is swathed in stunned horror. Sarah sobs uncontrollably.

Jessica stares at me with the same look the dog gave me just as I lifted him from his paws: stark terror.

"Did he kill it, Mom? Is it dead?" Sarah wails.

Alma reaches out and hugs her daughter close, shielding her from me.

I cannot think. I cannot act. My mind's so scrambled I have no inner censor, and words form that I cannot control.

"If you think this is bad, you ain't seen shit."

The family reacts as if I've struck them. Jessica bursts into tears. Why would I say that?

I drop my gaze. The adrenaline flushes from my system, replaced by mounting shame.

How are you going to fix this?

I have no idea.

I turn away to examine my leg. Blood pours from my calf. Cujo bit me good, and now as comprehension returns, the pain strikes.

It feels like I've been struck with a baseball bat. The wound throbs, just like the one I had in Fallujah.

"Same leg, too," I mutter to myself.

"Jeremiah! You're bleeding!" Alma cries out in alarm.

"Yeah."

"Sarah, run inside and get a towel."

Sarah doesn't want to leave the protection of her mom's arms, but Jessica shouts at her and gets her moving.

I stagger toward my adopted family. The one place I always felt safe. Now they look at me like I'm somebody to fear. I cannot bring my eyes to their faces. Instead, I keep my head down and stare at the ground.

Sarah rushes back with a towel. Von and Alma try to staunch the bleeding.

"We've got to get you to the hospital," Von says.

With their help, I limp to the car. After a quick drive, I'm hustled into the ER. The docs go to work on me. They shoot me full of painkillers and start stitching me up. An hour later, lying on a hospital bed in the twilight between consciousness and sleep, the Beal family files out of my room.

The last thing I hear before my brain shuts down is Alma talking to her husband from the doorway.

"What's happened to him?"

Von's voice cuts through the twilight. "I don't know. Something snapped in him." He pauses, then adds, "Did you see the look in his eyes?"

"Yeah," Alma almost whispers.

"I've never seen anything like that in my life."

"He scares me to death."

Von's voice drops an octave. "You and me both."

I retreat into myself and shut them out. I close my eyes, but all I can see is my stepfather holding down my own rotty, Bart, and putting the barrel of the .22 to the back of its head.

The memory triggers a long, post-adrenaline shudder.

Please God, I don't want to become my stepfather.

As I drift away, I understand now things will never be the same again. There will be no going back.

Chapter Twelve

DISCONNECT

June 2006
Richwood, Ohio

NIGHTTIME, BUT I don't know where I am. Is this a dream? Is this real? I have no idea. I feel carried along, a drug trip gone so very wrong. Lights spin a kaleidoscope of colors around me—reds and oranges, yellows, white and black. They swirl and blur my vision and lack definition. I have no idea what I'm looking at.

"Where am I?" I hear my voice say. It sounds distended and disturbed, like a distant cry from an open grave.

I try to move, but no muscle obeys my commands. I feel cold, so cold my hands could be solid ice. I sense that my feet are bare and standing on concrete. There's something bitter in my mouth that makes my tongue swell.

I still see nothing but the daze of colors, their luster fading as blackness surges forward.

I try to touch my face, but my fingers do not come. I can't even see my hands. Then my fingers send my brain a message: I'm holding something chilled and slick. What is it? I can't tell.

My ears detect voices, but they're far away and muted, as if they were shouted through a stadium tunnel after a game.

"Who's there?" I try to ask, but nothing comes out but a high-pitched grunt.

People cry my name. I can't distinguish voices, can't recognize who calls my name. I just hear it over and over, like a pain-wracked lament.

I want to answer with more than a grunt. I want to know what is happening. But my throat burns; my stomach churns and leaves me so weak that the effort to speak becomes too much.

Something squeezes between my lips. It is as cold as an Ohio winter. The coldness spreads across my face, down my shoulders, and into the tips of my fingers and toes, as if I've just been touched by Death itself.

Chapter Thirteen

EIGHT-THOUSAND-MILE SNIPER SHOT

June 2006
Richwood, Ohio

THE DINNER HOUR arrives and I'm feeling pretty good. This morning sucked. I cracked my eyes open and felt only that too-familiar sense of self-loathing. But as the day wore on, my spirits lifted little by little. I lazed around the Beals' house, reading and watching TV. For a change, everyone left me alone. Well, not really alone. There were times I sensed somebody watching me, and I'd look up to see Jess or Von or Alma peering in through a doorway or window. They'd duck away guiltily when I'd catch them out of the corner of my eye.

At first it puzzled me, but what the hell. Everyone's worried about me since I choked the neighbor's dog. That night, when we came home from the hospital, Jessica stayed up all night, just to make sure I wouldn't go back and finish the job. When the Beals got me to the car, Cujo woke up and crawled under his trailer to lick his wounds. Now, every time I go into the backyard, he hides and mewls.

At least he'll never bite me again.

I park the Tacoma in one of the last few slots left in the Denny's parking lot. The Beals wanted to meet for dinner here.

Today, I've been thinking a lot about my future. At first, I considered the Corps a stepping stone in my life, a first foray into adulthood that would give me the grit and gristle I'd need to become an Ohio state trooper. In Iraq, though, everyone figured me for a lifer. Truth be told, a career in the Corps still appeals to me. Those careless words in the psychologist's office aside, I could see myself doing twenty years. Not at Parris Island, of course, but somewhere else for sure. If it were up to me, I'd never go back to the Island.

I want to rejoin the fleet and be safe back among my brothers—warriors understand one another. There'd be no more confusion, no more uncertainty, just a code of honor and our flag on our shoulders. That elegant simplicity seems glorious compared to the messy reality of life here at home.

The thought of deploying again doesn't scare me. In fact, in some ways, it would be a return to normalcy. Besides, my knowledge and experience in the field could help keep alive some of those green-as-grass Marines I saw at Parris Island.

Maybe my future lies in combat.

College is an option, too. If I apply for Officer's Candidate School and go that route, I'd eventually need a four-year degree. That's a challenge I'd like to tackle. If I graduated, I'd be the first Workman ever to get a bachelor's degree.

I shut the Tacoma down and bail out of the driver's side. A smile crosses my face. The fragile happiness I felt earlier in the month is starting to return.

Having goals again—that's what it is all about. Without them, I've just been drifting with the wind, letting the PTSD dictate what happens to me. But not now, not anymore.

Maybe I'm over the hump. I'd love to be able to toss all these prescription meds away and start fresh, just me and Jessica and the Corps. We'd live together again, moving from post to post as my career unfolds. Hell, I'd even love to have kids someday. But only after I know I'm okay.

I reach the front door and step inside. The Denny's is busy tonight. Servers bustle about. Elderly couples fill the booths closest to the entrance. One of them is griping about the food.

Duh.

In the back, Von's head and linebacker shoulders tower over a booth.

"Just one tonight?" a perky teenage hostess asks me.

"No, I see my party over there."

She smiles, and I step past her.

A sudden strangeness hits me, like a dissonant note in a symphony. *What's wrong?*

I have no idea.

When I reach the booth, I'm surprised by who greets me. Von stands up to shake my hand. My mother is next to him, face red and eyes full of emotion.

Jessica is not here.

I hardly realize I'm shaking Von's hand.

"Jeremiah, have a seat," he says.

"What's going on here?" I ask cautiously. This scene strikes me as suspicious. My mother almost never hangs out with Von.

"Have a seat, please," Von urges as he slides into the booth.

"Where's Jess?" I ask.

My eyes go from Von to my mom.

"Please, honey," says my mom.

I sit down and stay silent. Nobody moves. Nobody speaks, but I feel their eyes crawling over every inch of my face. I'm getting inspected, and the sensation is enough to make me want to unzip my skin and flee.

Instead, I stare back with barely concealed hostility.

Goddamn, a perfectly good mood blown to hell again.

Von diverts his gaze to glance at my mother. She refuses to return it. We sit in awkward silence.

"Would you like something to drink?"

Startled, I look up. A server stands ready to take my order.

A double shot of Wild Turkey would be real nice about now.

Damn Denny's no hard liquor policy.

"Um, I'll have a Coke, please."

The server plasters a phony smile on her face and flounces off.

I realize Von and my mother are still locked in some sort of silent, eyes-only argument.

"Okay, what's going on?" I ask again.

Jess is leaving me.

Jess has had enough. That has to be it. She can't do this anymore. Can't pretend that we're okay and go through the motions and in the process make a mockery of what we once had been together.

Oh shit. My heart starts to fall. I want to be pissed, but I can't really blame her.

"Jeremiah, we need to talk," Von begins.

"So talk."

He winds up, takes a deep breath—

—And the server brings my Coke.

Damn. What do I need to do to coax this man to talk to me?

Don't make it easy on them.

"We think you have a problem."

Oh come on, Von, that's the most mealy-mouth line of crap you've ever fed me. Where's the man-to-man straight talk you laid on me back in high school?

"Yeah I have a problem. I have a big problem coming here and getting ambushed by the two of you then having to sit here wondering what the hell's the matter while you say nothing."

Okay, that came out a little more harshly than I intended. My mom looks stricken. Von's composure cracks, too.

"We need to talk about last night."

"What? What the hell for?"

My mind searches for a reason. I'm confused. What happened last night? We ate at home. The conversation was a little stilted. Everyone sort of kept an eye on me like they have since the dog incident. Big deal. We watched some TV, then I went to bed with Jess.

"You must know what I'm talking about," Von says, his voice warbling.

"I don't have a clue. And I'm getting pretty *damn PISSED OFF*!"

Von can't even keep his eyes on me now. He looks anguished.

"Okay, I'm gonna ask one last time, then I'm outta here. What the FUCK is going on?"

"You tried to kill yourself."

The words are like a slap. Enraged, I bark, "Bullshit!"

"Jeremiah, please! Keep your voice down," my mother pleads. Silent tears wet her cheeks.

"Jessica told us . . ." Von begins, but I cut him off.

"Jessica's full of crap!"

"Jeremiah, listen to me."

"This is crap."

"I saw you myself. I got the gun out of your mouth."

A sudden sensation, like cold steel against cracked lips, sucks all the fight out of me.

"I don't know what you're talking about." The words are softly spoken and full of fear. Was that even my voice?

You don't want to hear this, do you?

No.

But you must.

NO!

"We heard Jess shouting. I got up to see what was going on."

"I don't remember any of this," I say with genuine confusion.

"You'd taken a bottle of pills."

"What?"

"In the downstairs bathroom."

A sudden fragment of memory burbles out of my subconscious. *Bitter on my tongue.*

Von presses, "Jessica tried to stop you, but you went into the garage."

Cold feet on concrete. I remember that.

Oh shit.

"You went to the gun cabinet . . ."

NO! I did not do this, would never do this.

". . . got the .22 Marlin, the semiautomatic with the gold trigger . . ."

My mother starts to sob.

". . . and put it in your mouth."

Cold as steel between my lips.

Face it, this happened. You've got fragments of the entire thing spinning around in your fucked up head.

"I don't want to hear anymore."

The waitress scores a double play in the bad timing department. She shows up, hands and arms full of plates. She can tell something's seriously wrong here, but keeps her perky smile plastered on her face anyway.

"Can I get you folks anything else?"

"No."

She beats a hasty retreat. As she does, my eyes sink to my food. I stare at it and realize I have to face the truth. There's no way Von would ever say these things unless they happened.

"Jeremiah, you have a problem. We want to help you. All of us," my mother says.

Von picks up where he left off when we got interrupted. "We got the rifle out of your hands. Then Jess . . ."

"I don't want to fucking hear any more of this!"

Von ignores me. "Jess stuck her finger down your throat."

Throat burns.

"She made you throw up over and over. Finally, you went back to bed."

I stare at the food in front of me, as if Denny's peas are the most interesting things in the world.

You have to face this.

"Tell us what is happening. We're here for you," Von implores.

"I'm in a really dark place right now, Von."

"We'll get you out of it."

"How?"

"Let's talk about getting you help," Von says flatly.

Help? What help can save a man who has tried to kill himself in his sleep?

"What pills did I swallow?" I ask shakily.

"An entire bottle of eight hundred milligram Ibuprofen."

Well, at least it wasn't a whole bottle of Clonopin.

"Jeremiah, why did you do this?" my mother asks. She sounds like she's pleading.

"I didn't know that I was doing it, Mom," I say miserably.

"You can't do this to me."

"I'm sorry."

"No. That's not good enough. You can't do this to me. Not again."

"What do you mean?"

"Your grandfather killed himself when I was six. He swallowed a bunch of pills."

I don't even know what to say. The revelation leaves me shocked.

"I . . . can't . . . live with that again. I won't survive. Please, don't do this."

My mom erupts in tears. I've torn her apart.

"Your grandmother told me he came back from the war a different man. He drank. He got violent. . . ."

The pieces finally fall into place. This is why we didn't venerate Grandpa as a hero, even though he was one. In the end, he died a coward's death and shattered everyone around him.

The magnitude of what I almost did sinks in.

"I'm sorry, Mom, I'm so sorry I've done this to you."

A single tear escapes each eye. They streak my cheek and shatter my façade for good. My head hits my chest and I start to cry.

Von reaches to me. "Jeremiah, what's going on? Talk to us."

"I'm hurtin', Von. I'm hurtin'."

"Look, Jeremiah, you've got a lotta years left. A lotta good years ahead, you know?"

"I hate waking up in the morning."

"Well, we've got to fix that, okay?"

"Okay."

"Nobody wants to see you hurt. Not me. Your mom—or Jessica."

I give up. Fuck it. I'm beyond caring now. There is no bottom, is there? Just deeper degrees of humiliation.

"Jeremiah, you have to promise me you'll never hurt yourself again," my mother entreats.

How can I do that when I didn't control what happened last night? I can't promise to do what I can't control.

The war still rages here. It didn't end at the Kuwaiti Frontier, it just changed shape. And if I die now, it'll be an insurgent victory, like an eight-thousand-mile sniper shot center mass.

I feel cold steel on my lips. My mouth forms an *O*. The sensation makes me shudder. I feel like vomiting in my peas.

Yet, one look at my mother's weeping face shows me how much pain I've inflicted on her. She's breathing hard, trying to stay quiet and not make a scene in our local Denny's, but her face shows crystallized despair.

For a second, I'm back on my hooch outside of Fallujah, talking to my mom on a cell phone. We always got better reception on the roof, but that day, my timing really sucked. We were in midconversation when an AK-47 round cracked past me and slammed into a nearby palm tree. Before I could even duck, a car bomb exploded at our compound's front gate. Mom heard it all half a planet away and went crazy.

"What's wrong? What happened? Oh my God, Jeremiah, are you okay?"

I did my best to reassure her as I hit the deck. "Yeah, everything's fine. No problems here, Mom. Nothing to worry about."

But worry she did. It made her age, and now that I'm home, losing me would be the cruelest of ironies.

"Okay mom," I say, my voice still weak with emotion. "Okay. I promise. I want to live. I don't want to die. But I need help."

"Well, let's go to the hospital and get you some help," says Von.

Food forgotten, I stand up and walk for the door. My mother reaches my side and throws her arms around me. As we step into the parking lot, I'm not sure who is leaning on whom.

Chapter Fourteen

THE GHOST OF IRA HAYES

June 2006
Richwood, Ohio

"JESSICA?"

"Yeah?"

"Why do you stay with me?"

Jess and I lay on my mother's wraparound couch. We're both curled up under blankets, our heads meeting in the middle of the couch's *U*. The lights are off, but I can still see her face clearly. Our noses are only inches apart.

"Why do I stay with you? Why do you stay with me? Haven't I done enough damage, too?"

"No fair. You go first."

She smiles and shakes her head. "Always so damn stubborn."

"I'm a Marine."

"I know, I know."

She reaches up and runs her fingers through my hair. I've been away from Parris Island, so I've let it grow out a little. A little meaning about an inch, anyway.

"Come on, after last night, you've got to be wondering the same thing," I coax.

"I don't know . . . I've loved you since I was fifteen years old. Isn't that enough?"

"We have been together a long time," I muse.

"Ever since my dream."

God, I had forgotten about that. When I was a junior, Jess was a freshman. She had been in the stands the night I got hurt and was carried off the field with my knee injury. One day, while trying to maneuver around the campus on crutches, I noticed her at her locker. Mine was not far away. I couldn't help but stare at her. She was so beautiful and fresh-faced, I couldn't tear my eyes away.

Her friends noticed. A few days of this and one of them came up to me and said, "Hey, Jessica had a dream about you the other night."

Boldness was never a problem for me. Later that day, I walked right up to her as she busily stuffed some books into her locker and said, "Hey, heard you had a dream about me."

All of fifteen. She flushed red and could hardly speak, and her reaction told me everything I needed to know. She felt the connection, too. We had something before we even said hello to each other.

"Say, what was that dream anyway?" I ask. It dawned on me I never bothered to find out.

Jess smiles. "I've been waiting for you to ask that. Took you long enough."

"Sorry."

"We were in a car coming back from Prospect after going out for ice cream."

Her words are a blow. Prospect was the next town over. As small as Richwood, its only attraction was a little ice cream shop downtown.

"We did that!"

"Yes we did," she agrees.

Her dream was a prophecy. It led us to this moment.

"It all started so well, Jess. And it all fell apart."

"Yeah. It did, but when we're good, we're great, you know?" She thinks for a moment, then adds, "We're comfortable together."

"We drive each other crazy," I say.

"Well, it hasn't been good. Doesn't mean it can't be."

I roll over on my back and look up at her. She lays her head against mine.

"I just want you to get better."

True confessions time, Jeremiah. There's no sense in hiding or lying to anyone anymore.

"I don't know how," I tell her.

"I know, but we'll figure it out, okay?"

"Tonight, the chaplain said something to me. . . ." I begin, but then my voice stalls and I fall silent.

After the Denny's intervention moment, my mother drove me over to Marion General Hospital. A nurse took my vitals, then left us alone in a room in the ER. I had expected rubber walls and a straitjacket after everything Von had told me, but it didn't work out that way. Instead of a shrink, a chaplain my mom knew came by to talk to me. At that point, I was beyond caring who knew how far I'd fallen. When he asked me how I was doing, I said, "I'm twenty-three years old and totally satisfied with everything I've done in my life. I feel like there's no need to keep going."

My mother didn't like that at all.

"What did he say to you?" Jessica asks.

"I guess he works with the local police department. He says he sees a lot of cops who've lost their faith in life. You know, they show up on some call and the scene's pretty horrific. That affects a guy. The chaplain told me some stories that made me realize that there are a hell of a lot of people in my shoes, and they somehow get out of bed and get through the day."

"Did it help knowing that?"

"I suppose I already knew that. After that group therapy session and all. . . ."

"What group session?" I'd forgotten I hadn't told her about that. Come to think of it, I haven't told her much about anything this past year. I tell her about it, and she grows very still next to me. The idea that so many people suffer from PTSD is a new concept for her. Hell, it is for me, too, really.

Cops. Veterans. Firefighters. The chaplain connected the dots for me. No wonder the divorce rate is so high in all three professions.

"Did he tell you what to do?" Jess asks.

"No. When we finished talking, he asked me if I planned to hurt myself after I got home."

"How'd you answer?"

"I told him no." What I didn't tell him was I had no intention of dying—at least, no conscious intent.

Jess rolls on her stomach and puts her lips against my ear. "Jeremiah, tell me how I can make things better for you."

"Bring back Raleigh, Eric, and James," I say without thinking.

She starts to cry softly in my ear. "I can't do that. And I can't undo what I did. All I can do is tell you how sorry I am."

"I can't undo anything either, Jess. But sometimes I wonder if we've done too much damage to each other, you know?"

She doesn't answer.

"We've hurt each other a lot."

"Just tell me how I can make it better," she says again.

"I don't know. I'm in a dark place right now. But I want to get out of it."

"Does getting out include me?" she asks, her voice wavering.

"You know, all I ever wanted was somebody who would love me."

I feel her hand slide across my cheek. She cups my chin, her upside-down face appears over mine, and she kisses me. I cradle her neck with my right hand and kiss her back.

That's the other thing that's kept us together: The chemistry is unreal.

"I love you," she says as she moves back and rests her head next to mine again.

"I love you, too. But I feel like I'm betraying myself for doing it."

"I know. My husband tried to kill himself last night, and all I kept thinking was this was my fault. I drove you to it."

"That's not true."

"Tell me that again," she whispers.

"It isn't. You need to know what it's like for me now."

"What do you mean?"

I rise up on my elbow and face her. Her eyes are wet with tears. "It doesn't matter where I am or what I'm doing, I see Raleigh, James, and Eric every moment, like they're overlayed on my life today, you know?"

She shakes her head slightly.

"Right now, I blink, and I'm back on a 998 Humvee, looking down at them."

"Jeremiah . . ."

"No, you need to know this," I insist.

"They are with me every second. It's like my mind's a broken record and the needle's stuck right there on December 23rd, about lunchtime. Over and over, I see it. I can be eating breakfast, and I see them. Driving. I see them. Working, trying to sleep. They are always there. And I always feel the same thing."

"What?"

"Shame. Guilt. Horror."

"What can I do? Jeremiah, please, tell me there's something."

"Jessica, I don't know what anyone can do. I'm at war with my own mind, you know? If you and your dad hadn't stopped me, I would've been another casualty of Fallujah. The insurgents would've won after all, like an eight-thousand-mile sniper shot."

"Isn't that reason enough to live? To keep them from winning?"

That hits home. "Yes," I say after a long, thoughtful pause.

"What about the future? What do you want?" she asks.

I slip back down onto the couch on my back and stare at the ceiling. "The future? Jess, I'm just trying to make it through the day."

"Jeremiah, don't you want a family?"

"Yeah. But come on, what kind of father can I be now?"

"Not now, but in time when we're ready," she says.

"Will we ever be? Jess, I haven't exactly had the best role models for fatherhood, you know? Where would I even start?"

"Start with what's inside you. I know you're a good man. I've seen that in you."

"The things I've done . . ."

"Shhhh. You're not going there. Neither of us are. Not tonight, okay?"

"Okay," I agree.

We lie in silence for a long moment. I feel her cheek pressed to mine, eyes side by side. It is so intimate, yet I feel so lost. I have no idea what to do.

"Remember when you first came home?" she asks.

"Yeah."

That was an amazing, confusing day. We'd all been so excited when we boarded the plane in Kuwait. But the closer we got to the States, the more nervous I became. Jess and I hadn't communicated much, especially after the 23rd of December. We had about a month to go in that country, and I sent her an email and we reconnected. Can you imagine that? A husband in Iraq having to reconnect with his own wife?

"I knew right away that you'd changed. I didn't know how, but I thought I knew why."

By the time we landed in California, I was so nervous I wanted to go back to Iraq. Looking around at the other men in my platoon, I sensed some of them felt the same way.

"How had I changed?"

They bussed us to our own private corner of Camp Pendleton. Fire trucks sprayed out arcs of water over our path, like aquatic crossed swords. Banners flew. Hundreds of people lined our route holding signs and waving furiously. The guys on the bus with me would shout out, "Hey! There's my wife!" or "There's my folks!" as they pinpointed their loved ones in the crowd. We sang "Ninety-nine Bottles of Beer on the Wall" and sucked on orange slices and tried not to explode with anticipation. Or nerves.

One big sign read, WEAPON'S CO.: THIS WAY TO HOT CHICKS AND BEER→.

"Remember that old movie, *Crocodile Dundee*?"

"Yeah."

"Remember when Paul Hogan goes to New York?"

"Okay," I say.

"You were like that."

"What do you mean?"

"Oh come on. You sat on the bed and stared at the television like you'd never seen one before. Then you sat and watched all the traffic."

"Yeah, I was amazed nobody was getting blown up."

"No, it was like you had come from a primitive country and had never seen all this stuff we have here."

She nailed it. I spent thirty minutes in the bathroom just flushing the toilet, amazed to see running water again. "Reverse culture shock, I guess. But how'd that make me different?"

"I don't know. I just sensed a sea change in you. Like you'd come home a different person."

"I am a different person, Jess. I don't like who I am now. That's part of the problem."

She starts to cry again, and her tears oil the space between our cheeks. "Do you like who I've become?"

There's a loaded question. From the moment I got off that bus at

Pendleton, I wasn't sure whom I'd face: Jessica, my high school sweetheart, the girl I fell in love with at prom, the wife who promised to send me letters every day, or the bitter woman whose words were like vicious right hooks to an open wound.

What had she become? As I stepped off the bus, I saw her waving at me. All around us, Marines were locked in bear hugs with wives and mothers and children. A sea of humanity celebrated our survival. It was a moment of total euphoria for most of us.

Jess approached me, arms wide, grinning wildly, sunglasses covering her eyes and her hair dyed black, like she'd gone Goth from guilt.

I shook her hand.

"Answer the question, Jeremiah. Please." Jess sounds almost desperate.

"I think we're still getting to know each other again." That's the best I can do. I leave unsaid what I'm really thinking:

I don't know if I can love you, Jess, and not hate myself.

I add, "We don't trust each other anymore."

She's quiet. I'm content to let the silence linger. My mother's long asleep in her bedroom upstairs. The couch is comfortable, and I'm exhausted. After all that's happened today, I'm just ready for some sleep. Still, we haven't been this honest with each other in years. Part of me wants to just crawl in my shell and let it all pass. But Jess has always had a way of coaxing me to talk. I used to love sitting next to her, just shooting the breeze about anything that entered our heads. We had many long nights, many talks till dawn in high school. We fit each other perfectly, and even as we grew up together, I knew back then that I'd found the only woman I could ever really love. Now part of me feels trapped by that reality.

"Well, if we need to get to know each other, let's do it right. Okay?"

"What do you mean?"

"We haven't lived under the same roof since before your deployment."

"That's true."

"When your leave is over, we'll both go back to Parris Island."

"Are you sure?" I ask.

"Yes. But you have to try, Jeremiah. Since you've come home, we've all been walking on eggshells."

"I know. I'll try, okay?"

"I can't tiptoe around you all the time, wondering what's going to set you off next. We've got to learn to relax again."

"I'm not sure how."

"We'll work on it."

"Okay."

She sits up and looks down into my eyes. "Okay? You don't sound convinced."

"I want to get better. But it's been pretty bad, Jess, I don't want you to kid yourself. I may be a lost cause."

"You're my cause."

"We can't bullshit each other. I'm going to be dealing with PTSD for a long time. That counselor from our group session? He was a Vietnam vet. He's had PTSD longer than he was normal. That'll probably be me."

She looks uncertain now. Does she have the strength for this? I think we're both silently asking that question without knowing the answer.

Am I strong enough for this?

I have to be. I can't repeat my grandfather's life. I can't be that war hero whose life sinks deeper and deeper until death is the only way out.

"Ira Hayes," I suddenly say. I sit up at the recollection, and the connection. My sudden movement startles Jess.

"Who's that?"

"That old song. You know, the guy who always wore black?"

"Johnny Cash?"

"Yeah, that's right, Johnny Cash."

"What about him?"

"He sang about Ira Hayes."

> *Call him drunken Ira Hayes*
> *He won't answer anymore*
> *Not the whiskey drinking Indian*
> *Or the Marine who went to war.*

"God. If I'm not careful, that could be the story of my life."

"Okay, I'm confused. I don't know the song."

"Jess, Ira Hayes was one of the Marines who raised the flag on Iwo

My sophomore year, we played Ridgedale High and beat them soundly on our way to a 9–1 season. Here I am trying to break a tackle after a ten-yard gain, wearing the great Tom Rathman's jersey number. Like Rathman, I played fullback that year and gained about five hundred yards. My junior year, the coaches switched me to tailback and linebacker, positions I played for the rest of my high school career.

COURTESY OF *THE RICHWOOD GAZETTE*

Jessica and me at her senior-year high school prom, 2003. I managed to get leave so I could drive home to Ohio and be her date. It was the longest I've ever had to travel for a night on the town!

AUTHOR COLLECTION

My dad and I at Columbus International Airport the day I left for Parris Island and boot camp in 2001. I had just graduated from high school. Throughout school, my dad and I remained quite close. But after I joined the Corps, he all but disappeared from my life.

AUTHOR COLLECTION

Jess and I on our wedding day, seen here leaving the church as our friends blew bubbles at us instead of tossing bird seed or rice. Not long after, the wedding party fractured as a disagreement arose at the reception, and we spent our first married night apart. AUTHOR COLLECTION

My platoon touched down in Iraq in the late summer of 2004. The C-130 Hercules carried us from Kuwait to the Anbar Province. We soon found ourselves in heavy combat. AUTHOR COLLECTION

My 81mm mortar squad. Kneeling left to right: Lance Corporal White and our medic Doc Sunny. Standing left to right: Corporal Ryman, Corporal Levine, Lance Corporal Mullins, Corporal Smokes, and myself. This photo was taken on the outskirts of Fallujah in November, 2004, just as the battle kicked off. We fired thousands of 81mm rounds into the city with our tube as we supported the marine infantry battling house to house. The enemy tried to knock us out several times with counter-battery rocket fire.
AUTHOR COLLECTION

A marine M-1 Abrams main battle tank thunders past my Humvee at the head of a long column of tanks and armored amphibious personnel carriers bound for their final staging point before we launched our offensive into Fallujah. The ground shook and the fillings in our teeth rattled as these massive vehicles passed us. It was a display of power I've never seen before or since.
AUTHOR COLLECTION

For weeks I had heard nothing from home. One day at Sac-town, I scribbled this note and an Iraqi soldier snapped a photo of it for me. I sent the picture in a letter to Jessica just before we left for Fallujah. She never replied.
AUTHOR COLLECTION

Mimoso and I prepare to saddle up for another Fallujah patrol. Our Humvees weren't armored, but we used them every day inside the city. Here were are holding our full stock M16A4 rifles. Both of us had four power scopes instead of iron sights, which made long-range shooting much more effective, but at close quarters they were useless.
AUTHOR COLLECTION

February 1, 2005. Gardiola and Kraft pin my chevrons on my uniform as I am promoted to sergeant. It was one of the most meaningful moments for me in-country as these two men I respected and loved honored me in front of the rest of the platoon. AUTHOR COLLECTION

Kraft and me on the roof of a damaged building at Sac-town, prior to the Battle of Fallujah. We spent hours up there in the heat, watching over an Iraqi police station. We never trusted the IPs, and we kept an eye on them as much as we did the enemy. AUTHOR COLLECTION

In Fallujah, the enemy used the local mosques as supply dumps and rallying points, hoping that we would stay out of them. Instead, our Iraqi Army allies searched the mosques whenever possible, and they almost always found massive weapons caches within their sacred walls. Doc Sunny and Eric Hillenberg are standing on the back of one of our Humvees. AUTHOR COLLECTION

Left to right: Hillenberg, Doc Sunny, and Phillips stand with two "Swannis"—ex-Iraqi Special Forces soldiers who professed loyalty to the United States. We never trusted them, though we did patrol with them from time to time. Later, during the Battle of Fallujah, some of our Swannis were captured while fighting against us. It was that kind of war. AUTHOR COLLECTION

Our living quarters in Fallujah. We lived in a battered apartment complex. Kraft is sitting at right, watching an old Iraq television set he found somewhere. Meanwhile, Gardiola shaves with his canteen cup and a mirror. AUTHOR COLLECTION

Our three fallen brothers were not honored with a memorial service until just before we left Iraq in April, 2005. Our grieving was delayed four months by combat and circumstance. Once we did assemble to say our final goodbyes, it served only to reopen half-healed wounds. AUTHOR COLLECTION

On patrol in downtown Fallujah after the battle. Engineers stretched barbed wire along the sidewalks so civilians would not get into the streets and disrupt our vehicular patrols. We saw plenty of children on days like this—most wanted candy, but some saluted and waved. These houses were pretty typical of Fallujah: mini fortresses with many hiding places for enemy fighters waiting to ambush us. AUTHOR COLLECTION

The effect of American firepower on downtown Fallujah. We patrolled through the city's ruins for days in December, 2004, without seeing hardly another soul alive besides our men. It was an eerie *28 Days Later* sort of feeling being in a city hollowed out by such destruction. AUTHOR COLLECTION

My Navy Cross ceremony at Parris Island evoked strong and bitter memories for me. We lost three men that day, and each one deserved that award more than I did. AUTHOR COLLECTION

Left to right: Me, Jessica, her mom, Alma, and her stepdad, Von, at a meeting of the Ohio chapter of the Daughters of the American Revolution. This night was one of the first times I spoke about Iraq in public. I touched on patriotism and sacrifice, and spoke about the bravery I saw around me every day while we were in-country. AUTHOR COLLECTION

Easter Sunday, 2007. Jessica and me with our boy, Devon, who was two months old at the time. Jess, being a hairdresser, loves to change the color of her own hair. Here she is as a new mom with a new brunette look.

AUTHOR COLLECTION

Devon and I on the north lawn of the White House in late 2007. Devon's birth gave me renewed energy to face each day and continue my battle with PTSD. I live for him and Jessica now, and their love gives me the strength to overcome the memories of December 23, 2004.

AUTHOR COLLECTION

Jima. He was a Pima Indian. And a national hero. He came home and got invited to the White House. He went on a tour all over the country."

"So?"

"So, he came home with what had to have been a real bad case of PTSD. He couldn't take it."

Comprehension flares in her eyes. Hesitant, "Did he kill himself?"

He died a drunk one morning
Alone in the land he fought to save
Two inches of water in a lonely ditch
Was a grave for Ira Hayes.

"No. He drank himself to death." They found him facedown, smeared in his own blood and vomit. There was no dignity in the way he died. He'd suffered for ten years and rode a long slow ride downhill that ended in defilement and a senseless death. Truth be told, what he saw on Iwo Jima mortally wounded him in 1945. It just took ten years for the liquor to finish him off.

Maybe December 23rd is my flag raising. Am I dead and don't even know it? I haven't felt truly alive since Fallujah. And I'm in a long slow slide of my own.

"Oh."

Yeah. Oh. Like oh shit. That ditch could be my fate, too.

I remember standing by the bus, shaking hands with Jessica, at a total loss of words for the moment. Suddenly, Kraft appeared and interrupted our awkward moment. He introduced me to his grandfather, the FBI agent, code-talker, and full-blooded Navajo. His grandfather stepped close to me and regarded me. He was elderly, his face lined and weaved with age.

"Thank you for protecting my grandson," he said.

I didn't know what to say. We looked out for each other.

"He comes home to us, thanks to you."

"No, I'm here because of him."

Grandfather Kraft smiled at that. Then he pulled out a small pouch. He opened it and began to streak my face with cornmeal. As he did, he sang a song in a language I'd never heard before. At first, this invasion of my personal space caught me off guard, and I thought it strange and rude. But as Grandfather Kraft continued, I felt a surprising surge of peace. I realized he was blessing me in Navajo. When he finished, I tried to thank him for this honor, but did a very poor job of it.

I wonder if Ira Hayes underwent a similar ceremony by his own people when he returned. Unfortunately for me, the blessing didn't take. It just served as a signpost along the way of my own downward road.

I grow morbid now. "Then there was Chesty Puller's son."

Jessica looks questioningly at me, but doesn't ask.

"Chesty was a legend in the Corps. Fought at Guadalcanal, all through World War II and Korea. He was the most decorated Marine."

"What happened to him?"

"The Corps gave him five Navy Crosses."

"Five?"

"Yeah."

"Did he kill himself?"

"No, but his son became a Marine officer. Fought in Vietnam. Highly decorated. He stepped on a land mine that blew his legs off. I think parts of both arms, too."

"Oh my God."

I continue, "He came home. Went to law school. But he had huge ups and downs. Drank hard. Wife couldn't take it, she left. He killed himself right after that. Sometime in the nineties, I think."

"Jeremiah, why are you telling me this?" Jess looks stricken.

"It's hard to be a 'hero' in the Corps, Jess. It means you went through a hell of a lot. You know?"

"Okay."

"They had PTSD. Maybe we all have it to some degree."

"What are you getting at?"

"History isn't on our side. You need to know that. I'm just saying there aren't a lot of success stories here."

"Well, then we'll have to be the first one."

Chapter Fifteen

A MOMENT IN THE TROUGH

July 2006
Richwood, Ohio

WARM NIGHT. Humid, too. Fireflies buzz around the fruit trees in Von and Alma's backyard. I've stepped outside to have a moment alone. Of course, the minute my feet hit the back patio, Cujo fled to the sanctuary under his trailer next door. He's so wary of me now that he knows the sound of my footsteps.

The night sky and its panoply of stars stretch overhead. I'm struck by how this awesome beauty is so universal. This sight was my ceiling for all those nights outside Fallujah before we went into the city.

I sink into a plastic lawn chair and study the stars.

I've tried to be good these past couple of weeks. I've taken my meds and I've worked to watch what I say. Still, Jess and I have had our fights and flare-ups. The lack of trust cripples us, and I'm not sure how it can be fixed.

Trust. That's been a hard thing to find in my life. I trusted my mom, until she married a monster. I trusted my dad until he vanished after I joined the Corps. I trusted Jess . . . once.

When we headed to Iraq, I thought I was the luckiest Marine in the battalion. I had a hottie for a wife waiting for my return, who promised to write me every day. My home front—yeah, that was totally secure.

We rolled into Anbar Province and made a temporary home of Camp Fallujah. When we arrived, we were sitting at the front gate in unarmored seven-ton trucks. Kraft and Levine were sitting next to me. Mimoso, a New York–born Puerto Rican and one of my best friends, sat across from me. We'd gone for hours without water, and by the time we reached our new base, we were all suffering from dehydration headaches. It felt like a wild animal was trying to tear its way out of my head.

"Hey, Mo? What the hell's that?" Kraft asked, pointing to the sky at a tiny flare climbing starward.

Mimoso turned to study the phenomenon. "That a rocket!" His Puerto Rican and Bronx accent mingled together to create a bass version of Rosie Perez.

The rocket sizzled right over our convoy and exploded deep inside Camp Fallujah. We later found out that it scored a direct hit on a regimental command post, killing the communications officer, wounding the CO and several others.

Mo watched the impact's fireball twist upward into the night and said, "Holy shit. Welcome to Iraq."

The next day, a package arrived from Jessica. The men kidded me, but I knew they were jealous. One day in country, and my wife was already taking care of me. She must have mailed the package before we left. It was full of cookies and little treats. I shared them with my platoon.

"Jeremiah? You okay?" Alma calls to me from the back door. Behind her, I can see Von watching me.

"I'm fine, just enjoying the night."

"Let me know if you need anything."

"I'm good, thanks."

That package was the only one I received during the deployment.

I started to sense something was wrong before we'd left, but I didn't want to face it. Jess had started to hang out with a wild crowd around Camp Pendleton. It caused some friction between us, but nothing so severe that it would lead to being ignored. Forgotten.

"I'll be here, waiting for you. I love you." Those were her last words to me.

One day, when we were outside the wire near a little suburb of Fallujah we called Sac-town, I struck up a conversation with an Iraqi cop. He seemed like a nice enough guy. He and I shared a brief Coalition moment when he stumbled upon my foxhole.

"Shit. It's hotter than two rats fucking in a wool sock," I said to him as I took a long sip from my camelback and wiped sweat from my brow.

The Iraqi policeman (IP) regarded me with good-natured incomprehension. He smiled at me. I smiled back. I felt like I needed to share something with him, so I pulled out a photo of Jessica and showed it to him.

An honest grin split his face. "She veewy good! Veewwy good!"

Hard not to like an Iraqi who thinks the love of your life is an A-list babe. I shrugged in an *aw, shucks, thank you* sort of way and he laughed.

I had an idea right them. "You take picture for my wife?" I asked him as I pantomimed clicking a camera. He nodded eagerly. I dug out a spiral-ringed notebook and scrawled, "I LOVE YOU JESS WITH ALL MY HEART" on it. Then I handed the IP my little 35mm grocery-store throwaway push-here-dummy. He stepped back and shouted, "Cheeses!"

I didn't smile. It was too hot to smile. Instead, when the photo came out, I had a tight-lipped stare going. Half my face was shadowed by my booney cover. It wasn't the best photo taken of me over in Iraq, but I knew that we were heading into Fallujah soon, and I wanted to send Jessica something. It really was worth a thousand words—at least, I hoped it was at the time. I had thousands of words I wanted to share with her; I didn't know where to start. Marines don't do sap.

I sent the photo home, but I never heard from her. She didn't write. She didn't email. Before Fallujah, she hardly ever picked up the phone when I tried to call.

Broken trust. Story of your life.

I fear intimacy. Don't we all, really? It leaves us so vulnerable.

I trust Kraft. I trust Mo. I trust Levine. I know those three men would do anything, anytime for me. I would do the same for them. That's part of the blood brotherhood of the Corps. As I reach for a cigarette, the words from one of Bon Jovi's songs off their *New Jersey* album comes to mind.

> *But if I get that call in the dead of night*
> *I'll be right by their side.*

Big hair and all, they got that one right.

I light the smoke and take a deep breath. It's after ten and I'll need to take my meds soon. That'll put me to sleep; the Clonopin takes care of that. For the moment, I'm in a nice little trough—long enough removed from my last dosages that I actually feel a little human, but not too far to start craving the Clonopin. I'm at my most "me" here, and I find I can think clearly. It also lets me remember, which is just about a fifty-fifty blessing and curse.

I enjoy the moment—and the smoke. Don't tell anyone, but us leathernecks stocked up on Newports in Fallujah. They gave us a minty fresh mouth, or at least that's what we thought. Anything beat our normal foul breath, which is why I started the habit in the first place over there.

I miss Kraft and Levine, Smokes and Mo. If we'd all stayed together after we came home, this *Best Years of Our Lives* time probably would have gone easier for all of us. I know it would have for me, anyway. But within a few months, the Corps peeled my unit apart and we went our separate ways with empty promises to stay in touch. Even if you do make the effort, it's never the same again.

We found ourselves among strangers in uniform, men and women who didn't have our frame of reference. After seven months together in combat, we had become a family. Nothing stateside can match that.

Okay, that's a rose-colored way of looking at it. At our best, we were a dysfunctional family with guns and disgusting senses of humor.

We stayed at Camp Fallujah only a short time before moving to another satellite base on the edge of a lake. For whatever reason, the SeaBees set up our Porta-Johns right down there at the water's edge.

I exhale a cloud of smoke and start to laugh. Kraft was always such a priss when it came to his personal hygiene. I mean, we lived in filth, sat in those Porta-Johns amid clouds of flies, and Kraft would obsess over his hair. He carried his own bottle of hand sanitizer, and he used it constantly. For the rest of us, that just seemed like tossing bricks in the Grand Canyon. What was the point?

One day, Kraft headed over to the Porta-Johns. Mo and some of the other guys decided to play a prank on him. They pushed a Dumpster up against the side of the one Kraft was in. They used it to climb atop the shitter. I came out of my hooch and saw them rocking Kraft back and forth, the Porta-John swaying like a pendulum as he screamed holy hell at them. No amount of hand sanitizer helped him after that.

That lake was something else. It gave us a beautiful view every morning as we emerged from our beachside hooches. When people think of Iraq here at home, I've found they have images of endless sand dunes and camels, and blazing heat. For me, I see verdant palm groves, sunrises over our lake, and the skeletal remains of a sandstone-colored city.

And I smell corpses. Once you get a whiff of that, you never forget it.

Raleigh Smith loved our lake. He'd actually brought a fishing pole with him from Camp Pendleton. His best friend, Jerrad Hebert, also packed one in from California. They had to be the only two Marines in Anbar Province with graphite rods and Zebco reels. Either they knew where we were headed before the rest of us, or those two had a flash of intuition. Between our missions, Raleigh and Hebert would go down and drop a lure in the lake. They caught some butt-ugly fish, that's for sure. I swear those damned things looked like Blinky, the three-eyed radioactive fish from *The Simpsons*.

I counted on them. They counted on me. Not everyone in the platoon measured up, but most did. Levine and Kraft and Smokes—they set the bar pretty damn high on that front.

Mimoso did, too. Although, when we got home, we were bad influences on each other. We tom catted together. We partied and got wild on the town every night. He was my partner in crime. In the summer of '05, after I'd come back from my Ohio leave, I was pretty sure things with Jess were over. Mo and I hit the bar scene hard, but I decided I needed a better car. In one totally irrational moment, I drove my '03 Mustang GT over to a BMW dealership and traded it in for a sixty-thousand-dollar M3. While I signed the papers, Mimoso cleaned out my 'Stang and tossed my stuff into the Beamer's trunk. Then we hopped in and went tearing down the freeway, Mötley Crüe's "Kick Start My Heart" blasting at full volume from the Beamer's ten speakers.

All that partying was just a dodge, though. We didn't want to face what we'd become, so we hid from ourselves in the party scene. The drunken nights, the women, the craziness—it was an artificial high that wore thin even as we sank deeper into it. I had to get out before it swallowed my conscience completely.

How do you get your values back after you've drop-kicked them out of sight? I'm not sure, but when I figure that out, maybe I'll be able to trust myself again.

"Hello, you." Her soft voice comes to me through the velvet night.

"Hi Jess."

"Ignoring me?" she says as she slides into a chair nearby.

"No, just out here thinking."

"No more thinking. Time for bed."

"You don't have to ask me twice."

Together, we head back into the house.

The Clonopin awaits, and I'm starting to need it again.

Chapter Sixteen

LOST MOMENT

July 2006
Richwood, Ohio

SOMETHING'S SHAKING ME. Groggy, dazed, and drug impaired, I want to ignore it. I tuck the covers over my head and try to return to that zeroness of a Clonopin coma.

"Wake up!"

"Go away," I mumble. My head throbs and my arms feel like lead.

"Jeremiah! For God's sake, will you wake up?" Jessica's voice. She sounds excited.

Am I dreaming? I'm rocked back and forth, like a boat in heavy seas.

"God! You're intolerable! Get up!!!"

I peel one eye open, still unsure if this is real or a dream.

Jess grins at me and starts to dance around the living room and our makeshift bed.

What the hell?

"Jess, you look like a hummingbird on crack!"

"Are you awake? You're not going to believe this!"

"What? What's going on?" My voice sounds like I'm talking from a bathysphere four miles under water.

"I'm pregnant. Jeremiah, you're going to be a father."

What?

Did I hear my wife right?

No way. No . . . way.

"Baloney."

"Yes! I just took the test!"

"You misread it."

She skips out of the room and returns a moment later, waving some stick-looking thing at me.

"Ahhgh! Get that thing away from me. You peed on it!"

"Look! For God's sake, see for yourself! It's blue!"

Yes, blue. Yes it is.

Somewhere deep inside of me, I know I should react. At the core of whatever I am, I feel something stirring, something big. Then the Clonopin, Saraquil, and Zoloft all conspire to slam that door closed.

I feel nothing, just that empty numbness my crazy-man's cocktail provides.

"You are going to be a father!" Jess repeats. She's so excited she can't sit. She leaps off the bed to her feet and starts dancing around again. "And all because of a dream I had my freshman year!"

A teenage prophecy.

I roll over and stuff a pillow over my head. A small kernel of concern forms in my gut, but I don't have the capacity to care. The drugs have lobotomized this life-changing moment, and I'm okay with that.

In seconds, I'm out cold again. The Clonopin coma. It feels all right.

At ten, I'm released from its grip. The living room's empty. Jess has long since left for school. She's going through our local beauty school, learning how to style hair and whatnot. She's good at it, and has excellent fashion sense.

I rise from the sack, feeling hungover and sluggish. As usual. I begin another morning as a drug-induced zombie. God I hate this feeling. Every morning—nothing. Just slow dopiness, like I'm some sort of junkie addict.

Well, maybe you are.

No, we won't go there this morning.

A vague memory slaps me around. Jessica dancing. Waving a white stick and telling me she's pregnant.

—That was a dream, right?

Fuck all. On this stuff, I can't tell what's real and what's not.

I chalk it up to a dream. A shave and shower later, I head upstairs for breakfast, where I find Von and Alma in the kitchen.

"Morning, Jeremiah!" Alma says excitedly. That's strange. Dim alarm bells sound in my mind.

Von nods his head. He looks concerned.

Oh hell, have I done something again? I wrack my brain. Any crazy fragmented memories?

No. Just Jessica dancing around the bed.

"How's it feel?" Alma asks.

"How's what feel?" I ask in a flatlined voice.

"Why, Jeremiah, you're going to be a dad!" Alma bursts out, all smiles and a delighted look in her eyes.

"That wasn't a dream?" I ask.

Von shakes his head. He's the yin to Alma's yang. He's looking into the future—which contains what for his grandchild?

Another upwelling of emotion stirs inside me. A thousand thoughts dump into my brain simultaneously.

You're not fit to be a parent right now.

Guess I'll have to get fit.

A stab of panic pierces the drug cocktail's zombie-cloak. It recedes as quickly as it came, and I'm left feeling nothing again, but sensing a raging sea somewhere way inside.

"Aren't you excited?" Alma asks, a demi-frown now etched on her face.

"Sure! I've always wanted to be a dad!" It feels forced and overly happy; the zombie does Broadway. She doesn't look convinced. Von's frown deepens.

I grab a quick bite to eat before retreating to the basement living room. I spend the day trying to think. But I'm swimming upstream against the meds, and I find no clarity, only a muddy mess.

Jess comes home in the evening. She hugs me so hard I fear she'll crack her back.

"What do you think?" she asks, eyes bright. I know her. Underneath the excitement, she's worried, too. Terrified.

"I think I've got one more reason to get my shit together."

"Good. That's what I want to hear." She pauses, kisses my cheek, and adds, "You'll be a great dad if you aren't a depressed asshole."

"There's an endorsement. Thank you." I can't help grinning.

It's late, and the edge is off the meds again. I'm in that wonderful trough, becoming human again with all the frailties and emotions that go with it. The more my system flushes this crap out, the more I feel.

"If we have a son, will you let him play football?" I ask.

"Of course. If we have a daughter, will you promise not to cheat when we take her out golfing?"

We both bust out with our first real laugh of this leave.

Back in high school, Jess played on the school golf team. She has a killer swing, powerful and accurate, and whenever we played, she mopped the green with my ineptitude. The truth is, I've been programmed to win at everything I try. Getting my tail kicked by my girlfriend inflamed my inner Cro-Magnon chauvinist. So, I used to cheat.

One time, I had fallen many strokes behind. She enjoyed her dominance thoroughly, and as she teed up on the next hole, she flashed me a quick, sidelong glance. Her lips were curled in an *I own you, Bub* sort of smile. I couldn't suffer that, even if the glance made me want to sweep her into my arms and kiss her right there on the fairway. As she prepared to swing, I sidled over to our golf cart and hit the horn. The unexpected noise caused her to flinch in mid-backswing.

She looked up at me in mock anger. "Stop that!"

"My bad. Sorry!"

"Yeah, right."

I tried my best to look hangdog and apologetic. "Okay. I'll be good."

She settled back into her stance and concentrated on the ball. Just as she lifted her club, I threw the golf cart in reverse and went speeding off. Then I switched gears and raced back up to her.

She waited for me, hands on her hips, club at her side. She let out a long, exasperated hiss and said, "You only do this stuff because I'm better than you and you can't handle that."

With just the right amount of humility I let her be the alpha dog, at least for a second. "I know."

"You're a bad actor, Jeremiah," she scolded.

"Just take the shot, Jess."

She returned to her stance, lifted the club into her back swing, and just as she came down on the ball, I coughed.

Sliced it. Furious, she stared at me.

"Sorry! Had something in my throat."

"The hell you did!"

Her face glowed crimson, but even in her anger she looked absolutely stunning.

I chuckle at the memory, but then it recedes and vanishes.

"What makes you think I'll let our daughter golf?" I ask.

"Why wouldn't you?"

"Well, I doubt they'll have a golf team at the convent I'll send her to when she hits puberty."

"Oh, you think?"

"Yeah, that way she won't run into the likes of me."

"You were once so suave."

"Well . . . it worked on you, didn't it?"

She turns serious. "You're going to be a father."

"You're going to be a mother," I echo.

"Yeah. A mom. That's hard to get my mind around."

"Tell me about it."

She curls her arms around me and puts her head against my chest.

"Is this what you want?" she asks.

"Well, it's a little late to ask that, isn't it?" I say.

"Okay, the timing isn't the best. Still . . ."

We fall silent, holding each other next to our makeshift bed in her parent's basement.

"What do you see in our future now?" she asks.

I'm on the far side of my drug-free trough now. The first twitches of my Clonopin craving start to kick in.

"Not sure," I say honestly.

A ditch. Ira Hayes died in a puddle of blood and vomit.

The thought sends a shudder through me. Jessica hugs me harder. My arms come up to her back. I caress her hair.

"What do you see? You're the one with the prophetic dreams," I ask.

"What I want is barbeques on lazy summer days. Softball games. Christmas trees and birthday parties."

"I'd like that."

"I don't want things, Jeremiah. Diamonds won't do it for me, even if we could afford them."

"What do you mean?" The craving's crawling and scratching around in my head now. I've got to take the Clonopin soon.

"That BMW you owned? That's so not me. I just want us happy and healthy. An all-American family."

"Sounds nice."

"And I want you to be my best friend again."

I kiss her hair. I realize she's dodged my question and laid out instead what she wants our future to be. She's just as scared as I am. Maybe more so.

"You're my Angel," I say. That was our song, "Angel" by Aerosmith.

A moment later, I break our embrace and disappear into the bathroom. My hands shake as I search for the Clonopin bottle. I pop a tablet in my mouth and suck water straight from the sink's faucet. The trough is getting shorter and shorter. The cravings are getting harder and harder—and more physical.

I brush my teeth, and return to the living room. Jessica's already tucked in bed. I slip in beside her, the Clonopin starting to kick in. A sheet of drowsiness enfolds me. The world goes round, edgeless. Emotions fade to nothing. No corners. No worries. A dark tunnel of dreamless sleep looms on my horizon.

Vaguely, I feel Jess snuggle close. She's warm against me. I'm limp, clutched in the dead embrace of a Clonopin high.

"Tell me it'll be all right?"

"Jessica, I'll do my best. That's all I have for you."

The last thing I hear before the tunnel engulfs me is Jessica's voice, tinged with trepidation, "Just make sure your best is good enough, okay? There's two of us depending on you now."

Darkness. A void. No concern. No worries. Just a placid faux emptiness that leaves me sated. I drift away . . .

. . . To nothing.

PART
III

Chapter Seventeen

RETURN TO THE ISLAND

Late July 2006
Parris Island, S.C.

"HEY, DOG!"

I turn around to find myself face-to-face with Staff Sergeant Shelby.

"Hello, Staff Sergeant."

"I saw you getting out of your rig there." He points at my Tacoma. "Thought you and I might have a talk."

This is the last man I want to talk to right now. I've been back at Parris Island for about two weeks. Honestly, it hasn't been nearly as bad as I thought it would be—at least not yet. But Shelby in my face again threatens to kill my relatively good mood this morning.

He reads my face and can tell I'm reluctant. Last time we were this close to each other, he slammed a recruit's cover down across my nose and I wanted to tear his lungs out.

"Won't take long," he says with faux cheerfulness. I realize he's nervous.

"Okay."

"Good, come with me for a few minutes."

We leave the parking lot and I follow him into the barracks. As we enter his office, I can't help but take a long look at the red bench outside his door. A flutter of anger rises in me.

Stay calm, Jeremiah. Remember what Doc Radford's told you.

I've seen Doctor Ann Radford twice since I've been back. Both times, I've emerged from our sessions feeling much better. Toward the end of our first session, I explained the dog incident to her. When

I finished, she said, "Jeremiah, we've got to find better ways for you to channel your anger. We can't have you attacking neighborhood pets."

We still haven't found the right outlet, but I'm working on it. Anger management should be a graduate-level degree for us veterans.

"Have a seat, Sergeant Workman," says Shelby. He sounds even more nervous now.

I catch myself looking around the room for something to smash across his head.

Stop it. Give the guy a chance.

Part of me doesn't think he deserves a chance. I have to force myself to sit down.

Shelby takes a seat behind his desk. I'm surprised to find he's looking directly into my eyes.

"Hey, Dog. I have some things to say," he begins. I nod and just let him talk. His tone siphons away my anger.

"Look, I had no idea you had it so rough over in Iraq." The comment injects a dose of anger right back into my system.

What did you think? That it was a frat party?

Keep your mouth shut. Let him talk.

"I heard about some of what you went through. I didn't know . . ." His voice trails off.

"It wasn't a walk in the park."

"Yeah. Well, listen . . . I want to . . . I need . . . to . . . apologize to you. What I did was fucked up and wrong."

The anger abates. Shelby's making an earnest effort to set things right.

"Okay."

"It was wrong. Sergeant Workman, I'm sorry for what I did to you."

"It's okay." That's all I've got for him. I want to forgive him, but I'm not sure I really can right now. The memory of that humiliation is still too raw.

"Right. Well, uh, do you have anything for me?" he asks.

"No, not really."

"We're good then?"

"Yeah, we're good." We're not good, but this is a step in the right direction.

He stands up and offers me his hand. I get on my feet and shake it. Firm. Eyes locked. We'll never be friends, but I can't help but respect a man with the stones to admit he screwed up. In his place, I'm not sure I'd be able to do that.

As I head for the door, he adds, "Workman, if you need anything . . ."

"Thank you, Staff Sergeant. I appreciate that."

I duck into the hallway, pass the red bench, and exhale. It feels like I've been holding my breath since he cornered me in the parking lot.

A short walk later, I reach my new boss's office. Since I'm no longer a drill instructor, I report directly to First Sergeant Lewis. He joined the company while I was on leave, but he and I already have an awesome working relationship.

I step inside, and find him behind his desk, buried in paperwork.

"Mornin', First Sergeant."

He looks up from his stack of reports and smiles. "Sergeant Workman, how the hell are ya?"

First Sergeant Lewis stands about six feet tall. He has graying hair cut at a medium rake with dark, expressive eyes and a Caribbean accent. I've never asked him where he's from, but scuttlebutt has it he's either from Trinidad or Barbados.

I can't help but grin. "Livin' the dream, sir. Livin' the dream."

"Excellent. As soon as Staff Sergeant Edds and Allen get here, we'll go over what needs to be done today."

"Sounds great."

"Pull up a chair," he says to me. I find a folding metal one and swing it in front of his desk.

"Been meaning to ask you, First Sergeant, but is that you in the photo right there?" I point at a picture of a young African-American Marine charging off the ramp of an amphibious tractor. The photo was taken somewhere in the desert.

First Sergeant Lewis looks over his shoulder and nods. "Yeah, that's me all right, before I got old."

"Where was it taken?"

"Gulf War. I was just a kid, right outta school."

"Infantry?" I ask.

"Yep."

A look of understanding passes between us.

Before I can ask him anything more about it, Sergeant Allen comes through the door. We greet him, and he grabs a chair and sits next to me. Edds comes in a few minutes later.

All three of us have been reassigned to headquarters. Edds and Allen moved over after our recruit platoon graduated last spring. Both of them are having trouble at home, so First Sergeant Lewis pushed them up to HQ so they could spend more time with their families. Drill instructors have the highest divorce rate in the Marine Corps.

Given how high it is in the infantry and fleet units, the rate here must be damn close to ninety-five percent.

Among these three Marines, I feel comfortable and at home. They don't baby me, they don't condescend. They don't offer pity, or stare at me like I'm a freak. Nor do they try to suck up, which some of the others have done since I received the Navy Cross.

No. Edds and Allen and First Sergeant Lewis, they treat me as an equal. They treat me like a man, as if the mess hall incident never happened.

What a relief that's been. Coming back here, I dreaded what I'd find. The first day I got up and drove back here, all the dark thoughts returned. Part of me just wanted to spin the Tacoma around and head back to Ohio.

Instead, I found out I still love the Corps and love being a Marine. After about my first week back, I discovered that Doc Goldberg had started the process to have me medically discharged from the Corps. I'd be a civilian again; Jessica and I would be free to do whatever we wanted.

I didn't want to leave. The Corps is my home, and facing the reality of not being in it anymore forced me to recognize I've got no backup plan. The Ohio State Police are not going to take on a medically discharged Marine as a cadet, that's for sure. I don't have any marketable skills for the private sector. I mean, since when does Microsoft or General Motors need men who know how to assemble and fire a mortar? Hewlett Packard has no need for an employee who can shoot a hole in a quarter with an M16 at a hundred yards. I've been in the Corps my entire adult life, and it has left me singularly ill-equipped for a life outside its ranks.

I could probably go to the VA and draw one hundred percent disability for my wounds, hearing loss, and PTSD. But what sort of life would that be for my family? We'd collect two grand a month for the rest of my life, which would allow me to squander the time Eric and James and Raleigh never got.

I can see myself in ten years, addicted to that disability check, a couch potato moving only to refill the chip bowl or reach for the remote.

That's an empty hole I don't want to fall down.

Doc Goldberg called me one day to tell me he had finalized the paperwork. I'd be processed out in a couple of months.

"Please, Doc, please don't do that. I want to be a Marine." I practically begged him.

Reluctantly, he granted my wish. Instead of a discharge, he kept me on limited duty.

Yesterday, I heard he was retiring himself. Letting me stay on was one of the last thing's he'll do as a Marine.

"Okay, guys," First Sergeant Lewis says to us, "we've got a lotta work to do today." He grabs a clipboard and starts reading over a laundry list of maintenance, chores, and paperwork that's got to get done. Instead of micromanaging us and giving us specific duties, he lets us work out who does what among the three of us.

When he finishes up, Edds, Allen, and I split up the work.

Ten minutes later, I'm outside in the broiling South Carolina heat. The temperature has to be well over a hundred degrees, which isn't bad in and of itself. But when you layer the humidity on top of the summer sun, it feels like I'm swimming through a sauna gone haywire.

Everyone thinks Iraq is the same way, but it's not. There were times we shivered in the frigid winter nights outside Fallujah. That came as a definite surprise to me.

I reach a little equipment shed in the courtyard of our company headquarters building. Inside, I find a gas-powered weed whacker. Today, I took the lawn boy duties. The grass around our H-shaped barracks needs to be cut down. I'll be working on the spaces above and below the horizontal bar, which is so cluttered with machinery, air-conditioning units, and heaters that a mower won't fit.

I walk over there, sweating already with the effort. The grass stands over a foot tall. It looks like a field of asparagus. Time to get to work.

The weed eater cuts with a little plastic cord, not a metal blade. This makes for slow going. The grass survives the onslaught well, and I have to rake an area over thoroughly before the stalks sever in half. I can't start at the bottom, either. The grass is too thick down there, and the weed whacker doesn't have the power to slice through it. Instead, I work from the top down.

My body burns with heat. The humidity makes breathing an effort. I've got a water bottle with me, but I don't have the energy to stop, walk over, and get it. I stay on the job instead, losing my cammie top to work in my green T-shirt. Within minutes, it is sweat-soaked and sticking to my skin.

A stream of perspiration swan-dives off my brow and stings my eyes. I pause and try to blink it away. That doesn't work, so I rub them furiously with the bottom of my T-shirt until the discomfort ebbs. When I open my eyes again, I'm staring at Raleigh, Eric, and James again. They're overlayed against the lawn. I look away, and I see them outline against the barracks wall. Eyes hollow. Faces contorted.

Come on. You've been through this before. You need to make your peace with what you see.

I get back to work, scything the grass and doing my best to admit these three ghosts into my daily existence. What's the point of resisting it? That'll just make things worse.

An hour passes. My pants are now streaked with sweat. My T-shirt looks like its been submerged in a pool. Tiny clippings of grass cling to me. I must stink to high hell. I remember that old Stephen King novel, *Night Shift*. There's a short story in there called "The Lawnmower Man." It was nothing like the movie. Instead, King wrote about a middle-aged guy who just needed his grass cut. He called in a mowing service, and the dude who shows up turns out to be a psycho fetishist who eats the grass clippings his mower produces. The middle-aged guy watches him eat a chewed up rodent and flips out.

The lawnmower man runs him over and leaves his pieces in a birdbath.

That used to be my kind of entertainment. Not anymore. Not since I saw pieces of people in Fallujah. No novel in the world can do that scene justice, let me tell you.

Now I wonder what kind of sick mind can come up with that stuff. Even worse, what kind of sick person wants to read it.

The weed eater runs out of gas. It takes a minute to refuel it, giving me time to catch my breath in some shade. How people do this for a living down here in the South is beyond me.

Since coming back to Parris Island, the press has been after me again. The History Channel called. Some of the reporters who talk to me have asked some totally illogical questions. They know nothing about the Corps, and their ignorance shows with the sort of things they ask me. I don't know how to answer them. Now, I don't return their calls.

In fact, I didn't even wear my Navy Cross ribbon at first. I still don't feel like I deserve it, and wearing it seemed like a betrayal to my three friends who didn't make it home. But one day, a general asked me about it. When I told him I didn't feel comfortable with it on my chest, he said, "You've got to wear it, Sergeant Workman. You owe it to the men you lost over there. You can tell their story and make sure they are not forgotten."

After that, I wore it.

Back to work. Another forty minutes, and I'm halfway done and twice as sweaty and grass-speckled. My head starts to buzz from the heat, which prompts me to finish off the water I brought with me. That doesn't help.

Get the job done. That's what we're trained to do; it doesn't matter if it is storming a beach or cutting a lawn. A Marine takes pride in whatever he does.

If those reporters could see me now. Sergeant Jeremiah Workman, Navy Cross recipient, national hero, chopping grass. I'm sure somebody would have a comment or two about "oh, how the mighty have fallen."

I don't care. Actually, I don't mind the work. It gets me out of the office and keeps me in shape. Besides, it is all about pride. I'm not too proud to believe some work beneath me. That would be a betrayal of my Richwood roots.

Another hour passes. I'm smoked. The heat and humidity suck the energy right out of me. I'm filthy and can smell my own stench, but I'm almost done. One more corner near an air conditioner unit will complete the job. Then I'll change and go find a nice cold drink.

The weed whacker saws off the last stalk. I put the tool away and spend the next twenty minutes raking up the cuttings. When I'm finally done, I check my watch and shake my head. This took twice as long as I thought it would. The entire lawn's done. It was a hell of a lot of work, and I feel kind of sick to my stomach, but I've knocked a task off our list.

I turn to head back to the shed. I'm confronted by a single blade of grass, which sways slightly in the midafternoon breeze. It towers over the otherwise trimmed and neat lawn and looks like a solitary asparagus with its foxtail of seeds at its tip.

A step . . . two . . . one more.

The smell of fresh cut grass.

Heat beating down. So brutal. Relentless as a silent killer.

Another step. My head floats. Sweat on my brow.

A flood of anger.

A flush of shame.

I try to take another step. Instead, I fall to my knees and stare at the single blade of grass. It sways lazily, mockingly. It has survived as a triumph over my best efforts. It is a symbol of my shame.

My head explodes with rage. Somewhere in the back of my brain, the sudden surge of fury blows a fuse. For a moment, I'm struck completely blind.

> *Then Ira started drinkin' hard;*
> *Jail was often his home*
> *They'd let him raise the flag and lower it*
> *Like you'd throw a dog a bone!*

Cutting grass, is that my bone?

Failure. Again. Not again.

Mowed lawn. Ripe smell, like summer in the suburbs.

Or Fallujah in November.

"No!" I hear myself yell.

Vision returns, but everything's dull and lifeless, like the summer sun's sucked all the lushness from the colors around me.

I want to reach for that stalk of grass, tear it up by its roots and cast it aside. I can't move. My arms hang limp at my side. Panic rises, mingling with my anger and shame. I'm paralyzed.

"Oh my God," I hear my voice again. Did I say that, or think it? I can't tell.

"I can't even mow a lawn right. I'm such a fucking failure."

Who's talking? I want to look around, but my neck feels sheathed in lead.

Sobbing. Gasping. A wail of despair.

Who? Me? Where's that coming from?

I flop on my stomach, the blade of grass inches from my eyes.

"Workman! Come on! Come on!"

Kraft? Where are ya, buddy? I can't move. Help me.

"Move it Marine!" It's a husky voice, deep and authoritative.

Major D.?

Phoomp! A grenade explodes behind me.

My ears ring. Head buzzes, stomach flips.

Major D., leave me.

Leave me. Please let me die here.

Not another step. I have failed and deserve no other reprieve.

The world contracts and spins. Gunfire sputters. Grenades burst. Men shout. I scream.

Eliminate the threat.

Hoarse and lost, I keen like a wounded beast. At least, I think that's me. I'm not sure, and I've gone blind again.

Failure. Men died. You did not measure up.

"Kraft? Smokes! Help me. Please, we can't leave them up there. We can't abandon them!"

Trust them. No one else will see you through.

No ammo.

Naked with fear.

A machine gun chatters. The earth quivers.

I try to rise to my feet, but not a muscle responds. Surrounded by a world gone black, my body refuses to obey.

Smoke. Cordite. Blood. A musky hint of sweat-soaked men.

Pain. That's the one thing I can ignore.

Leave me. Let me die. I'm ready.

I blink once more. A pinpoint of light ahead, like I'm looking through a tube.

I scream and sob. Nothing's right.

A single blade of grass: That's all I see.

Chapter Eighteen

BROTHERS

December 23, 2004
Fallujah

A PATCH OF GREEN in the smoke. I lie on my stomach, choking, throat burning and eyes afire. Boots near my eyes, tan once, now gray and mottled with Fallujah filth. The world spins—am I upside down?

Darkness and green. Boots and blackness. My vision fails to focus. The colors pinwheel every time I open my eyes.

I feel myself being dragged across a carpeted floor.

Shouts and screams. I recognize voices—Smokes and Kraft and Doc Sunny. But like my vision, my ears have taken too much abuse, and I cannot tell what they're saying.

I squint. Blink. Painful tears wash away the grime.

Eyes open now. Blurry shapes move and pitch around me. No focus yet, but I see light ahead. And green—a vibrant and vivid green. It seems terribly out of place in this hellhole.

"Workman! Get up. We gotta go!" Kraft's voice calls to me. It sounds like he's inside a giant pipe a thousand yards away.

I want to get to my feet, but I still can't see. My eyes sting so bad I want to rub and scratch them, but somebody's holding my arms.

I crack my eyes again. More boots ahead of me now, striping the light with their shadows. Smoke plays across the scene.

The machine gun upstairs rips off another long burst. AK's join in.

Come on, Jeremiah, you can't fight if you can't see.

I tear an arm free and wipe my dirty shirtsleeve across my eyes. Dry now, I try again.

Focus returns. The smoke shrouded green is the manicured front lawn, trimmed and neat, a sign of a conscientious owner who once took pride in his work. The edges are sharp, corners well defined. If it wasn't for the bullet-divots stippling the turf, this could be a yard in Oceanside. Here, it seems so out of place.

I'm only a couple of feet from the front door, staring outside. There's a concrete step beyond the doorway. Along its edge, a few rogue blades of grass stretch above the others. The owner missed a spot.

We have to cross that lawn to get back out on the street. The moment we clear those rogue blades, we'll be in the kill zone again.

"Workman, you ready?" Kraft screams over the gunfire.

I nod. Smokes looks grim but resolved. Levine, even though his blood-filled eye and blackened face make him look like a bad Halloween mask, continues to resist Doc Sunny.

"I wanna fuckin' fight! Get off me, Doc!"

Doc Sunny holds on to him.

The machine gun upstairs rips off another long burst.

"Who the fuck they shootin' at?" Smokes yells.

I shrug. "No idea."

I struggle to my knees, then Kraft helps me to my feet. The stack moves. I'm last man this time. I watch their boots stampede through the doorway. The tuft of taller grass gets trampled flat. My men brave the kill zone.

Back to the door, weapon on my shoulder, I watch the stairwell to make sure no insurgents countercharge us. Secretly, I pray I'll see Raleigh, rifle blazing as he bounds down those stairs back to us.

Nobody comes.

I'm alone in the house now. Time to leave. I step out into the sunlight, and charge across the lawn. My boots sink into the soft turf. This would be great grass for a football field.

The machine gun cuts loose. AK's bark. Is that a SAW firing? I'm not sure. There's so much shooting now that everything's so overlapped and intermingled it becomes one continuous noise. Whatever the case, nobody shoots at me, thank God.

I hit the wall, spin ninety degrees, and make for the gate. Nothing comes my way. Not a bullet spangs off the wall, not a single new divot's torn from the once-immaculate lawn.

Where are they shooting? Whom are they shooting?

Are our guys still on the second floor? How can that be? I never saw a soul.

Through the gate and out onto the street. I pivot a hundred and eighty degrees and move to use the wall as cover. Up the block, the rest of the platoon's spread out in a ragged line as our sprinters pull away from the middling athletes. Our rigs are about a hundred yards away.

I pause to catch my breath, leaning on the wall for support.

Come on, Jeremiah! Move. A hundred yards ain't nothing. You've got plenty in your tank.

The noontime heat beats down on me. The house offered protection from it, but now its strength assails me. My head throbs, the world spins again.

Without warning, my stomach contracts. Vomit sprays from my mouth and streaks the wall beside me.

"Jesus Christ," I hear myself say.

Another spasm and I spill bile onto the street. I'm so dizzy that I'm not sure if I can even walk.

You've got to try. There's a battle raging upstairs, and you have no business sitting here indulging your body.

I take a step toward our vehicles; it feels unsteady, almost ethereal, like I'm trying to run on a cloud.

Another step. I swoon forward, stagger-step twice, then regain my balance. Using forward momentum for balance, I keep my legs pumping. Faster. Harder. Faster.

Fourth quarter of a football game. That's what this feels like, only worse. Legs are rubber, head's shot. Vision blurry again. I put my head down and charge.

I gain speed, gritting my teeth as I force my body to obey my will. Soon, I feel like I'm flying down the street.

That's it. Keep going. Another ten seconds and you'll catch up to the rest of the squad. Breathing hard now, gasping really. Keep it up. Don't slow down. Don't give in to your body.

When I look up, I realize I'm still ninety yards away. The sudden incongruity of my effort versus my progress throws my focus off. I'm confused, and my body takes that moment to fail me. I lurch sideways, drop to a knee, and nearly fall facedown into the street.

A pair of hands grab me just as I throw up again.

"Workman, you okay?" Kraft says as he pulls me to my feet. The world shifts and I feel like I'm trying to stand on the side of a skyscraper.

"Whoa! I gotcha," Kraft says as I nearly keel over again.

"Fuck this. Let's go," I manage to say.

Kraft pulls me forward. My legs engage. I half run, half lean on my Marine brother. His presence comforts me, takes my mind off my failing body.

Stagger, listing, world spinning, time slows to a crawl. The vehicles loom, but the distance we cover doesn't seem to get us any closer. Frustration boils; we've got to get back into the fight.

"Come on, Workman. We can do this. Keep going. That's right."

I miss a step, and we both almost go down. At the last minute, Kraft saves us. His raw strength and force of will keep us on our feet.

Suddenly, I'm slammed against metal; it takes me a second to realize Kraft's pushed me against the side of a Humvee.

"Thanks," I manage.

Corporal Ray, one of our drivers, runs past me shouting, "Where's Raleigh? Raleigh? Where are you? Anyone seen him?"

Everyone's shouting over one another. Their words are indistinct, just a babble of frightened, excited, and adrenaline-infused men.

Corporal Ray and Raleigh Smith are best friends. Ray looks stricken with worry. He stops to look at me, then takes off into the crowd.

"Get all the ammo you can carry!" Kraft shouts over the cacophony.

Leaning against the Humvee, I slide to the back. Men are passing out fresh magazines. I grab them, two and three at a time and stuff them into every pocket and pouch. Then I drop the one still in my weapon and slide a fresh thirty rounder in its place.

Everything's so remote, unreal, that I'm not even sure how many mags I've got. I forgot to count. I do know that my uniform is bulging with ammo now. I can fight.

Levine's suddenly beside me. His eye is a fright, but his expression seethes with murderous intent.

"Let's go kill those fucking bastards," he growls in his Bronx accent. He slaps a magazine home and turns for the house. Other Marines start to do the same thing. The sight reenergizes me.

Be a leader. Come on, Jeremiah.

A long pull from a bottle of water and I'm ready to go as well. At least my heart is, anyway. I don't trust my body.

Take care of yourself. You're dehydrated. If you go down from heat exhaustion, you'll be a liability to the platoon.

Another gulp returns some more strength. I swish the water around in my mouth, spit it out, and take one last drink.

Kraft bounds up to me. "QRF is on the way. We'll have tanks here in a minute."

"Accountability?" I ask.

"Not sure. But we're missing at least five, maybe six. We've got guys all over the place. Some of the platoon's still down the street. They've set up a support-by-fire position in another house," Kraft tells me.

"Let's go find 'em," I say.

I push off from the Humvee like a swimmer launching from a pool wall. Kraft strikes out after me. Together, we sprint for the house. I don't know how long this resurgence of energy will last, but I've got to use it to find our brothers—and lead my men.

We're in front now, the gate stands open twenty yards away. We must look like heavily armed keystone cops. There's no order, no military formation. We're just a big gaggle of pissed off, ready-to-fight Marines spread out along a sidewalk.

We don't even pause at the gate. Instead, we buttonhook through it, and fly across the lawn. My boots touch the concrete step just behind Kraft, who pauses in the doorway and turns to watch the men behind us.

I screech to a stop in the hallway, duck my head into the living room, and clear it. A quick spin, a few steps, and I get eyes on the kitchen, too. Nobody's downstairs but us. Behind me, the men stack up again as they come through the front door. Everyone's panting for breath, but I can see fury in their eyes. We've got to find our men.

Overhead, the firefight rages. The usual sluggish-sounding AK reports entwine with that damned *Tatatatatatatatatata* of that machine gun. Every few seconds, I can hear the sharper, more distinct crack of an M16.

I join the stack. Kraft's right behind me; I'm at the front. He knees my ass and I bolt for the stairwell.

I hit the landing without getting shot at—something of a minor miracle. Our return must have caught the enemy unawares. I swing around, past the now-broken window on the back wall of the landing. Its glass crunches under my boots. Two big bounds and I grab the corner at the top of the stairs again. Kraft and Snell are right behind me.

We're met with a hurricane of fire. It all seems to come from the far room. I can see the couch again, and muzzle flashes flaring in the gloom.

The marble floor, already gutted and torn, explodes as the insurgent machine gunner aims too low. He overcorrects and laces the stairwell wall well over our heads. Somebody goes full auto with an AK-47. The wall I use as cover reverberates from multiple bullet impacts.

Snell kneels next to me and triggers off a full magazine from his AK. Kraft opens fire as well.

Okay, no more spraying and praying. Make the shots count. Let's get up here this time.

I shoulder my M16 and take aim at the couch. Three quick spasms on the trigger and I see more stuffing explode out of the furniture. I rake my fire back and forth. Surely, if anyone's behind it, my bullets must be hitting them.

Levine starts firing from below. His rounds crack and snap past us. Snell drops his empty mag out of his AK and reloads. Kraft covers him, snapping off rounds into the far room.

Click. My M16 runs out of ammo. Ducking behind the wall, I discard the empty mag and grab a fresh one. As I slam it home, I pause to survey the foyer. The desk is splintered and pockmarked with bullet holes. Streaks of something dark scar the marble floor. Blood? I can't tell. The door to the balcony hangs open. Light from it filters through the sheen of smoke still lingering in the air.

There's no sign of Raleigh, or any other Marine.

Okay, ready. Weapon hot.

I lean forward and get my rifle trained on the bedroom. Three muzzle flashes wink back at me. Surely there's more than that, though, given the amount of return fire we're getting. I try and suppress the ones I can see. One winks out, but the other two keep flashing.

Out of ammo again. I drop back, reload, and drain another mag. We must achieve fire superiority if we are to assault forward. The problem is, the enemy has the upper hand again. We simply can't match the amount of lead they throw back at us.

"Fuck!" Kraft screams. "This isn't working!"

What can we do?

Grenades. I have an M67 frag in a pouch on my flak vest. This is a dangerous gambit. If I blow the throw like the LT did downstairs, we can get hit by its shrapnel. Worse, we don't know where our Marines are. They might still be up here somewhere, and an area effect weapon like an M67 can't tell the difference between friend and foe.

If I accidentally kill one of our own guys, I couldn't live with that.

Shoulder on the wall, I try to think this through. The risks are high, but we've got nothing else that can level the playing field here.

Okay. I drop my M16 and pull the frag out of the pouch on my flak vest. The rifle's barrel drops, but the weapon hangs at my side thanks to my three-point sling.

A meat grinder of machine gun bullets sweep across the top of the stairs. Everyone ducks. Marble flies. Concrete chunks explode around us.

Damn, that was close.

Grenade in hand now, I start to prep it. Without my rifle, I feel totally exposed, naked in a firefight. My hands start to shake. If the Muj come out after us, I'll have no time to grab my M16.

Slow down. Think this through. Okay, slip the grenade into your right hand.

Good.

Standing up, I stay hidden by the corner of the wall. Its edge is jagged and gouged, evidence that the machine gunner and his buddies have come close too many times to count.

Left hand up. Right on. Pull the thumb clip. That's right, keep going.

Kraft sees what I'm doing and tries to lay down some covering fire for me. Snell joins in. Levine and the others shoot from the landing and the first stairwell. We're at our maximum firepower level now. Surely, we'll be able to hose them down now, right?

Grenade is prepped, just need to pull the pin. Slip it out.

The ring falls from my fingers and pings off the concrete stairs.

All right, how's this going to go down?

I'm holding the spoon, suddenly unsure of myself. To stay the most protected, I should throw it with my left hand. That way, I'll only expose a bit of my left shoulder, hand and arm. The problem is that I'm right-handed. There's no telling where the damn frag will go if I chuck it with my left. If I use my right, I'll have to come off the wall, sidestep to the left side of the stairs, and be totally exposed for several seconds.

What's it gonna be, boss? Safe and who knows where the thing will land, or bet the farm and try to fire it home before they cut you in two?

I glance at Kraft. He's watching me over the top of his M16's receiver, waiting for me to make my move. Snell's laser-focused, snapping out bursts with his AK. Its barrel must be white-hot by now.

A deep breath brings a sudden sense of peace. My hands stop shaking. I know exactly what to do.

Fuck it. I've got nothing to live for anyway.

Jess?

Come on. No word from her in weeks.

Grandma?

Dead.

Dad?

Vanished. Abandoned.

Mom?

Her son died proud.

These men here with me? They are my family now. We are brothers, and I will die for them, just as I know they will die for me.

Do it.

I push off from the wall and slide sideways. Kraft and Snell hold fire. I twist so my shoulders are square with the stairs. Something buzzes past my ear. A bullet sends a chunk of marble tumbling across the shattered foyer. Two or three stitch across the railing to my left. Another one ricochets up from the floor and spangs into the ceiling. I slide and slide, feeling as naked and vulnerable as an infant surrounded by wolves.

As soon as I come to a stop, I side-arm the grenade straight through the far doorway. It sails over the couch and disappears. Just as I kick back for the cover of the wall, the frag explodes.

The machine gun stops chattering. The volume of fire dips.

Right on! That did some damage.

We Marines pour the fire on. Smoke billows out of the far room, concealing the couch. The foyer grows dim from it.

I prep a second grenade. Kraft and I watch each other. On a silent command, I swing out again and toss this one into the smoke.

Damn! I didn't see where this one landed.

An AK looses off a long, almost frantic-sounding burst. Snell and Kraft respond. Another AK joins the fight.

The machine gun suddenly roars to life.

The firefight swells to its previous intensity. I look back down the stairs to see Smokes and Levine reloading. Doc Sunny's blazing away with his sidearm, an almost comically intense expression branded on his face.

Snell drops his mag out. As he reloads, it dawns on me that I've got an AK as well. It's been strapped across my back this entire time. Damn it. Time to use its full auto feature.

With my M16 dangling at my side, I grab the AK's strap and pull it off my body. The wood stock feels short and uncomfortable compared to the M16's more ergonomically friendly one. The weapon's a little heavier as well, and it has no broomstick handle. I have to hold it old-school style with my left hand clutching the wooden foregrip. The thing feels foreign to me, but right now we need to put lots of rounds down range—heavy ones with lots of stopping power. The AK and its larger bullet fits the bill.

Right hand flies up to the metal safety lever on the side of the receiver. One click down is full auto. Full down gives me single fire. I set it to full auto and lean out from behind the wall.

Smoke coils twist out from the far doorway and rush along the foyer's ceiling. I see no muzzle blasts, but I can hear them firing back.

A smooth curling of my fingers sends a spray of bullets into the air. The AK bucks furiously and gets ahead of me. The barrel climbs before I can correct and keep it down. My shots tear into the far wall and knock plaster from the ceiling.

Shit! This thing's impossible to control. *Tink-tink-tink.* Its empty shell casings catapult out the right side of the receiver and bounce off the wall and stairs.

The AK clicks on an empty chamber. I drop back against the wall, reload, and rack the bolt back. Pivoting on my right boot, I bring the weapon to bear. This time, I try to hold the barrel down, but as it rocks and rolls in full auto, the spastic recoil throws my aim off again. Who knows where that volley landed.

I go through three more magazines with the AK. It doesn't seem to suppress the enemy at all.

Somebody taps my shoulder. When I look back, I find Kraft standing behind me, holding a fragmentation grenade. I drop the AK and take it from him. It's already prepped, I just need to pull the pin.

I do so at the same time I move for the left side of the stairs. Through a hole in the smoke, I watch the grenade disappear into the far room. The whole house shudders when it explodes.

The incoming fire dips again. Perhaps that one did the trick.

Kraft hands me another grenade. I throw this one, too. All down the stack, men are passing grenades forward to Kraft and me. We prep and throw three more in quick succession. Only a few AK's are firing now. This is working.

Finally.

I pitch another frag. It skids along the marble and vanishes into the smoke. A second later, it bowls straight back for us, gyrating wildly as it skips and bounces over the shattered floor.

They've kicked it back at us!

"DUCK!" I scream, but it is too late.

Chapter Nineteen

BLEEDING LOVE

December 23, 2004
Fallujah

The explosion sweeps over us. It catapults me straight into Kraft and Snell. We all tumble down the stairs, legs, arms, guns flailing as we fall into a camouflaged heap on the landing.

My grenade knocked everyone off their feet. I see Levine mouthing something as he picks himself up. Doc Sunny's saying something, too, but all I hear is a persistent ringing. Ears are toast again.

Kraft, Snell, and I disentangle and find our weapons. We all look shaken, but nobody's wounded. What sort of a miracle is that?

Kraft shouts something. I shake my head and shrug. "Can't hear!"

He leans close, and his voice penetrates the ringing. "You good?"

I give him a thumbs-up. He offers a stiff smile then nods his head toward the top of the stairs.

With you brother.

Together with Snell, we bring our weapons to the ready up position and climb the stairs. I discard my AK-47. I'm doing no good spraying the ceiling and walls with the thing. The M16 feels cool and comfortable in my hands, even though it is too long for this sort of work. A good M4 Carbine with a collapsible stock would be the perfect weapon for a close-quarters fight.

I start shooting into the far room as soon as I grab the corner. Then the smoke engulfs us, and we start gagging from its acrid, burning taste. I duck low, but still inhale a lungful of the stuff. I feel like I'm standing in the middle of a campfire.

Snell moves up to my left shoulder, even as I choke and hack. He's focused, determined, and wanting to kill. Between bursts from his AK, I see him spitting up vile-colored phlegm. If we survive this nightmare, we'll probably all die of some crazy form of cancer.

Kraft taps my shoulder and hands me another grenade. Through the buzzing in my ear, I vaguely hear him say, ". . . milk . . . it!"

"Roger!"

I flip the pin out, release the spoon, and count. Our frag grenades are supposed to have a three-second fuse, but who trusts that? That's what makes milking one of these things so bloody dangerous. It's like playing Russian roulette with a bomb.

One . . . two . . .

I slide left past Snell, who holds his fire, and launch the grenade. It flies into the doorway and blows up in midair. The concussion punches my chest and stomach, leaving me gasping for breath.

Jesus that was close.

This is not a game we can keep up. Sooner or later, we'll find a frag some tired worker back home screwed up by cutting the fuse just a hair short. That'll be the end of me, Snell, and Kraft.

Kraft hands me another frag. "Last one!" he shouts.

Pin out, spoon spins off into space.

One . . .

God I hope this thing has a long fuse.

Two . . .

I slide and chuck. The grenade doesn't even make it to the doorway this time. It explodes at the far end of the foyer. Shrapnel scythes the air around us. Bits of the stuff pepper the wall next to me.

The machine gun opens up again. This time, its bullets stream just past Snell, who ducks forward for the cover the last steps provide. I hug the wall, Kraft close behind me.

A wail of rage and pain bursts through the ringing in my ears. Snell twists back to look over his shoulder, and I see his blackened face contort with horror.

Oh no. Oh shit. Somebody's hit.

"Motherfucker! Motherfucker!"

I want to pretend this isn't happening. My heart battering rams my chest so hard it feels split open and horribly exposed.

Turn around. You've got to see what's happened.

No, please no. Not my men. Not my brothers.

The machine gun pans left, raking the floor, wall, and corner. I ball up and make myself as small as possible. Bits of debris cascade down over my Kevlar and fleck my flak jacket. Something strikes my left hand. A tiny, smoking hole appears in my Nomex glove.

Doc Sunny shouts frantically. The din of battle swallows his words, but not his sense of urgency.

As if in slow motion, I force my head to swivel left. A half inch. Something stops me. I can't look.

Self-discipline. It is the cornerstone of every good Marine. Own your fear, Jeremiah.

Dread. Hate. Worry. I'm almost hysterical now. I'll fight all day long and face my enemy's bullets, but just don't make me face this.

The screams are fury-laced and wracked with pain.

My head turns another inch. Then another. My field of vision sweeps to the landing.

"NO!!! NO! NO!!!" I've lost control of my voice. Panic spurs my instinctive cries.

Levine's slumped against the landing's far wall, a jagged, burnt hole in his cammie sleeve just below his shoulder. Blood spurts through it, which Doc Sunny furiously tries to staunch.

"NO!" The sight splits me open. I love this man, our Bronx-born warrior driven to the Corps to mete out revenge for the people he lost on 9-11.

The Corps taught me how to love.

"We gotta get him outta here!" Kraft bellows into my ear.

Betrayal is all I've known. Except here, with them.

I bleed away inside, my own wound impossible to staunch.

Levine's face is painted with rage and angst. Beneath the grime and smoke stains, his skin drains to an ashen gray. Blood spills across the landing and drips down onto the first flight of stairs.

"Leave me alone! I wanna fuckin' fight!" he shouts.

Another burst from the machine gun sends us all flying for cover. A bevy of AK's follow it up with a swarm of bouncing, ricocheting 7.62 rounds.

Doc Sunny turns his face to us. He's gravely concerned, eyes wide, hands and arms slick with Levine's blood. He mouths "We've got to go!"

Kraft nods. The entire stack opens fire with everything we've got.

Bullets fly, men scream. Levine begs to stay put. He tries to bring his M16 to his shoulder, using only one hand, but the effort exhausts him. Doc Sunny and Smokes grab him and drag him toward the first flight of stairs. His boots toe through a puddle of blood and leave dual parallel streaks, like tire marks before a car wreck.

Kraft, Snell, and I lay cover fire. The rest of the men move with Levine, Smokes, and Doc Sunny, weapons blazing. When they reach the first floor, we displace off the top of the second flight and back down to the landing. Kraft inches over until he's got eyes on the foyer. Standing calmly, he unloads an entire magazine with hummingbird-quick trigger pulls on his M16. The insurgents apparently can see him, and a sudden hail of bullets demolish the wall behind us. Amazingly, he isn't hit, but he runs out of ammo. As he sidesteps to reload, Snell takes his place and faces the same fusillade.

Can there be any braver men? Neither of them even flinched.

Snell moves for the ten-step kill zone. Kraft and I slip into the line of fire and give him all the cover fire we can. Then Kraft and I back down the stairs, firing and loading as we go. At last, our boots hit carpet.

Doc Sunny and Smokes have Levine between them. His wounded arm hangs over Doc's shoulder, spraying blood down the back of his flak vest. The three of them stagger out through the door with the rest of the men following in support.

We're rear guard again. Nobody comes down the stairs, so we burst out into the midday sun. A pickup-truck-configured Humvee sits parked in the open gate, and one of our transport guys mans a SAW balanced on the canvas roof over the crew compartment.

Kraft screams, "On three, start shooting!" The gunner nods and gets down behind his light machine gun. Just then, Levine stumbles away from Smokes and Sunny.

"Doc! Doc!"

He staggers back toward the house, determined to get back into the fight. He starts to fail in front of Snell, who catches him. Doc and Sunny scoop him back up. Levine's lost a lot of blood and he's getting weaker. We must get him out of here.

Kraft shouts, "One! Two! Three!"

We start moving across the kill zone, but the SAW gunner doesn't open fire.

"What the fuck?" somebody shouts.

The gunner pulls the trigger but nothing happens. Suddenly it dawns on him that he's had the weapon at Condition Three. He racks the charging handle, which loads a round into the chamber. As we lurch across the yard, trampling the manicured, incongruously lush lawn under our boots, he finally gets his weapon on line. It spews 5.56mm rounds into the upstairs windows.

God I hope our guys aren't still up there.

Overhead, a volley of incoming fire rips into the branches of the trees standing near the outer wall. The men ahead of me reach the gate, maneuver through it and past the Humvee. As they disappear, I breathe a sigh of relief. They're safe in the street.

Kraft and Snell duck through the gate next. I'm last and moving very slowly. The adrenaline rush that the firefight kick-started drains out of my system. All the aches and pains crash down on my nervous system. I start to limp.

The afternoon sun sits perched high above us, its brilliant light drowning out the morning shadows and shade. It has to be a hundred and ten degrees now. We're left cruelly exposed.

Ahead of me, the rest of the platoon section reaches our vehicles. Kraft and Snell catch up to them while Doc Sunny tears open Levine's shirtsleeve. Hopefully, somebody's called a medevac so we can get him to the cloverleaf east of town where a medical unit has set up shop.

Suddenly, my vision blurs. Sweat in my eyes again. Raking my filthy shirtsleeve across my face takes care of that. A few blinks and I see . . .

Hebert?

To my left, a figure stumbles out from between two houses. He takes awkward baby steps, his arms dangling limp at his sides. He looks like a marionette with half his strings severed.

"Hebert? Is that you?" I shout.

His head lolls over to one side, and he baby-steps twice. He's fifty feet from me, face stained and saturated with grime.

". . . Work . . . man . . ."

"Hebert! Hang on."

Limp-running toward him, my wounded leg drags me down. I feel like I'm trying to break an ankle tackle but the defender refuses to let go. Ahead, Hebert sways unsteadily and tries to turn for me. His knees buckle, and his forward momentum falters.

I have a fleeting vision of him grinning like a kid, hoisting a fish he'd caught on his latest expedition to the lake with Raleigh Smith. They took turns posing and snapping photos of each other and their butt-ugly catches with their digital cameras. The only two Marines in Anbar province with fishing gear.

". . . help, me . . ."

He reaches the sidewalk, forty feet away. I tug and pull my wounded leg, but it feels like I'm running on flypaper. Thirty feet. Hebert's mouth is open, jaw slack, arms disturbingly lifeless at his sides.

"Hold on, brother. Hold on," I call. It doesn't register on him. Through his orange Wiley X's, I can see his eyes now. They're unfocused, crazy. I realize I'm seeing the thousand-yard stare—the same look of Iwo and Peleliu vets, like those spooky Tom Lea paintings I've seen in books.

"What happened?" but my words are lost in another torrent of gunfire.

Twenty feet. Hebert stutter-steps over the sidewalk, trailing something. What is that?

Blood. I see it now, rich and crimson in the Fallujah sun. It stains the sidewalk like red paint slopping from a can. His pant legs are soaked black.

A panic-driven sense of urgency spurs me forward. Fifteen feet. He starts to lose his balance. One arm, zombie-like with lifeless fingers dangling, raises up for me.

". . . help . . ."

"I gotcha, man," I say as I collide with him. A bear hug keeps us on our feet. He pitches almost limp against me, forcing me to prop us both up with my wounded leg. A new spurt of adrenaline suppresses the pain.

". . . Workman . . . thank . . ."

A bullet ricochets off the sidewalk not even an arm's length away. Holding Hebert, I look back over my shoulder. Somebody's got eyes on us, but we're not in view of the house.

They've got reinforcements, Jeremiah. You've got to move. MOVE NOW!

I start to bull-rush Hebert toward the vehicles, but we stumble and lose our balance. That's not going to work.

Another bullet zings off the asphalt.

". . . They're still . . . shooting . . ." Hebert sighs. He sounds barely conscious.

Jesus. God. Help us. Help us.

Hebert sags through my arms and falls to the street. I hear a crack and a whine. Another near-miss. Somewhere up the block, a sniper ranges in on us.

"Hebert, can you walk?" I ask.

His body trembles. He shakes his head like a ten-shot drunk.

He's a hundred and sixty pounds without his gear. Close to two hundred with his weapon and flak vest. We're a good hundred and twenty yards from the vehicles. I can't carry him; I simply don't have the strength anymore.

A branch snaps off a tree in the yard Hebert staggered out of a minute ago. It falls to the sidewalk with a rustle of leaves.

"Okay, bro, I'm gonna drag you."

". . . hit . . ."

I grab a strap off his flak vest, and let out some slack from its buckle. When I have enough, I wrap both hands around its end and spin around. Hebert comes off the street, his back presses against mine. I heave and bring him up a little farther.

"Okay, here we go."

". . . keep . . . firing . . ." he says dreamily.

Shit. He's gone into shock. Move. Move, Jeremiah. Everything you got. Lay it out now.

I once saw a video of Virginia Tech's star quarterback, Jim Druckenmiller, as he pulled a station wagon across a football field. Leaning forward, every muscle popping, he seemingly defied the laws of physics with brute force and will.

That's how I feel right now. Hebert's heavy on my back. I'm staggered by his load, my leg refusing to fully function. My arms are taut as I hold him in place, the strap over my left shoulder.

A solid heave and we move forward with a lurch. My knee gives way, and I collapse to the pavement.

"Hold on, I got you," I say, more to myself than to Hebert.

A bullet hits the street right in front of Hebert's blood-speckled boot. ". . . gotta get . . . outta . . . here . . ." he cries weakly.

I tug hard and surge forward onto my feet. I'm hunched over almost double now, which causes Hebert to slide down my back. I have to pull the strap down with all my strength to keep him from falling off me.

Another bullet sings overhead.

I take a step, then another. Each move bleeds energy, erodes my strength. But I am not going to fail this man. I will die first.

I lean farther forward, balancing his weight against me. I trip and have to release my right hand, which slaps against the grainy asphalt for balance. I'm so low now, that I must look like a defensive lineman in a three-point stance.

Weight down on my right hand, left leg crab-walks forward. Right leg pushes off. Weak now, barely functional. Another push, a spike of pain. Hebert slips to the small of my back. Left hand coiled around the strap, I jerk it hard against my ribs. Hebert's head pulls up an inch.

I scream from effort, teeth grinding, muscles straining, body taught and taxed.

Hebert scrambles backward with his boots. It gives me a little leverage. I take another step.

The sniper lays a bullet right beside us. There's no cover here. No hope if my body fails. Our erratic movements must be the only thing saving us.

Right hand down for balance, left burning with the burden of Hebert's weight. I hold on with everything I've got left and duck-walk two more steps.

We'll never get to the vehicles.

"Workman . . ." Hebert moans, his voice borders on delirium.

It propels me forward. Two more duck-steps, hand slapping for purchase on the hot asphalt.

Fourth down. Goal to go. Carry the load. When the chips were down, I always wanted the ball. I knew I could break through the line and get that score, even if it meant dragging linebackers with me.

Desperate now, I pull Hebert along. My head's down so low, my Kevlar helmet scrapes the ground with every forward surge. From between my legs, I can see we're leaving splatters of blood in our wake from both our wounds.

The sniper takes another shot. Not even close this time, but the sound of the bullet passing sends a sudden bolt of energy through my muscles. It carries us another two or three yards, but then my right knee fails and we go down again. Kneecap on asphalt, I push up to get us going again. My knee comes up an inch . . . two.

Come on. Come on. Come on.

Ping! A bullet hits the sidewalk to our left.

My knee gives out again, and this time I go down hard. Only my right hand prevents a sagging face-first belly flop onto the asphalt.

I raise my head to see how far we've got to go. Bad move. The sudden change of perspective sends my stomach into a death spiral. Sweat pours off my brow, stinging my eyes. Vision blurs. Stomach spasms and I heave up another mouthful of bile.

I try to rise, but my stomach betrays me. I vomit and gasp. Strength fading, my vision tinged with fuzzy black edges, I start to run empty on hope.

You cannot fail this man.

I will not fail this man.

Get through the line. How'd I always do that? Pump your legs, they are your engine. Never let them stop.

I drop my head with no idea how far I am from the vehicles. One . . . two . . . three . . . I piston my legs, my knees jerk off the ground and we're up and moving. One step, another. I drag Hebert forward.

The sniper's found the range. A bullet embeds in the asphalt right next to me. I lurch crazily, changing directions. I used to be good at that. In the open field, I'd zig and zag and drive the defense crazy. Now, my life depends on it. So does Hebert's.

Another crack. Will this ever end? I zig wildly, shambling, staggering sideways then forward. I feel warmth on my back. What is that?

Hebert's blood.

Holy shit, keep going.

I want to call for help, but I have no breath for it. Besides, nobody will hear; we're too far away and the gunfire is simply too overwhelming. Back at the house, I can hear the Humvee's SAW gunner laying down long, uncontrolled bursts of fire. He's a transport guy and doesn't know how to use his weapon like we do.

Hebert tries to say something, but only a strangled gurgle comes out. He suddenly gets heavier. Looking between my legs, I see his hands dragging limply by his sides. He feels like deadweight.

No. No.

I pull him along, half dragging, half carrying him on my back. Knees are shot, calves succumb to the strain. Right hand forward, for balance at first, now my fingers claw for purchase on the asphalt. I drag us forward on my fingernails.

Keep those pistons moving!

We shuffle forward. Bullets whine past. I puke and pull, gasp and gag as rivers of sweat waterfall off my downturned face. My body feels like rubber. Hebert doesn't move. His body goes slack against mine.

Oh Jesus, don't let him be dead. Don't let my brother go.

My heart's an open wound, bleeding, beating, pain-wracked and crazed.

Love.

The bond between us like a sword gutting me out.

"Hebert? HEBERT?"

There's no answer to my anguished cry.

Chapter Twenty

THE DARK SIDE OF THE BROTHERHOOD

Late July 2006
Parris Island, S.C.

"Hebert!"

No answer.

Crushed flat, knees throb. Hands dug deep in soft turf.

Turf?

I can't move. Hebert's deadweight keeps me pinned on my knees and hands.

"Hey, you okay, Dog?"

"Kraft . . . help me!"

My eyes are open now. No Kevlar weighting my head. I see a solitary blade of grass standing high among a fresh cut lawn. Every muscle burns from overuse.

Am I back in front of the house?

Hands reach for me.

"Get Hebert!"

"What? Who's that?"

An unfamiliar face stares at me. He looks shocked and concerned, and I don't recognize him at all. Whoever he is, he pulls me to my feet.

I'm not back at the house, I'm behind the barracks. A discarded rake lies a few feet away.

"Come on, let's get you inside."

"First sergeant's office," I mumble.

Arm around this stranger, we limp inside the barracks.

"It doesn't matter."

"Why?"

"The war's going to throw curveballs at you. Even here. Even years later. I saw it in my own unit from the Gulf War."

"So what matters, then?"

"The fight. That's all you got to keep you going now, Workman."

"What do you mean?"

"Other guys'll give up. They'll eat a bullet or take some pills. That's the easy way out. You know what? It disgraces the men we lost."

I flush with guilt. He senses it.

"They didn't have a choice. We do. We either man up and fight for this gift—time, living, breathing, having kids—or we fucking pussy out. They didn't have that option. And to do anything *but* fight for what they didn't have is like pissing on a grave at Arlington."

I feel like I've been smacked. I wish I had the first sergeant's clarity.

"I feel so lost."

"Then stay on your feet until you find your way."

"How?"

"Did you risk your life that day?" he asks harshly. "And don't bull-shit me. It's just the two of us in here."

I drop my eyes to the floor. "Yeah. I suppose."

"You either did or didn't, Workman."

"I should have died." I didn't mean for that to come out. It slipped through my lips like an oiled snake.

"No, goddamn it! Nobody *should have* died anywhere. It's pure luck of the draw. Fate . . . God. Whatever."

"I wanted to stay and fight."

"Were you ordered out?"

"Sort of."

"Did you pussy out and run away?"

"Fuck no."

"Then you have no reason to be guilty. None. Did you give every-thing you had?"

"And then some, First Sergeant."

"Then hold on to that. Take pride in that."

"It wasn't enough."

"That's the way it shakes out sometimes. Nobody's best could have saved those men on the second floor. I've heard the story. It was a terrible situation, but that's war. Men die despite our best. We can't train for it, we can't be prepared for it. It just *is*. All we can do is accept it."

I don't want to believe that. The randomness of it all makes me feel out of control, and I hate that sensation. Marines—we dominate. We own land and we take what we want. To think that fate can deal us an unwinnable hand is to admit a level of human frailty we've been programmed to reject.

I finish the second bottle of water and feel more alert. "So now what?"

"Now what? You get back on your feet, Workman. You get the help you need and you keep moving forward. If you stop—if you punch out on me, so help me God, I'll kick your ass."

We both start to laugh. "Roger that, First Sergeant."

"You getting any counseling?"

"Yeah, over in Beaufort."

"Wanna go over there now?"

"Probably should."

"Okay, take the rest of the day, but then I want to see you here first thing in the morning, ready to go, got me?"

"Yes, First Sergeant."

We both get to our feet. Just as I turn for the door, he steps forward and engulfs me in a fierce bear hug. It almost cracks my fragile self-control again.

"Keep fighting, Workman. That's all we got. You hear me?"

"I promise, First Sergeant." The words sound hollow.

"Don't let those men down."

Again.

Now that's the rub, isn't it?

"Don't let *me* down."

As I leave his office, I feel his eyes heavy on the back of my head.

PART
IV

Chapter Twenty-One

THE WRONG FIGHT

September 2006
Quantico, Virginia

SEPTEMBER. ALL I'VE done is fight, mainly with Jessica. Just after she arrived in South Carolina, I received orders transferring me to Marine Corps Headquarters in Quantico, Virginia. What began as a fresh start for both of us quickly turned toxic.

Since leaving Ohio, my troughs of humanity have grown shorter and shorter at night as my craving for Clonopin increases. Everything that's happened drives me to seek solace in its emotion-deadening power.

Besides, I'm at my worst now when I'm in the trough—angry, spiteful, and mean. Cruel, really.

Tonight's battle began with what? A fight over how clean our place is? Who would really care about that? Truth is, I came home looking for a fight, and found it in the nitpicking I know drives Jess so crazy.

The Corps has turned me into an office clerk. That is not me, and I hate my job. I boil and fume all day, counting the minutes to come home. When I do, there's no peace, only a bitter campaign between Jess and me.

I miss Doctor Radford. I always felt better after talking to her. Here, I'm seen twice a month by docs who don't seem to give a shit. There's a whole lot of us in the same boat, and going over to the clinic makes me feel like I'm on a conveyer belt. We're mass-produced PTSD cases, and the docs here simply ask us if we're thinking about hurting ourselves or others. If we say yes to either question, they up our dosages and send us on our way. "See you in two weeks."

This isn't care; it's a stay of execution. They're keeping us doped up—zombified—so we don't become headlines. IRAQ VET KILLS FAMILY, SELF.

Sooner or later, it's all going to boil over.

I've been a bastard. No way to deny that. Every chance I get, I find myself lashing out at Jess. Her pain gives me a bitter sense of pleasure, like I've dished out a little of what she did to me in Iraq. Now that she's pregnant and even more vulnerable, well, I've taken advantage of that. Part of me wants to destroy her, just as she did with me.

So much for her all-American family.

"What's left to say here?" I ask from the bedroom doorway. The lights are off, and I can see only Jessica's silhouette by the window. She's sitting in a chair, staring off into space.

"I don't know. Haven't you done enough damage tonight?" Her voice is bitter-laced and weary. Her makeup kit lies overturned and spilled across the bedroom floor. I threw it there about an hour ago.

I push off the doorway and walk into the bathroom. I need my Clonopin. As I fumble around looking for the pill vial, I hear her say, "Jeremiah, you're a fucking addict."

"Shut the fuck up!" I shout.

"Father of my unborn child's a druggie. That's right, get your hit."

My fist slams the bathroom wall so hard the house shudders.

"I can't live like this. You're such a psycho, Jeremiah."

"You have no idea, bitch!"

I hold the tablet in my hand. I want so eagerly to pop it in my mouth, swallow it, and make all this go away. I'll be out in no time, feeling none of this rage and pain.

I hear her crying now. "You said you'd change! You swore you'd try!"

"And you swore you'd wait for me. Not even a fucking letter, Jess! You wouldn't even take my calls!"

"How many times can I tell you I'm sorry?" I step into the bedroom, pill clenched in my fist. She's got her face in her hands. Her hair's a mess.

"There aren't enough times. Believe me. Words don't mean anything anyway. Especially not from a lying slut like you."

Jeremiah, you just called the mother of your child a slut. Have some restraint here.

Fuck that. I want to destroy her. Living together again was a terrible mistake. It just evoked all the old pain, resentment, and anger. Once betrayed, there's no going back.

"Oh, do you really wanna go there? Who's the liar here, Jeremiah? I know her name for God's sake. I went to her house!"

"You had no right to do that!" I had no idea she knew I was unfaithful.

"You see her again, I'll leave you. I swear to God, I will."

"You don't have the guts."

She gasps and starts to sob.

"Why do you resent me? Why do you hate me?"

"Because I can't leave you!" I roar and kick the wall. "I'm trapped, don't you get it? First you destroyed me, then you trapped me. I'm like a fly hanging in your web. You've sucked me dry, Jess."

She falls silent.

"I can't believe you just compared me to a spider."

"I can't help but hate you."

"I thought you loved me! You tell me that every day."

"That's the trap. I do. God help me, I do," I say as I slump down the wall.

"Then why do we keep thrashing each other?"

"Love is pain."

"You are really twisted if you believe that."

"It isn't me. It's life."

"No, no it isn't. Not for normal people."

"Well, Jess, you just said I'm a fucking addict psycho. Where's the normal in that?"

"Goddamn you. Goddamn you." She pulls at her hair with both fists.

"You know, you've never asked about what happened."

"I don't want to know," she says through a half-choked sob.

"Why not? I don't get that."

"For God's sake, how can you not get that?" Anger flares in her voice now.

She turns to look at me.

"You don't give a shit, do you?" I accuse.

"I can't survive the guilt," she wails.

Careful. You've got to back off. Don't say anything more.

"You deserve it." My own voice sounds viperous.

"We just go round and round, don't we? This will never end."

My body starts trembling. The stirrings of a headache form in the back of my head. I need the Clonopin. When Jess turns away to stare out the window again, I thumb the pill in my fist, playing with it. I want to pop it into my mouth. I *need* to do that. But I have too much pride to do it in front of her.

Pride? Pride you arrogant ass? Look at what you're doing to her!

There's a sheet of armor down inside me so thick I can't begin to care. Maybe after this is all over, I'll feel something. Right now, I'll admit nothing, give her nothing.

Bullshit, Jeremiah. You're slitting your own wrists every time you tear her apart.

Like I care.

"Jeremiah?"

"What?"

"Part of me wants to run to your arms and beg for forgiveness." Her voice is high and broken, her words suffused with despair. "But part of me wants to run out the door and never come back."

Don't do it. Don't do it, Jeremiah. For God's sake, this is your chance to end this. Fix it.

"Go."

Her sobs form her reply.

For a long minute, neither of us say a word. Jess stares out the window into the night. It's drizzling outside, and the pane is speckled with raindrops.

I lean against the wall and focus on the floor in front of me. We don't look at each other—can't look at each other.

At last, she stands, a silhouette against the window. For the first time, I notice that she's starting to show.

"I wish I'd never had that dream," she says softly, almost to herself.

Dream, or prophecy? It led us here.

The moment the front door slams shut, the armor inside me shatters completely.

Run after her! Go! Now.

My legs won't move. The words I've said tonight can't be taken back. The damage can never be fixed, can it? I slashed and burned and destroyed the only woman I've ever loved. And now, I'm left with nothing.

What am I doing? I've betrayed my pregnant wife. There is nothing more vile than that. Still, I'm defiant. Part of me screams that she brought this on herself. She started this war of emotional destruction with eight simple words spoken across three continents.

The affairs are so easy. No emotion. Just the chase. No pain. No history. Just anonymity and a quick thrill.

Hollow thrill, and at great cost, to be paid in full on nights like this one.

Is this the sort of man I want to be? Is this the father my kid will have?

My stepfather. Just the mention of his name injects a pure serum of hate in my soul. Abusive. Always screaming, calling my mother unfathomable names. I once saw her on the living room floor, him atop her beating her senseless. I was in fourth grade. What could I do? I threw something at him to distract him. He came after me, shouting and screaming and filling me with terror. I fled upstairs and grabbed a curtain rod. As he came after me, I surprised him in the hallway and struck him with all my preteen strength. The blow stunned him long enough for me to flee the house.

There was no safe haven for me.

There's no safe haven for Jess.

I am destroying her. And part of me loves that.

You scream and yell and control her through fear.

She earned this fate.

Don't lie to yourself. Every time you do this, you burn away another part of whatever good is left inside you.

"I don't care!" I shout to the empty house.

Then there will be nothing worth saving in you. You'll be beyond redemption; you won't deserve it.

Hell? Is that what you're talking about here? 'Cause if you are, I can't imagine it is any worse than my life right now.

You know what I'm talking about.

Fucking conscience. If I had an M16, I'd drill you right here.

I'm your last hope. Ignore me and you'll be lost.

Screw you. I'm a lost cause, and I don't have it in me to care anymore.

A sudden vision strikes me. I see my stepfather in our backyard, my dog at his feet. He's holding a .22 and I'm pleading with him not to do it. He cocks the weapon. The barrel falls slowly until it rest on the back of his furry head. My dog's oblivious; he stares happily at me.

My stepfather turns to look at me, a wicked smile on his face.

With cold terror, I see it's my own face. It is my finger on the trigger, and now I'm looking at my only son.

Dead inside. I don't care, just like tonight. Whatever I feel after this is over, I'll drown it in liquor and drugs. I pull the trigger and watch with fierce satisfaction as my son's face collapses with grief and trauma.

I fly to my feet, screaming at the top of my lungs.

That is your fate if you keep this up. This is the man you are becoming.

Panic-stricken, I run for the front door.

All you have to do is open it. Go after her. Make this right.

My headache grows. My fingers quake on the knob. I've got to take the Clonopin. It will erase everything, make this nightmare go away. I sag chest-first into the door.

I look down at an open palm. One little pill awaits. I toss this on my tongue, and all of this goes away.

No it doesn't. It's just a dodge and you know it.

Jessica's right, I am an addict.

Go through the door!

I bring my palm up to my chin. With jackal eyes, I regard the Clonopin.

Take it. Everything will be better. Everything will be fine.

You keep taking this shit, and you'll never move forward. Never.

Total peace. Nothingness awaits. I ache for it.

Forget Jess. Forget your son. And the Corps? You'll be the most decorated clerk in the Marines. No more schools. No more achievements. You'll just mark time and punch a clock.

My left hand comes up of its own volition. I don't control it and watch with fearful fascination. Its fingers scrabble along my right hand's upturned palm. I feel the pill between my thumb and index finger. The sensation is irresistible. One little jerk and the pill will be in the back of my throat.

I want this more than anything I've ever wanted in my life. I need it, like air. Like food. More than anything.

More than your son?

"SHUT UP! SHUT UP!"

There's only one hope for you now.

"Oh yeah? What's that?"

Forgiveness.

The corrupted, putrid side of me that relishes all this hate and cruelty bucks in revolt. It feels like physical blows.

"No. Not anymore. This ends now."

The pill falls to the carpeted floor. Door open now, I rush into the rainy night. Maybe, just maybe, I'm not too late.

Chapter Twenty-Two

BOOTSTRAPS

October 2006
Quantico, Virginia

So this is what hitting bottom feels like.

Take the Clonopin.

No. Stay the course. You're almost through this.

My skin crawls and jumps. I lay sprawled on my bathroom floor, the buzzing of the interior fan my only company. How long have I been here? An hour? A day? Time has no substance anymore. I just endure.

A spasm wracks my body, and for a moment I curl fetal on my side as I suffer through it.

Take the Clonopin. I NEED it.

I threw all my Clonopin away, probably four days ago. My body has punished me ever since.

You gotta do this to get your life back. Jessica. Jump school. Achievements and family.

"My life? What is my life now?" I'm talking to myself out loud again.

There's a knock on the bathroom door.

"What?"

"Jeremiah, are you okay?"

"Stay out of here!" There's no way I'm going to let my wife see this.

"How're you doing?"

"I'm fine." I'm not fine. My body screams for its fix. I'm slathered with sweat even though I shiver uncontrollably from imagined cold.

I'm lying right next to a heater vent, and even its hot air seems frigid on my skin.

"Just remember, jump school. You gotta do this to go to jump school."

I've waited my entire Marine Corps career to parachute from an airplane. I just got a slot at Fort Benning. The school starts in a few weeks, but the flight surgeon who examined me won't clear me to jump unless I'm totally med-free.

"I know. I know. Jesus, Jess, please. You gotta just leave me alone, okay?"

I hear her press against the door. Has she turned her back to lean on it? "I love you."

"I don't know why," I say through chattering teeth.

"Why? The man you were. The man you still can be."

Jump school. This is my stand, my chance to climb out of this miserable life and find my way again. If I can just get through this, I will become a man that Jess can be proud of again.

My body seizes up. Every muscle contracts. A colony of tearing, scratching insects scrabbles under my skin. The sensation borders on unbearable.

I barely make it to the toilet before I throw up. Again.

"Jump school," Jess says through the door.

I'm doing this for you, too.

And our child. Boy or girl, I don't care. I just want to be a good father to a healthy kid.

Face in the toilet, I hear Jess say something else, but the words are lost in a dry heave. A moment later, my stomach goes slack and I sag back onto the floor.

"I love you," I manage, unsure if my voice will carry through the door.

"Call me if you need me," she says. I hear her walk down the hall to the living room. A moment later, I hear the babble of the television.

Who is the man Jess thinks you can be?

For two years, I've just wanted to return to normal, be who I was before Fallujah. I've fought and lost that fight. My PTSD is like an immovable stone wall. I've pushed and flung myself against it with growing desperation, but it still bars my path back to who I once was. That struggle has earned me nothing but more scars.

The overhead fluorescents start to hurt my eyes. Weakly, I reach up and flip the switch off. A thin beam of light from the hallway shines in from under the bathroom door, but otherwise I will suffer in darkness now.

The heater blasts my skin, but I still feel as though I'm lying on ice.

Keep fighting, Workman.

I see First Sergeant Lewis, his face hard and determined. He knows what he's talking about, but what's the point of fighting if you don't gain any ground? That just becomes as futile as the Somme, or Verdun.

Worse, what's the point of fighting if you aren't fighting to get anywhere? It simply becomes a battle in a vacuum, a struggle for life that's filled only with the fight and nothing else. That's a rootless, hopeless existence that can only lead to oblivion.

And here you are.

And here I am.

There has to be something more than the fight.

Jess. Jump School. Fatherhood.

The man I need to be.

Another sudden flurry of shakes grips my body. I flop around on the bathroom floor like one of those fish Hebert and Raleigh Smith pulled out of our lake. When the seizure passes, I'm slick with a fresh sheen of sweat, every nerve exhausted.

I can't go back to who I was. There's no denying that. I've tried for two years and failed. I've denied the truth, bucked against it. That stone wall will never be shattered. But maybe there's another way.

Evolve.

Yes. I have weapons left for this fight. Self-discipline. Determination. Strength.

Reason to try.

Withdrawal is my first test.

JUST TAKE THE CLONOPIN.

My body's like a vicious, jilted lover. Now that I've denied it what it most needs, it strikes back with no restraint.

I start to doze. The television clicks off. The light coming from the hallway through the crack under the door suddenly disappears. I'm left in total darkness, just me and my conscience.

Evolve through this. That's the only option. That's what a Marine would do.

Yes. I can't fight PTSD forever. But I can fight for a fresh start, a new life where I move forward and grow. That will give me meaning and substance.

A purpose.

For a fleeting moment, I see myself back in that group therapy session. I understand now what that Vietnam vet who was our counselor tried to tell us. We can't be ashamed. We can't try to deny our condition. We can only embrace it, absorb it into who we are and what the war has made us become.

Hello, my name is Jeremiah Workman, and I suffer from PTSD.

No shame. No guilt. Only resolve to be a man my child can respect and love.

Somewhere in the future, I see myself in front of a school. I'm holding a tiny hand and smiling. I look down and see a mop of hair—my son? My daughter? It doesn't matter. I am this child's father.

Suddenly, we're in front of a classroom full of kids. The teacher stands in back, primly dressed and a warm and welcoming expression on her face.

This is my dad, Jeremiah. He's a Marine. He served in Iraq against terrorists.

The pride in my child's voice is fuel for the fight.

That's where I want to be, that's where I have to get.

From our bedroom, I hear soft music playing. Jess has turned the radio on as she gets ready for bed. The song swirls around me even as another bout of the shakes sweeps through my body.

> *I'm alone*
> *Yeah, I don't know if I can face the night*
> *I'm in tears and the cryin' that I do is for you*
> *I want your love—let's break the walls between us*
> *Don't make it tough—I'll put away my pride*
> *Enough's enough, I've suffered and I've seen the light*

This is our song. We danced to this in high school. I told Jess I loved her for the first time while these words washed over us.

And in Iraq, to win her back when things went so far astray, I copied down the lyrics and mailed them from Fallujah. It was my last-ditch attempt to save us.

Aerosmith. "Angel." Our first wedding dance.

The darkness melts into my past. I see Jess and me walking hand in hand. I'm in an off-the-rack rented tux, Jessica looks stunning in a dark green and black dress that falls to her calves. Prom night, 2001, my senior year. We're in the last months of normal small town life, before the towers fell and the bodies of our generation's warriors returned to Dover, Delaware, en route to their final resting points.

We lived life in a bubble, unsullied by the realities of what loomed on the horizon. Prom night was the biggest thing in our lives.

At first, we couldn't even recognize the gym. The place was covered with trees and vines. A rock wall dominated one corner, and a waterfall spilled into a pool set beneath it. It looked like we'd just stepped into the Amazon rainforest. Our folks had even paid the Columbus zoo to bring down some exotic animals. As we moved to join our friends out on the dance floor, monkeys and lemurs capered around us. There were even a few penguins waddling about.

I asked the disk jockey to play "Angel" for Jess. We held each other and swayed to the music, just two young American high school sweethearts with our entire lives before us.

The insects race around under my skin. I quake and twitch, the bathroom floor feeling like a glacier beneath me.

Get through this for yourself. Get through this for Jess. If you really still love her, you've got to make it.

I can almost taste a Clonopin tablet on the back of my tongue. My body aches for it. I find myself sliding on my back toward the door.

What are you doing?

I've got to have some.

No. You've got to rebuild this mess of a life.

This is too hard. My body's joined my brain and gone to war with my resolve.

My hand reaches up to the doorknob. Somewhere, there's got to be a hospital or a dispensary that will refill my Clonopin prescription. I'll drive until I find one.

Raleigh and Eric appear before me. James Phillips stands behind them. Three Marines, denied this gift, this torment.

Other guys'll give up. They'll eat a bullet or take some pills. That's the easy way out. You know what? It disgraces the men we left over there.

My hand falls off the knob. First Sergeant Lewis is right. I can't disgrace myself to these men any longer.

My body punishes me with a brutal wave of the shakes. Minutes later, I'm weak and dry heaving again.

I will not give up. This is my stand. From here on out, I grow out of this hole. I will achieve. I will be the winner I always was and need to be again.

That's right, Jeremiah. Jump school is only the first step. You know what you have to do next, right?

I know. And it will be far harder than anything I've yet gone through.

Maybe, but you do it, and you'll set the foundation for your future.

I'm back on the floor, but now it is broiling hot. Even in boxers and a T-shirt, I feel like I'm lying on a grill.

I have to forgive myself.

Yes.

It is the only way to exorcise the guilt.

Yes.

I will never be able to forget, but maybe I can absorb, forgive, and move forward.

Did you risk your life that day? And don't bullshit me. It's just the two of us in here.

"Yes. I did." My voice is hoarse and frail.

In the background, I hear our song still playing.

> *Without your love—I'm nothing but a beggar*
> *Without your love—a dog without a bone*
> *What can I do? I'm sleeping in this bed alone*

Jess. I have to forgive her, too. And I'm not sure I can.

If you can't, you've got to stop savaging her for what she did. Can you do that?

There's so much bitterness in me. It is poison to the soul.

You have to let it go.

I've tried to reject all the things Fallujah did to me and deny the damage it has done. Now I know that if I don't integrate that experience into who I am, I will always be a fractured and malfunctioning human being. That is the only way around the stone wall PTSD has thrown across my future.

Okay then.

If I'm going to go forward, I have to first go back and walk through it one more time to examine everything I did that day. Could I have done more? Could I have saved those men?

Part of me recoils at what I might find, but if I don't go back this night will be for nothing. Jump school will forever be out of reach, and I will trail in circles until I share Ira Hayes's ditch.

Are you man enough for this? Can you survive the answers you seek?

A tiny hand in mine, a toothy grin, and a child's embrace. We stand in front of a classroom of kids, whose dads are insurance salesmen, tax attorneys, and accountants. There's nothing wrong with that. But my kid's dad is a Marine, proud, strong, a breed apart. Different. I realize as I look into those innocent eyes that I am my child's hero.

That's where I want to be someday.

Okay, then you've got to do this.

I know.

You've got to go back.

The floor suddenly goes glacial again. I shiver and shake and sweat. My skin crawls with angry, biting bugs. I'm weak and drained, but still up for this fight. But I know the biggest one lies ahead inside my own mind.

I am ready.

The darkness evaporates. The bathroom vanishes. Colors and light play around me. I close my eyes. For two years, I've been at the mercy of these memories. Tonight, I'll take control of them once and for all.

Chapter Twenty-Three

SCORCHED EARTH

December 23, 2004
Fallujah

Weight on my back. I'm stooped so low all I can see is the gray-black asphalt of this forsaken Fallujah street.

Desert heat pounds down on me. My head spins, ears ring, my lungs are still full of smoke.

"HEBERT??" I'm frantic now.

No reply.

I crab-walk sideways and forward, my brother hanging from the strap I've thrown over my shoulder. How far from the vehicles are we? I've got to look, but the last time I tried it cost me.

Kevlar heavy on my head, neck aching from its weight. I'm not used to moving with my head down, and it has taxed my muscles. I raise my head. The world tilts, but this time, I don't heave and puke.

Thirty feet away stands our seven-ton truck. Inside the cab, one of our transport guys sits and watches me, one arm resting on the driver's door.

Why is he just sitting there? His sloth enrages me. I scrabble a few more steps and shout, "Why the FUCK aren't you helping me?"

The transport guy looks stricken. He jumps from the cab and runs for me. A bullet whines overhead. He sprints for me and pulls Hebert off my back. His head flops to one side, carried by the weight of his helmet.

"Doc! Doc!" I scream with a hoarse, smoke-seared voice.

Together, the truck driver and I pull Hebert to safety behind one of our Humvees. Wherever the sniper is, he can't see us here.

Doc Sunny's working on somebody's arm when we arrive. At first, I assume he's treating Levine.

"Doc, you gotta help Hebert!" I shout again. Doc turns away from his patient, and I see it isn't Levine at all. He's working on Richeson, one of our missing Marines. His cammies are bathed in blood, and his arm's been wrapped like a mummy. He looks dazed and shares Hebert's thousand-yard stare.

I haven't seen Richeson since we first jumped out of our rigs to search this neighborhood. He was with Kraft's squad. I wonder if he was among the missing who had been trapped on the second floor. If that's the case, maybe all our Marines are safe now.

Doc finishes up with Richeson for the moment and rushes over to Hebert. He leans down and checks his pulse.

"He's alive," I hear Doc say. A flood of relief follows his words.

Doc turns Hebert onto his stomach and starts examining his wounds. Like Levine, he's lost a lot of blood. I can see he's been hit all along the back of his legs. Shrapnel? Bullet wounds? Maybe both. I move away to the back of another Humvee, where I start stocking up on fresh M16 magazines. Kraft stands nearby, stuffing mags in pouches. Down the street, the firefight sounds like it has grown and spread, like we're fighting an entire neighborhood of insurgents.

"Hey, Workman?"

I turn around and see Levine leaning against the wall of a nearby house. He's only a few feet away, looking Casper-white and gaunt. Blood flecks his face and darkens his flak vest. Doc wrapped his wounded arm and put it in a sling. It hangs across his chest.

"Workman!" he shouts again. His voice rivals mine with its smoke-induced raspiness.

"Levine, are you okay?"

"Come here?"

I stuff another magazine into a pouch on my flak vest and run over to my friend. Before our command ordered us into the city, we spent three weeks just outside of it, supporting our fellow Marines with our 81mm mortars. At night, we slept beside a railroad embankment that served as cover for all the rockets and mortar shells the Muj fired back at us.

Levine and I slept side by side every night, talking about the future, home, women.

It seemed like our long talks always started the same way. Levine would take a long drag on a cigarette, blow the smoke straight up in the air so he looked like a steam locomotive working up a grade, and say, "Workman, we're hidin' behind these damn tubes."

"Come off it, Levine. We're killing our share," I'd tell him.

"Alls I'm sayin' is that I joined up to kill fuckin' bad guys. These mortars? It ain't personal enough. I want to see who I kill. You know?"

"You're nuts."

"Yeah, maybe. But I lost people on 9-11. You know? I feel like a coward."

"Levine. Shut up. You're no coward."

"Until we get into the city, that's the way I'll feel."

I always wondered about Levine. Was he all talk? Nobody else in the company had his level of bloodlust. He'd talk about looking his enemy in the eyes as he killed them until I couldn't take it anymore. It made me wonder if his bravado actually concealed a yellow streak.

Now I stare at him, a pizza-place owner turned thirtysomething Marine grunt, covered in his own blood. He's always had a civilian's heart: independent, defiant of authority, and totally incapable of putting up with rear-echelon chickenshit, like shaving and keeping his shirtsleeves rolled down.

This man is no coward. He more than proved that today.

Levine raises his unwounded arm. He's got a smoke in his hand and he takes a long drag from it. He exhales almost into my face.

"Workman, gimme a pistol."

"What? What the fuck for?" I reply.

"I'm going back in."

"I don't have a pistol, Levine."

"Go find me a fuckin' pistol, then."

I notice that he's bleeding through his bandage. His lips are tinged blue.

"Stay here," is all I can think of to tell him.

"Fuck that." He turns to the crowd that our platoon's become and shouts, "I need a pistol! Somebody gimme a nine mil!"

Our battalion sergeant major appears out of the crowd. He must have just shown up. I hope he brought reinforcements—and tanks.

"Sergeant Major . . . gimme your pistol!" Levine shouts fiercely.

The sergeant major stops and regards our Bronx Marine. "Levine, no fuckin' way. You're not going anywhere."

"Fuckin' A, I am! I got one good arm." Levine pushes off the wall and starts to hobble back toward the house. He only gets a few feet when the sergeant major stops him.

"Come on, Levine. You stay here. That's an order, Marine."

At that moment, Corporal Levine becomes my personal hero. No man I've ever met has this lion's heart.

Our friends lead him back toward the casualty collection point. I hear him shouting the entire way, "Just gimme a goddamned pistol! I can still fight! Doc, hand me your nine mil!"

Doc Sunny shakes his head and doesn't bother to reply.

Hebert's moving now. Doc's busy bandaging his legs. Maybe we can all make it through this nightmare. This bloom of hope feels like a battle dressing to the heart.

I gather some more ammunition. Kraft has filled his pouches with fragmentation grenades. We're going to get back into this fight and end it once and for all.

How much do I have left for this? My leg throbs with pain. I haven't bothered Doc about it—he's been way too busy with wounded Marines. Everything seems so floaty, surreal, and distant, the same way I used to feel after getting concussed on the football field.

My flesh feels burned, bruised, and sunbaked. I pluck a tiny sliver of shrapnel out of the back of my left hand. It's left a jagged, singed hole in my Nomex glove. My stomach still feels like I've got the worst case of the flu imaginable. We've been fighting for over two hours in hundred-plus heat, running and fighting, getting grenaded and suffering from smoke inhalation. I've never felt this level of complete fatigue, utter exhaustion. Every moment, however small, becomes a sheer act of will. If it were up to me, I'd collapse back here with Richeson and Hebert, flip the cap off my camelback's nipple, and just suck it dry before falling into a coma-deep sleep.

But if I did that, I'd never be able to look Levine in the eyes again.

How much can one human being take? How much can a single Marine endure?

I'm tapped out. Done. Smoked. But I will go back, pride and discipline will triumph over the frailties of the flesh.

A rash of gunfire erupts down the street. Gardiola and his crew in their support-by-fire position suddenly hammer away at a target. I hope it's the sniper that was shooting at Hebert and me.

I move down the street to get a better view. As I pass the back of a 998 Humvee, I notice boots. Somebody's lying in the back. What's that all about? I drop my weapon, find the hand-grip, and raise a weary leg until my boot slides onto the step just below the tailgate. I heave myself up and onto the bed.

There are two Marines here.

The sun beats down with relentless fury. I turn my face to it, and feel its raw power against my face. Its sheer intensity whites out my vision.

Don't look down, Jeremiah.

Why not?

I open my eyes. My vision flares, then returns to normal. Over the back of the cab, I can see some of our men starting to organize for another push down the street. My gaze falls lower until I'm looking at the men at my feet.

"Raleigh?"

How'd he get here? Last I saw he was on the second floor. He looks like he's asleep. One arm's cocked over his face to shield his eyes from the desert sun.

"Raleigh?" More concern in my voice now. When I get no response, I look over my shoulder and call for Doc Sunny.

Doc's still working on Hebert. He pauses and peers up at me, but says nothing.

What the hell?

"Doc! Doc! Get over here, now!"

"Don't worry about it, Workman," I hear him call back in a strangely strained voice.

"Doc, we've got wounded men back here! They need help, goddamnit!"

"Workman, they're okay."

I look down.

Raleigh's lips are twisted down. He looks like he's in terrible pain.

"Raleigh? You okay, bro?" I'm puzzled. Maybe he's unconscious, or sleeping.

I reach down and pull his arm. It sloughs off his face and flops to

the truck bed. I see that his eyes are closed. He is asleep. I pull my
Nomex glove off and tap his cheek with my right hand.

Nothing. It feels cold and slack.

"Doc! For God's sake, get over here now! Raleigh needs you."

"He's okay, Workman."

"DOC!"

"Workman, he's fucking dead!"

His words don't sink in at first. Then their implication sends a shock
wave through me that's so profound I'm rooted in place by it. Something stirs deep within me. A tumbler clicks into place and a vault
door falls open. Pure, toxic grief spills out. It burns away all that I once
was, and all that I hoped to be, like acid to the face.

"Raleigh! Raleigh!"

He's fucking dead.

I want to see Raleigh as he was just a few days ago when he threw
that grenade into the well. His eyes were bright, grin wide and puck-
ish, a jaunty step in his walk. He kept us laughing, even when we
found ourselves surrounded by the worst of sights.

His face is still and pain-stamped; no grin will ever stripe his face
again.

This can't be happening. My mind bucks and kicks against what I
see. The finality, the total destruction of this free-spirited kid who
called me his friend, sends my brain misfiring. A fuse blows, then another. I can't process anything, save the molten rivers of grief searing
me from the inside out.

There is another Marine here.

I don't want to look.

I have to find out who it is.

My eyes shift. I see a head turned to one side, like the man has
tucked himself against Raleigh's shoulder. I cannot see his face.

Who is this?

A bullet has shattered his temple. Blood covers the side of his head.
He died instantly, but that is no comfort. None at all.

His nametape reads HILLENBURG.

Oh God, not Eric.

He had only a few more months to go before his enlistment was up.
Five more months and he would've been in civilian clothes, back

home with his family and going to college. Instead, he lies next to his brother, Raleigh Smith, his head a picture of horror.

More fuses blow. The flow of grief suddenly collides with a paroxysm of pain. The two combust and flare with such intensity that it overloads every sensation, every neural pathway, like a string of lights hit with a power surge.

I stand over my fallen brothers, boots weighing three tons each, legs encased in concrete. I am a statue, paralyzed by what has happened inside me.

The overload fades. The cocktail of grief and agony morphs into molten rage. I throw my head back and scream as the last of me is burned away.

I break the paralysis and leap from the 998, screaming and howling as I barrel down the street one last time. I am a dead man running now, nothing left but a scorched earth soul.

Chapter Twenty-Four

HUMAN BOMB

December 23, 2004
Fallujah

THERE'S NOTHING LEFT of me but flesh now, and failing flesh at that. I run, stagger-step, stumble and weave down the street through a gaggle of pissed-off, screaming Marines. I pass Smokes and Kraft, then Major Todd Desgrossielles, our battalion executive officer. He's shouting and trying to get us organized.

A couple of times I almost fall. I wobble like a drunk on jelly legs until I get to the wall in front of the house. The Humvee is still parked in the gate, the SAW gunner now going cyclic with his rate of fire. Across the street, Gardiola's support-by-fire position is a mass of muzzle flashes.

I round the corner through the gate and onto the front lawn just as a burst of fire knocks chunks of masonry out of the second floor of the house. Halfway across the lawn, I slip and fall flat on my back. I land in the grass, a soft landing. This stuff would have been great for Friday night football. I turn my head to check the upstairs windows and make sure nobody's shooting at me. When I do, my nose makes contact with the turf, and I breathe in the sweet smell of fresh-cut grass, evoking memories of lazy summers, softball, backyard barbeques, and fourth downs with the game on the line.

I roll onto my stomach and push up onto my feet. The other Marines with me go through the gate; Kraft, Snell, and Major D. in the lead. I'm carried away by their tide, and before I can even breathe again, we're inside the hallway making another charge for the stairwell. This time, I don't bother to check the downstairs.

I sense Snell right beside me, Kraft hard on his heels. Everyone's shouting. Machine guns chatter. All I can think of is revenge.

Three great strides and I hit the landing, taking fire the entire way. An unsteady pivot on my left boot and I'm climbing the second flight of stairs.

"Allah Akbar!"

The voice sends a bolt of pure hate through me.

"Allah Akbar! Allah Akbar!" More voices join into the chant. Before I reach the last two steps to my corner, I can hear more of them shouting from the upstairs rooms.

Kill them. All of them. That is all you have left.

Dense smoke fills the foyer. I can't even see the desk. The door to the balcony has either been closed, or the smoke is so thick it blots out the afternoon sun.

A wave of automatic weapons fire slams into us. Snell, Kraft, and I are in the lead again, and we flatten ourselves on the steps. The bullets come from the far side of foyer and rip into the wall at the back of the landing. This is new. Every other time, they've come from that oddball angle out of the second room.

I flip on my SureFire light that's attached to my M16, hoping it will help me see the enemy. As soon as I do, the fusillade stops. Snell and I share a glance, and it dawns on both of us that Gardiola's Marines in the support-by-fire position across the street must have been hammering away at us by accident.

"Allah Akbar!"

I pop up on one knee and start shooting. I can't see anything or anyone, but I pepper the smoke with my M16. Snell starts shooting as well. Kraft and the others behind us lay down suppressing fire.

Muzzle flashes, like fireflies on an Ohio summer's night, dance in the smoke. I see at least six or seven at once.

"How many motherfuckers are up here?" Snell screams.

"Shitloads! Pour it on them!" Kraft yells back.

Behind me, I can hear Major D. shouting orders. The fact that a field-grade officer is right here in the thick of the fight is a shock. But that's Major D. About two weeks ago, he threw himself between an enemy grenade and two of our men. That's the kind of man I'll follow anywhere.

We exchange small arms fire with our enemy for another interminable minute. The noise, the smoke, the crazy flashes and colors play around me. I fire and reload like an automaton, but again we don't seem to be doing any damage.

Kraft grabs my shoulder. I turn and see he's offered me a frag grenade. I pluck it from his hand.

Do it.

I don't want to live with this pain. My brothers need something to get us upstairs. We need to make sure there are no other Marines up there. We need to win this fight and end it on our terms.

The grenade is prepped. I drop my rifle to my side and pull the pin out. The grenade's live, and I clutch it to my chest, hands firm on the spoon.

I'm naked now without a weapon at the ready. Should we be counterattacked, I'll have no defense. This time, I don't fear it. All I feel is rage and bitter hate.

Die fighting. There is honor in that.

End the pain. I'll carry the grenade and charge into the far room. I'll hold it out and die with the enemy I'll have surprised.

One . . . two . . . three . . .

I step around the corner and charge into the foyer.

There's a room ninety degrees to the right of the corner I've used as cover all through this fight. The entire time, I've never been able to get eyes on it. Now I see shapes moving in the smoke through that door.

And they see me. Christmas lights wink, bullets crack and whine. I'm standing exposed in a tornado of fire. Suddenly, my progress is stopped cold and I'm savagely yanked off my feet.

"Workman! What the fuck you doin'?" Kraft screams as he tugs me out of the line of fire and back to the cover of the wall.

Kraft just saved your life.

I don't want it anymore.

I hurl the grenade. Three seconds later, it explodes with a muffled *phoomph!*

Snell's eyes suddenly bulge and dilate with terror. His finger spasms on his AK's trigger.

"Allah Akbar!" Jesus Christ, that came from the foyer! I peer around the corner of the wall and see shadows drifting through the smoke.

Counterattack. Holy shit they're charging us.

Two figures, then a third appear. Snell's bullets smack home, but they do not stop. As they move, the smoke around them curls and spins, concealing, then revealing them.

Snell snaps off five more shots. The insurgents don't even look fazed. A bearded one reaches the center of the foyer. I see his outline in the smoke. He moves in slow motion, AK in his hands. I bring my rifle up, not bothering with my sights. Snell and I pump bullets into him, but he doesn't go down. Instead, he moves toward us, screaming in Arabic as we tear chunks from his body.

Five feet away now. His two comrades lurk in the murky darkness behind him. I pin my SureFire on him and we unleash hell.

He drifts to a stop, body jerking as bullets hit home. The smoke trailing in his wake suddenly streams around his body. Tendrils waft across his face, masking his features even as he screams on.

Snell takes careful aim and hits him center mass.

Go down! Go down!

No man can take this punishment.

Yet this one does. With preternatural calm, he turns around and walks back into the smoke. A second later, all I can see is his dim outline. His two comrades fade back with him, walking like they're in no more danger than if they were strolling at noon in Central Park.

They didn't fucking die. How is that possible?

Snell and I have no more targets now. Both of us shake uncontrollably. I can hardly keep my rifle raised. That was the spookiest thing I've ever seen.

"Allah Akbar!"

"They're coming again!" I shout, my voice drained of hate and revenge and filled now with only stark terror.

Chapter Twenty-Five

FIELD-GRADE HERO

December 23, 2004
Fallujah

"WORKMAN! WE'RE PULLING OUT!" Kraft shouts into my ear. I listen, but don't take my eyes off the smoke.

"Fuck that. I'm staying."

"Major D. wants us out!"

I wait, weapon pointed into the smoke, hands shaking, heart stutter-stepping, and feeling mortally wounded.

The smoke swirls and curls outward toward us. Something's moving in the back of the foyer, but I can't even see a shadow. I fire anyway, hoping for a lucky shot.

A tunnel of clear air furrows through the smoke. A split second later, I realize that it's been created by a flying object.

"Grenade!"

It hits the shattered marble floor after describing an arc from the far room's doorway. Another yellow monstrosity, oddly shaped, it spins and sputters while skipping across the fractured marble floor until it falls in a bullet divot just out of arm's reach.

I twist away from it and duck. When it explodes, a roiling ball of fire engulfs the entire foyer. Flames shoot out over the top step just above our heads. There's so much fire this time it creates a back draft, which sucks the oxygen from my lungs.

I feel myself falling down the stairs. I hit a step two or three above the landing, unable to breathe.

A sudden onrush of smoke fills the landing. Everything flammable now burns with a hellish glow. It casts crazy shadows through the smoke.

"Allah Akbar!"

Where's my weapon? I still can't breathe. My lungs feel compressed, like a balloon a child has squeezed hard and drained of all helium.

Find your M16, Jeremiah.

My hands play across the steps around me. They're stippled with shrapnel and broken glass.

Hurry! They could be moving across the foyer right now.

I look up for the top of the stairwell and half expect to see another figure swell out of the smoke. If that happens, I'll die on my knees without a weapon. Another stab of pure terror hits me.

I try to get to my feet, but I slip and fall. I have no balance. I'm reduced to crawling on my hands and knees. I tumble to the landing and sprawl chin-first into the broken glass under the window.

I still can't find my weapon. My eyes are open, but I don't see anything but a brilliant orange light.

My hand strikes cold ABS plastic, and my fingers confirm I've found the stock of an M16. I pull it close, but the effort leaves me dizzy.

I still can't breathe. The sounds of battle grow faint. The gunfire drifts away into a low background noise, like the hum of a stereo left on. The shouting fades until it merges with the sound of my heartbeat in my ear.

Soon, that sound is all I have to tell me that I'm still alive.

Eliminate the threat.

I have to go back up there. Even if I'm the only one.

I have the M16, but it barely rises off the landing before my arm gives out.

Like a dream, a scream pierces the background noise. An insurgent victory cry.

They're coming for you, Jeremiah.

I try to breathe but my muscles refuse to work. I'm suffocating. The last of my strength starts to flow away.

I try to roll on my side, but I make it only halfway before I pancake face-first onto the landing again. I feel the cool concrete and broken glass against my cheek.

The brilliant orange light winks out. I'm left in darkness now, unable to even gasp for air.

Dreamlike, ethereal voices penetrate the fog my mind is lost within. I hear somebody close. Have they come for me? Will I be their war prize? A hostage to torture?

No. I will not die a prisoner, executed in front of some jihadist's camera and my recorded death will spread across the Arab-language websites like a viral video on YouTube. That threat breaks the stranglehold on my lungs, and I'm able to get some air. It seems pitifully little at first, freighted with smoke and the coppery scent of blood.

My hand slaps for purchase on my M16 again. My fingers reach the pistol grip and grasp it. I pull it toward me. I might as well be pulling the *Queen Mary*. It refuses to budge from the landing floor.

GET BACK INTO THE FIGHT! DON'T DIE THIS WAY!

Both hands on my rifle now. I pull hard. The M16 slides into my stomach at last. I've got it now, even if I don't have the strength to raise it.

Get on your feet.

Not happening. I can only see a tiny shaft of light. It spins like a pinwheel, which leaves me sick and dizzy. I can't get my bearings. I can't see the top of the landing, and I can't tell where my brothers are.

Am I alone?

The tiny shaft of light grows, like a camera aperture getting reset. I can see a sliver of the landing slowly spiraling around and around.

Finish this. Get up there and die as you intended. Don't let them shoot you like a dog, on all fours without any hope of defending yourself.

I find the strength to roll back against the landing's back wall. My head hits my flak vest, and the spinning sliver of landing shifts until I see my own body, oscillating around the tube of blackness that dominates my vision.

My cammies are torn and blackened. My hands and arms are slick with blood. Now, I'm spinning away, floating over myself, a sprawled nightmare of a Marine lying in smoky rubble.

The light winks out.

The hum of background noise becomes a staccato melody of gunfire. I listen to it, unable to find the will to move, unsure if I am even conscious.

Am I dying?

A shape appears out of the darkness. An insurgent? Am I about to be finished off, or dragged to a fate worse than death?

No, it is my grandmother. Her face is placid and reassuring. She beckons to me and mouths the words, "Jeremiah . . . Jeremiah . . ."

Consciousness slips away like a ship in its death throes. One system after another fails as seawater snuffs them out.

A wave cascades over me. I feel loose, adrift. Free. I float away into the blackness.

I see my grandmother's face again. I want to reach for her. I know she'll give me peace.

I can't get back upstairs. I have nothing left.

Then die here with your rifle on your shoulder.

There's no better way to die, fighting evil. Fighting for something I believe in.

"Let's go Marine!" a husky voice bellows.

I open my eyes to see its source. I'm looking through a straw, with just a spear of light slow-rolling at its end.

"MOVE IT MARINE!" A sharp sting on my face.

No. Let it end here.

"Leave me."

Another sharp sting raps my cheek. The straw vanishes, and I've got a full view around me again. Major D. kneels in front of me, face blackened and blood-speckled.

Don't rob me of this. I've made my sacrifices.

"Leave me," I say again.

His hand comes up and slaps me across the face. I want to flail at him in response, but I don't have the strength.

A hail of gunfire erupts around us. Something explodes in the distance. More screaming. More shouting. Smoke unfurls down the stairwell. I cough and hack as Major D. grabs my flak vest.

My vision blurs again. The world gyrates, like I'm in a dryer looking through the little window in its door.

"ON YOUR FEET!"

No.

He clutches my flak vest and hoists me to my feet. The sudden movement causes my stomach to contract. My head falls forward and I vomit on myself in front of my XO.

I feel his arms clutch me against his own flak vest. I realize he's hugging me.

"Come on, son."

Fuck. I'm still alive.

"Can you walk?"

I shake my head. Now I see Kraft and Snell. They're standing in the ten-step kill zone, covering us with suppressing fire.

It isn't working. AK's bark. The machine gun laces us again. My Marines fight on without me.

A dagger of guilt strikes me. I should be shooting, too, and throwing grenades—anything to win this fight.

I can't even raise my weapon.

Major D. releases me, and I sag to my knees. I can't go any farther. "Allah Akbar!"

Major D. swings around me and snatches my Kevlar. Its strap is tight against my chin, so he uses my helmet to drag me headfirst across the landing. A solid yank, and I tumble down to the hallway.

"We're getting out, NOW!" he shouts. Kraft and Snell brush past. I see them as I look up from the floor, running for the doorway.

Major D. grabs my flak vest. I must weigh over two hundred with all my gear.

"I gotcha, Marine. I gotcha."

Chapter Twenty-Six

OBLITERATION

December 23, 2004
Fallujah

SUNLIGHT ON MY FACE.

Machine guns in my ear.

The once-manicured lawn, now torn and gashed, has been ruined beyond repair.

Major D. pulls me through the doorway and over the front porch. My boot heels scrape across the concrete as he shouts at me to hold on over the din of battle.

Bullets stitch the grass. Hunks of turf fly around us. We're under intense fire. Major D. lets go of me, spins and hook-shots a grenade over the balcony on the second floor.

"That'll teach 'em!"

"You have no clue, sir."

"Hold on, Marine!"

He grabs my flak vest again and tugs me across the lawn. I'm so weak, so nauseous, that all I can do is watch my limp legs trail behind us.

Major D. staggers as a bullet ricochets into his leg. He keeps going and doesn't let go of me.

Brothers.

Major D. probably doesn't even know my name. But he knows I'm a Marine, and it is enough. He risks his life for me, just as I did for Hebert. That's how the brotherhood works: If you wear the uniform and stand against this whirlwind, there will always be a connection so deep that men will give everything for one another.

Major D.'s the best of us. He is a father, a husband, a good and ed-
ucated man. One bullet and his kids lose their dad. That's what he's
laid on the line for me.

We get to the wall, still under fire. Major D. limps along until we
reach the gate, where a hulking M1 tank now sits in the driveway instead of a Humvee. Its gigantic 120mm gun barrel is pointed right at
the second-floor balcony.

A moment later, we're out on the street and Major D. pulls me to
my feet.

"You okay?"

"Yeah," I mumble.

"Listen, you guys did the best you can do," he says to me, Kraft, and
Snell, who've just shown up after covering our withdrawal.

"What about Raleigh?"

I'd always had a touch-and-go relationship with Raleigh Smith. He
kept us laughing, and there was no better mortar man in the battalion,
but trying to get him to do anything else could be like pulling teeth.
He'd duck out and disappear whenever a tough job came up. I remember getting particularly pissed at him once when we had to fill
hundreds of sandbags right after we arrived in Anbar province. He
wanted nothing to do with it, and vanished every chance he got.

None of that shit mattered. I know that now. All that counted was
what that kid had in him during a fight.

I never got to tell him what an incredible mortar man he was.

Major D. leaves me with Kraft and Snell. The M1 cooks off a main
gun round at point-blank range right into our former battlefield. A funeral pyre of smoke shoots up over the outer wall and coils skyward
over the house.

We stagger for our vehicles. I'm in terrible shape, but at least I'm
on my feet. I start throwing up again, and I know I've got to get some
water in me soon or I'll go down with heat stroke.

Twenty minutes later, Major D. pulls us back out of the neighborhood. My platoon withdraws on foot. We are bloodied, black, and
charred, so spent that we struggle to carry our weapons. Nobody says
a word as the wreckage of Weapon's Company, 3/5 Marines shuffles
through the shattered city's streets.

We find a house with a mostly undamaged yard and collapse in the
dirt. Somebody hands me a cigarette, and I take it eagerly. Soon,

we're all smoking in near-total silence. We're a broken bunch, our uniforms filthy, our bodies wracked by shrapnel and strain. After a short break, we start checking out our own wounds.

I drop my pants and see a hole in my right leg. I've got another one in my arm and elbow. My trigger hand has a small chunk of shrapnel sticking out of it.

The other men are hurt even worse. Doc Sunny looks us over as the sound of incoming jet aircraft grows in the distance.

"They're gonna nuke the neighborhood! Everyone down!" somebody yells. We take cover in the yard of a nearby house.

The jets swoosh overhead. As they pull up, the ground quakes as their bombs explode on the house we fought to clear for over three hours. Another pass, more bombs strike the neighborhood. Bits of rich Iraqi housing material tumble around us. A brick plummets down between Kraft and me. Bits of wood and concrete fall like rain. I lie facedown in the dirt, hands cupping my face.

You're still alive.

Another pass and the strike planes release a fresh salvo of bombs. The ground seethes as they explode.

All I wanted was to bring everyone home.

We didn't do it. We couldn't do it.

We failed.

The cataclysm continues. The attack jets smother the house and the surrounding neighborhood with bombs. When they finally finish, there's nothing left but heaps of rubble.

Chapter Twenty-Seven

CRATERSCAPE

December 23, 2004
Fallujah

WE DRIVE TO Camp Fallujah, the sun dropping lower on the horizon now. When we get inside the base, we climb out of our dust-covered Humvees looking like extras from a Hollywood horror film. We're smoke-stained, bandaged, and covered with blood, vomit, gore, dirt, and concrete dust.

The rest of weapon's company stands in a ragged line, anxious—no, almost desperate—to find out what's happened.

Mimoso sees me and rushes up with Sergeant Martin at his side. "Workman, who is it?"

"Smith, Hillenburg."

"Phillips," somebody adds.

Mimoso's face drains of color.

What else can I say?

Several of my Marines cluster near the back deck of our rig, talking in morose and hushed voices. ". . . Phillips almost fell apart. . . ."

I don't want to hear this.

". . . so many bullet wounds his gear's keeping him together. . . ."

I step through the huddle and say, "Let's go."

Our three fallen Marines have already returned. They're over at the morgue, body bags their shrouds, under harsh fluorescent lights.

The Humvees must be cleaned out. The back of the 998 that carried them home is a horror. Blood, gore, brain matter. The heat has congealed this all into one gelatinous mess. Gardiola steps up next to me and says, "I'll help." Kraft puts a hand on his shoulder. "We'll do it."

Kraft and I climb into the back. Ten minutes later, the nightmare task is done.

Lieutenant Butler, our platoon commander, comes over to us. I only saw him a couple of times during the firefight, but every time our paths crossed, he was fighting right alongside the rest of the men.

"Let's head down to Bravo Surgical," he says. That's our base's aid station. "Levine, Richeson, and Hebert are over there."

He starts limping away from the vehicles. One by one, we sling our weapons and trail after him.

Bravo Surgical is full of random people. Staff officers stand around looking forlorn. Other Marines I don't recognize are huddled in small groups, talking among themselves. As we arrive, our chaplain starts to circulate through our platoon. I see him take hands and whisper prayers with my men.

Phillip Levine, our Bronx lion, lies on an operating table in the ER. The battalion surgeon is just about to start working on him. There's a civilian standing next to him, back to the rest of us. Seeing him there sends waves of anger through me.

Fucking reporter! He's come to pick us clean.

Kraft nudges me. "Check that out," he says, pointing to the civilian.

I want to start shouting, but then the civilian turns slightly and I go from furious to hyper-emotional in the blink of an eye. Don Rumsfeld stands next to Levine. He's not interviewing him, he's giving him a few soft words of comfort. I see him reach inside a pocket and produce a coin. For decades, this has been a tradition among America's warrior class. Coins are a concrete means to express respect, and they come in many forms. We have our own battalion coins, regimental coins, division coins. Some of the men actually design their own and have them specially minted. The SECDEF has obviously done this as well.

He presses one of his coins into Levine's ghost-white hand. When he turns to leave, I see his eyes are wet with tears.

Richeson and Hebert are in the OR right now. I want to go see all three and sit with Levine, but the corpsmen tell me no. That will have to wait for later.

"Corporal, do you want to call home?" I turn to see somebody from the battalion staff holding a cell phone out to me.

"Home?" I say as if that's a foreign word.

"Yeah. Call your wife and family. Tell them you're okay. This will be all over the news soon."

I regard the phone with complete indecision. Part of me wants to refuse it. Who would I call? My mother? She's fragile, and if I tell her that I've been wounded, she'll fall apart. Since the day I called her from the roof of our hooch and that car bomb went off, she's been living in perpetual dread. Telling her what just happened would only inflict more torment.

Who else could I call? My father? Who knows where he is. I haven't heard from him since I graduated from basic training. I have no number, no address, and no clue how to track him down. At this point, I wouldn't want to, either. Why would I want to share this day with a man who walked out on his son?

Jessica. She's the only one.

I take the phone and flip it open.

Do you really want to do this?

Jess has always been there for me. When I got hurt in high school, she took care of me. When I graduated and couldn't go to college on a football scholarship because of my knee, she was there to console me.

But what about now?

Since I deployed to Iraq, I haven't received a single letter. Mail calls for me have been ordeals. I stand with everyone else, waiting, hoping to get a letter. Praying, really. By the time we left for Fallujah, I'd have been happy with a postcard that just had her name signed on the back. At least that would have been a sign I wasn't forgotten. When I sent her the lyrics to "Angel," each mail call afterward chipped away at the hope I had left.

What happened? I didn't understand. I'd dwell and grow angry, morose, and self-pitying. Then I'd get mad for even caring.

I just wish I understood why.

"I love you. I'll be here, waiting for you to get back."

Those were her last words to me. They seem like such a lie now.

The few times I've been able to call her have not gone well. She either hasn't answered, or has told me to call back later because she's in the shower. She always has an excuse. Once, I could tell from the background noise that she was at a bar. She's not even twenty-one yet, and it made me suspect that she's been sucked deeper into the party crowd that orbits Camp Pendleton.

Come on, Jeremiah, this is different. This won't be a "hello, how are you?" sort of call. No. This is the type of call marriages were created to handle. She'll know that. She'll be there for you.

That's true. No matter what, we've always been there for each other whenever we've faced a crisis. That's one of the bonds that we forged through school and beyond.

The staffer looks anxiously at me. He wants me to get on with this so he can pass the phone to another Marine, and my uncertainty leaves him puzzled.

"Gimme a minute," I tell him. He takes a step back and disappears into the Marines around me.

I need her right now. I need her more than any other time in my life. Surely, her voice will be able to ease some of this pain. All my life, I've just wanted somebody to love me. It's been like a hole inside me ever since I was kid. Then Jess came along, and her loyalty and devotion filled that hole.

I dial the number. As it rings, I wonder what time it is over in Ohio. I'm trying to do the math when she picks up.

"Hello?" Her voice sounds guarded and wary.

What are you going to say?

I try to speak, but I have no words.

"Hello?"

Tell her you love her. Tell her you need her right now like never before. Tell her she's the only one who can bring you back from what you became today.

"Jess?"

Ten thousand miles away, her voice goes cold. "What do you want, Jeremiah?"

"I . . . um . . . I was wounded today. We lost three Marines."

Static crackles and pops in my ear. I hang on her reply.

"Well, you signed the enlistment papers. You deal with it."

I hear a click as she hangs up on me.

A sudden searing pain, like a last hope cast into a fire, flares inside me. The tattered edges of who I am burn to blackness until finally, I feel nothing at all.

I close the phone and hand it back to the staff guy.

At least I know where I stand back home. I have no one.

Kraft comes up to me. "Hey, you okay?"

"You won't believe what just happened."

"What?"

"Jessica hung up on me."

Kraft scowls and mutters, "Well, you're with us. That's all that matters."

That's all I have.

Chapter Twenty-Eight

BATTLEFIELD REQUIEM

December 23, 2004
Camp Fallujah

"MARINES, ON ME." Sergeant Major Carlton Kent walks toward the center of our broken platoon.

"Huddle up."

We move around him and listen as he speaks from the heart. He's the senior staff NCO in the First Marine Expeditionary Force. Tall and proud, he has the slender, chiseled face of a true warrior. I've never met him before, though I know of him. He's a legend in the 1st MEF. He's charged with the well-being of something like sixty thousand Marines here in Iraq, but he doesn't hide on a rear echelon base and let himself drown in paperwork. Instead, he rolls out every day to check on his Marines. He shares our risks, and genuinely cares about us. Someday, he'll be the sergeant major of the Marine Corps. Of that, we have no doubt.

He speaks to us of love—love of the men we've lost, love for one another. That bond is what makes us Marines so strong in a fight.

"Every man here is a warrior, and I want you to know how proud of you I am. These Marines who didn't make it—they're heroes. We all know that. They died fighting for their brothers, and there's nothing more meaningful than that."

They didn't die for nothing.

His words are sparse, but well chosen. As he continues, I can see every one of us has choked up.

"I know it's tough right now. I know you're hurting. We all are. But

I want you to keep your heads up. We're in a fight with a determined, fanatical enemy, and I'm going to need each one of you in the weeks to come."

There is nothing we wouldn't do for this man. He understands us.

As he speaks, he makes eye contact with each one of us. "You'll have a couple of days off. Get some rest, then pick yourselves up and keep fighting.

"Whatever happens in the future, wherever you go and whoever you become, you need to do one thing: Remember their sacrifice. Honor it with your memory. Don't let these Marines disappear. They gave everything for us today and showed us the true heart every Marine has."

He looks us over. Our morale is shot. We're all in shock, depressed, grieving, and in physical pain. "You men fought hard today. There was nothing more you could have done."

He moves from Marine to Marine, hugging each one of us and sharing a few words. When he reaches me, he says, "Don't forget their sacrifice."

When he finishes doing his best to console us, he tells us, "Okay, go get some chow."

Behind our young Lieutenant Butler, we straggle off to the mess hall in silence. When we reach the front door, some rear echelon POG bars our way. His cammies are pressed and spotlessly clean, and he's got a booney cover on instead of the Kevlar that we have. "Hey!" he shouts at us with scorn, "there's no way you're coming in here looking like that. Go clean up."

Lieutenant Butler goes absolutely postal. His tirade sends the POG fleeing in retreat. Butler watches him go, then throws open the door and tells us, "Don't let anyone give you shit. Send him to me if you have to, but I want everyone to eat. That's an order."

Once inside, we sit together and practically dare the POG's to challenge us. The mess hall is full of them, and we stand out among their clean uniforms like a Steelers fan at a Browns game.

The entire platoon section suffers from shrapnel wounds, and as we try to get some food into our stomachs, we continue to bleed onto our cammies.

Wisely, everyone else in the mess hall keeps their distance.

"I can't believe I'm still alive," I say under my breath. Kraft hears that and just nods his head. I've never seen him so filthy. Usually, he'd be working himself over with a whole box of baby wipes by now. This afternoon is different. He doesn't care.

When we finish up, we leave blood splatters on the deck beneath our tables.

Don't forget their sacrifices.

I don't even know how they died. I just know one minute Raleigh was alive. The next, he's on his back with that frown of pain eternally etched on his face.

At some point, we'll all sit down and share our stories until we can make sense of the day. Right now, nobody has that in them. We're too shell-shocked.

I limp into my hooch and drop my gear. My flak vest will need to be hosed down, my weapon needs to be thoroughly cleaned, but I don't care. I toss them against one wall and collapse onto my cot. All I can do is stare at the ceiling, my mind moving so fast I can't make sense of a single thought.

Twenty minutes later, Doc Sunny comes in to check on me. "Workman, let's take a look at your leg."

"I'm fine," I lie. "How're Levine and Hebert?"

"They'll be okay. Richeson's in pretty bad shape, though."

"What the hell happened?"

Doc shakes his head. "I don't know, Workman. I don't know."

He steps to me and starts looking over my wounds. I have a decent chunk of grenade shrapnel in my right leg, and he digs around in it until he's able to extract it with a pair of forceps.

I'm so far gone, I don't even notice the pain.

Three hours. Three dead brothers. As Doc finishes cleaning out my leg wound, I realize that nothing will ever be the same. I don't even recognize myself now.

"Let me see that elbow," Doc orders. I hold up my arm, and he tells me to take off my cammie top. Stripped to my T-shirt, we both see that my arms are striped with tiny shrapnel cuts. A bloody piece of metal sticks out of my elbow. Doc plucks it out with his forceps and swabs the cut with iodine.

"Hold still," he tells me as he pulls another sliver out of my flesh.

"Thanks."

He finishes up and packs his instruments. "Hell of a fucking day."

"Yeah."

He leaves me to my thoughts. I stare at the ceiling, unable to make sense of anything that's happened today, until sleep finally overtakes me.

I wake up in the middle of the night with tiny shards of metal peppering the bunk under me. It feels like I'm lying on a cactus. I flip on the light switch and brush the cot clean. When I lie down again, I still feel prickly.

I have scores of splinter-sized fragments of metal in me. They're working back out of my skin and falling to the cot with me. When I run my hand along one arm, it feels like a porcupine's back.

The next morning, we are all so stiff and sore as to make walking difficult. Still, we have one last job to do. Kraft and I meet in Raleigh's room. He and Eric Hillenburg shared a hooch together. Its emptiness is overpowering. Reverently, we gather up their personal belongings—letters, clothes, souvenirs, and photographs.

Kraft says, "What do we do with these?" as he holds up two penis pumps.

Both of us try to laugh, but for me it feels like a sob. As a joke, we all bought penis pumps off the Internet and had them sent to us. The entire platoon carried M16's, mortars, and penis pumps with us to Fallujah. Now, the joke just underscores the grief and sense of loss.

"I think we ought to keep these here."

"Agreed." We set them aside and continue with this brutal task.

When we finish, we gather their weapons. We've got to turn them in so they can be reissued, probably to some Stateside Marines fresh from infantry training who'll fill the gaps in our ranks. The thought of that makes my stomach clench.

We carry the weapons to the battalion headquarters. As we walk, Mimoso joins us. "Hear what happened last night?"

"No."

"Lima Company went into that neighborhood after you guys left."

"What for?" I ask. There was nothing left of it. What was the point?

"Battle damage assessment," Mimoso explains.

"Okay. What'd they find?"

"The place was blown to shit. But they took fire right around the same house you guys were in. Or what was left of it."

Kraft and I stop walking. "You're kidding?"

"No. Lima lost a Marine."

"Unfuckingbelievable," I spit.

"Yeah. But they also found a live Muj. They pulled him out of the rubble and our guys just finished interrogating him."

"And?" Kraft says.

"The fucker was loaded on coke and atropine."

Kraft and I share a look. This explains why they didn't die when we shot them.

Lieutenant Butler joins us. He fills in some more details. "Battalion says that there were eight high-value targets in the house. At least twenty-five to thirty insurgents on the second floor."

We were fighting thirty men?

Mimoso nods. "Lima says they found forty bodies in the neighborhood, not counting the guy they took alive."

Our platoon section numbered less than half that.

We fought for three hours outnumbered and outgunned.

"There was some sort of a meeting under way in the house. We interrupted it."

I wish we'd known all this at the time.

We turn in the weapons. I still don't know all the details, but right now, I know enough. I know we failed to save our friends as they fought and died for us.

As we leave battalion headquarters, Kraft pauses and looks around. It's another sunbaked Fallujah morning. The sun is rising high again; the shadows are in full retreat.

"What next?" he asks.

"Let's go see Levine and Richeson before they send them home."

Together, we walk to Bravo Surgical to say our goodbyes.

Chapter Twenty-Nine

OCTOBER DAWN

October 2006
Quantico, Virginia

THE FIRST STREAKS of dawn filter through the bathroom window, bathing me in a curious orange glow. I lay on the floor, the heater still going, the fan still turning. I'm not shaking anymore. The sweats are gone.

I finally drifted off long after Jess killed the radio. Now, as I wake up, I wonder what sort of shape I'm in. I lay still and study myself.

The bugs are gone. My skin no longer crawls. I'm dry, no longer slathered in perspiration. I've got an appetite and find my empty stomach gurgling with hunger. I can't even remember when I ate my last meal.

Most important, I'm not craving Clonopin anymore.

You made it.

My strength has returned and my arms and legs don't feel like Jell-O anymore. There's something different, too, and I can't quite put my fingers on what it is.

I ease onto my feet and find myself in front of the bathroom mirror. This is the moment I most hate, it is the time I cannot hide from what I've become.

I reach for my razor, deliberately averting my eyes from the figure in the mirror. A little warm water, a washcloth, and some shaving cream, and I'm ready to scrape the stubble off my face.

But am I ready to look at myself again?

Who are you?

I am a veteran of Fallujah.

I find the courage to look into my own eyes.

I see a man, gaunt, deep circles, expression sad and tired. I look old beyond my years.

What truth have you found?

Visions of the firefight play across my mind. I see Levine, screaming at me for a pistol. Major D. pulls me across the torn and gutted lawn. Then I see myself, stooped over, looking like a crab with a broken leg, dragging Hebert up the street.

Truth? I gave the last full measure out there.

Your best?

Beyond that. You want the truth? Here it is: Love inspires a man to be better than himself.

And Jess? What about her?

My imagination sees her, sleeping soundly in our bed. My wife.

Your betrayer.

Yes, but I am equally guilty. No, more so. And we've been playing by a balance sheet of pain ever since I got home. That's a lose-lose scenario.

Can you stop hating her?

I want to try.

Can you stop loving her?

No. I'm hers and she knows it.

I lather up and run the razor down my cheek and jaw as if I'm scrubbing myself free of all that's happened since I came home. The stubble falls away into the sink. I feel like I'm emerging from a cocoon.

A chrysalis.

I stare into my eyes, unafraid. I feel different, like an unwanted companion has left my side.

What is it?

I am not ashamed to be alive.

I marvel at this new sensation even as I lather up again. Today's shave will be down to absolute bare skin. No rogue blades of hair, no missed tufts of stubble. Not one sign of anything other than perfection.

Why are you still here?

I don't know. Luck of the draw, like First Sergeant Lewis said. Or maybe God.

You should have died in that house.

I'm not afraid of myself anymore. I don't break contact and look away, suffused in guilt.

"Perhaps, but I survived. And I have to live for them."

For who?

"Jessica. My child . . . and . . . myself."

For the first time in two years I have hope. A glimmer of a smile appears on my lips. I feel exhausted, but reborn. Damaged, but not broken beyond repair anymore.

I am Sergeant Jeremiah Workman, I fought as hard as I knew how.

Three dead Marines say that you failed.

No, they don't. We stumbled into a fight we couldn't win with what we had on hand. It was a fluke. I know that now. We killed and killed, but they kept coming and used the bodies of their dead comrades as cover from our M16's. We later learned that the Muj sent reinforcements into the second floor from the roof of the house next door.

What do you see in your eyes, Jeremiah?

I see resolve. I see three Marine brothers, faces set. They know I'll live for them as well.

This isn't over.

"Hell no," I find myself saying to my mirror image. "This is just the beginning."

I finish shaving, my eyes never wavering, then I turn from my reflection and step into the shower. The hot water on my sore and tired frame feels exquisite. I linger as long as I can. The water beads over me. I scrub myself clean, then start over and do it again.

This isn't over, not by any means. But today is the first day I feel like I have a legitimate shot at making it work.

There's one thing left to do.

Jessica.

At last, I step back out and towel myself dry. I'm about to leave the bathroom when I venture one more look at myself. I square up with the mirror. The shower's made me look a little more human. I feel no guilt, and the lack of it feels like I've been set free from a cage.

I know the truth. I fought hard and only went down after my body had succumbed to all the abuse it endured. That said, I did not deserve the Navy Cross. Kraft, Levine, Snell, Major D., Raleigh Smith, Phillips, and Hillenburg—they all deserved my award. So I will wear it for them, and I will tell their story to whoever will listen. That's the only way I'll be able to make my peace with the ribbon on my chest. Maybe down the road, the Navy will see the light and give these men the medals they earned. I can only hope that wrong gets righted.

So who are you?

I am Jeremiah Workman, Marine, father-to-be, and husband, a veteran of Fallujah. We went to Iraq nine hundred strong. We buried nineteen of our brothers and carried home two hundred and seventy Purple Hearts.

I am a man who bore witness to their bravery.

Chapter Thirty

RECONSTRUCTION

October 2006
Quantico, Virginia

"JESS?"

She's asleep, curled on her side. I've put my uniform on and am almost ready to get to work.

"Yeah, Jeremiah? How are you feeling?"

"I'm through it."

She looks relieved and wary at the same time. I sit next to her on the bed and brush her bangs from her eyes.

"Jess, I'm trying my best to learn how to love you."

"I know."

"But I need an answer again."

She sighs. "Oh no. Here we go."

"Look at me."

Her dark eyes flash my way. She looks so wounded, so full of hurt and suspicion that I want to either hug her close or flee.

You have got to do this.

"I know I've asked you so many times you're ready to hit me, but I want to just take a step back and try to be an adult."

"Sounds encouraging."

"I want to forgive you. I need to forgive you. And I need you to forgive me."

Between us, we've got a lifetime of debts we owe to each other for what we've done.

"But I need to understand why you shut me off."

She pulls a pillow over her head. "Jeremiah, how many times do I need to tell you?"

"Don't do that. Look at me. We can't bullshit each other anymore."

She slides the pillow off her face and sits up.

"Why are you doing this? We're just going to go in circles again."

"No. I need to know if we can get past this."

"Are we being serious here, or just vindictive?"

I take her hand. "Serious."

"Okay," she says slowly. "You may hate me after I tell you, though."

Stay quiet and give her the space she needs to tell you.

"Part of me resented you. A lot."

"You did?"

"The longer you were gone, the more I started hating you."

"Why?"

She looks fearful. "When we got married, I was only eighteen. You told me how to dress, what to do, where to go . . . how to style my hair."

"It isn't easy being a Marine's wife . . . there are certain expectations," I say in self-defense.

"No, you were being overly controlling."

She waits for me to answer, but I don't know what to say.

Don't try to win or crush her. Just listen.

"Jeremiah, you dominated my life. When you left, for the first time in my life I had to think for myself. Before you, my parents took care of me. With you gone, I had to take care of myself. I didn't know how."

"So you partied."

"Yes. It got out of hand. I got in too deep and didn't know how to stop." She pauses, then adds softly, "I wanted to hurt you."

"Wait, who's being vindictive now?"

"You wanted the truth."

I have to fight off a wave of anger.

"What else?"

"I couldn't deal with it," she says flatly.

"What do you mean?" I let go of her hand. She looks even more nervous and vulnerable now.

"I mean like the man I've always loved—the only one I've ever loved—is suddenly torn away from me! For God's sake, do you have any idea what it was like wondering every night if you were alive or dead?"

"I got to the point where I didn't think you cared."

"Every day, there were Marines coming home in boxes, Jeremiah. That was too real. I was just a girl . . . for God's sake, I'm only twenty-one now! Everyone else my age was out having a good time, living life. Carefree, you know? I couldn't take lying in bed without you, wondering if somebody was going to knock on my door to tell me that you'd been killed."

"I'm sorry."

That breaks her rising anger. She suddenly bursts into tears. "No. Don't say that, I am so ashamed of what I did." Her hands go to her face. "I abandoned you. I broke trust."

"Yes you did. And when I came home, I did the same thing."

"With the affairs?"

"Yes. I wanted to hurt you. Punish you for all you put me through in Iraq."

Our relationship for two years has been based on mutually assured destruction. A thrash-fest with no bottom.

"It needs to end," she says.

"I know."

"We'll never make it otherwise."

I nod and clasp her hand again. "I know. I want to be with you, Jess. I want to be a good father."

"This is a good first step. Keeping your dick out of other women is a good second one."

I feel like I've just been slapped.

"I deserved that," I say with resignation.

"Yes, you did."

"And you need to stay out of limos with other men," I counter. On New Year's Eve, I called her again from Fallujah. She was in a limousine on the way to Las Vegas with a bunch of men. As I tried to talk to her, I heard them yelling, "She picked us, Fool! She picked us!"

The memory of that cruel moment makes me shiver.

"Okay, we can hack at each other all morning like this."

"That's the sad part. We can," I reply.

She pulls the covers over the swell of her pregnant belly. She's always been rail thin, and now that she's showing she's terribly insecure. "What now?"

"We move forward. We try to forgive."

"Can we leave it in the past?"

"That's the first step," I tell her.

I stand up and lean toward her. This catches her off guard and she recoils from me, unsure of what I'm doing.

We have a lot of trust issues to work though.

I kiss her blond hair and walk for the door.

"Jeremiah, where are you going?"

"To jump school, baby."

For the first time in months, we both smile.

Chapter Thirty-One

GENERATIONS

November 2006
Quantico, Virginia

THE DAY AFTER I return from jump school, Jess and I head over to the doctor's office. She has her first ultrasound appointment, and I'm dying to find out if we're having a boy or girl.

They take us into a back room and have Jess lie down. The ultrasound technician rubs some sort of gooey gunk all over her stomach until it shines. She gives me a look, but all I can do is shrug.

"You look hot," I whisper. The tech hears this and chuckles.

I mastered the art of flinging myself out of an airplane. It was invigorating, and I felt human again at last. I met some stellar human beings, too, from all branches of the service. We bonded and had a blast, even though I injured myself on one of the jumps.

The ultrasound technician runs a weird-looking gadget over my wife's stomach. The display on the little television monitor looks incomprehensible to me, but Jess and I are riveted by it.

I see a little hand.

"Okay, baby's lying on its side," says the tech.

"Can you tell if we've got a boy or girl?" I ask. If they can make sense of this stuff, they deserve a medal. All I see is fuzzy shades of gray.

"No, not yet."

I feel good for a change. I'm in the moment, eager to see what the future holds for my family.

"Well," the tech begins, "if I had to guess, I'd say you're having a boy. I'm having a hard time telling for sure, because baby's got the umbilical cord between its legs."

"His legs," I correct.

"Not sure," the tech replies.

I look at Jess. She knows I'm having visions of football games and peewee soccer.

"Golf, too. I'm going to teach him how to golf," Jess tells me.

"How'd you know I was thinking sports?"

"Come on. We've known each other almost half our lives."

I pester the tech. "Are you sure? Isn't there some way to be positive about this?"

The tech calls in a few of her peers for second opinions. Everyone stares over Jess's belly at the monitor.

"My guess is a boy, too," says one of the fresh arrivals.

"I don't know. I can't see anything," says another.

The first tech looks at me. "I wouldn't be buying any boy clothes just yet. This isn't a hundred percent. But everything looks good so far."

I have a healthy child. That's all that matters.

The next day, I start a new job as a docent at the Marine Corps Museum on the base at Quantico. It is an amazing place, complete with a series of in-the-set dioramas, called immersions, which capture some of the key moments in the Corps' history. The job soon gives me a renewed appreciation for the heritage of which I am now a small part.

And I am awed by the people I meet. Every morning, I come into the museum and take groups of civilians on tours through the exhibits. Every day, I meet graying Marines, veterans of Chosin, Iwo Jima, Khe Sahn, and younger ones who served during the Beirut crisis in the eighties and in the first Gulf War.

One day in early December, a frail, stoop-shouldered World War II veteran rolls through the door in an electric wheelchair. The museum's quiet, and it is just him and me.

"I've waited twenty years to see this place finished," he says after I introduce myself.

"Where would you like to go first?" I ask.

"I landed on Iwo Jima. I'd like to see what you have on it."

I lead him to the Iwo Jima immersion. It starts with a life-sized video screen showing color footage of the landing craft churning to the beach. The ramps go down, and the doors open onto the diorama.

The veteran gasps as he looks around. Tears well in his eyes. "Son, we lost half our company on that godforsaken place."

"You guys were warriors."

"So were the Japanese."

I show him the rest of the World War II exhibit. He grows increasingly emotional, and I can't help but feel the same way. Someday, if I live to be his age, will I come here to relive Fallujah one more time before I pass? Probably. I'll want to see if the Corps has kept the faith and done justice to the men I saw die there. That will be part of my generation's legacy, our contribution to the heritage of our uniform.

We finish up in the World War II gallery. "Show me your war," he says.

"Right this way, sir."

I take him to the Global War on Terror display, and he reads everything he can from his wheelchair.

"Were you in Afghanistan?" he asks me.

"Iraq."

He points to my uniform. "I see you have the Navy Cross."

"Yes, sir. I wear it as a reminder of the men we lost that day. They were the best."

He shakes his head. "I don't know how you boys have done it. At least we knew who our enemy was."

"Nothing we went through compares to what you did," I counter.

"That's not true at all." His wizened face shows utter sincerity. "I have nothing but admiration for what you new Marines have gone through over there."

As we exit the gallery, the veteran says, "Sergeant Workman, I need to use the restroom."

"Okay, sir. Right this way."

"I'm sorry"—he sounds desperately embarrassed—"but can I ask for some help?"

"No problem, sir. Anything for a fellow Marine."

I hold the door for him as he rolls into the bathroom. He parks in the handicapped stall, and sits there, looking ashamed. I realize he can't get out of his chair.

Without a word, I come to him and ease him over to the toilet. I help him get his pants down. He feels so frail, a warrior grown old, but still proud.

I will do anything to protect this man's dignity.

He finishes his business. "I can't reach," he mumbles.

"No worries, sir." I wipe him clean. A moment later, I ease him back into his wheelchair.

"Thank you, son."

"Marines stick together. I've got your back, sir."

He looks ready to cry. I walk with him to the museum's entrance. He pauses there, and spins his wheelchair around for one last look. "I came hoping that the men I served with would be remembered the right way."

"Is that what you've found?"

"Yes. And more." He lingers on those words before continuing. "I've found the Corps is in good hands. Your generation has done mine proud."

"Thank you, sir."

"No, thank you, son. You're keeping the faith. We'll all be gone soon. All we'll have is this place and the story you tell of us here."

He turns and motors for the door. But then he pauses and adds, "And one day, it will be your turn, too."

We are all Marines, no matter what our war. We share the bond.

Chapter Thirty-Two

SETBACKS

December 23, 2006
Quantico, Virginia

"JEREMIAH? ARE YOU going to get off the couch today?"

"Jess, just leave me alone."

"Come on, you're starting to stink."

"I feel like I'm in Fallujah," I say, rubbing the three day's worth of stubble on my jaw.

"Yeah, well, you're not."

"Thanks for the input."

She leaves the house to do some last-minute Christmas shopping. I haven't been out of the house in four days. I haven't showered in five.

Today is the second anniversary of our firefight in Fallujah. December 23, 2006. All I can do is wonder how Raleigh's family can enjoy the holiday. I know I can't.

The families learned their Marines were dead on Christmas Day.

Christmas. The Corps sent contact teams to their doors on Christmas morning. From here on out, the families will always associate trimmed trees and unwrapped presents with the death of their sons and brothers.

I hate Christmas.

I haven't gone into the museum, but they understand. They know I face a battle every day. Sometimes I gain ground, sometimes I lose ground.

For the past few weeks, the stairwell nightmare has returned. I wake up in cold sweats, Jess wide-eyed and fearful next to me. Apparently, I scream and thrash when I have the dream, and a few times I've hit her in my sleep. Because of that, I've taken to sleeping in a different room for now. The last thing I want to do is harm my pregnant wife.

I close my eyes and see Kraft again. He shakes me awake. "Merry Christmas, dude." His voice is dead.

Mine sounds the same. "Yeah, Merry fucking Christmas."

The season of love and joy, Fallujah-style.

It took me weeks to find out what happened on December 23rd. Hebert finally explained it all to me one night. I'd been sent back to Camp Baharia to talk to a retention specialist. I ended up having to spend the night, so I bunked down in Hebert's hooch. He was still pretty torn up and could barely hobble around. In fact, the Corps finally sent him back to the States for further treatment after we talked. He was loathe to leave us.

Levine tried to stay in theater as well. For three weeks, he fended off the Bravo Surgical types. He wanted to get back in the fight and be with weapon's company. Ultimately, he lost this one and got sent home. I heard he was medically discharged and went back to school somewhere in Southern California.

That night, we slept in bunk beds like kids at a sleep over. Through the darkness, Hebert filled in the missing blanks.

Kraft's squad entered the house, just as we went into the one across the street. Half the men started to clear the downstairs, while Richeson, Hebert, Smith, Phillips, and Doc Sunny climbed the stairs to check out the second floor. When they got to the foyer, they turned right to clear the first room.

Inside, they found sleeping mats stacked almost to the ceiling against one wall. Bedding and blankets were piled nearby. On another wall, a full bank of what looked like lockers dominated another side of the room. As our guys went to go search the lockers, concealed insurgents boiled out around them. Some had been hiding in the lockers. Others were hunkered down in the bedding and between or behind the sleeping mats. A sudden, Old West–style gunfight broke out where everyone shot from the hip.

Outnumbered, Smith, Hebert, Phillips, and Richeson shot their way out of the first room and took cover inside the foyer. That's when the insurgents in the second room opened up with AK's and that god-damned machine gun.

They were pinned down in the foyer when I came up the stairs and saw Raleigh. Hebert was in a corner, and I never saw him, but he saw me. As we talked, he thanked me several times for coming after him.

What else would we have done?

That first grenade the insurgents tossed into the foyer did most of the damage. After it exploded, the five men crawled through the outside door and got onto the balcony. Phillips covered them with a SAW and laid fire down on both rooms. Hebert was helping Richeson, who'd been wounded in both arms by the grenade. Hebert was hit in the back of the legs, so things were pretty desperate.

Raleigh Smith staggered onto the balcony, took three steps, and fell over dead. He'd taken shrapnel to the heart and had just enough life in him to get out of the foyer. There was nothing anyone could have done for him.

Phillips held off the Muj while Hebert and Richeson and Eric Hillenburg looked for a way out. Just then, Gardiola called down to them from the roof. He'd been able to get into the house next door and jumped from rooftop to rooftop with several other of our men. They'd been fighting a close range battle of their own, shooting into windows and tossing grenades at the enemy on the second floor. Major D. showed up and fought alongside them.

Hillenburg and Hebert handed Raleigh's body up to Gardiola. The fight suddenly intensified, so just to get away, Hebert and Hillenburg dropped Richeson off the balcony. Hebert went after him, and Hillenburg climbed onto the roof with Gardiola.

That's when the insurgents charged Phillips. At that crucial moment, his SAW jammed, leaving him defenseless. He tried to close the door and hold them off, but they pushed their way through and from mere inches away, riddled him with automatic AK fire. Hebert said he'd been shot forty-two times.

Exactly what happened to Hillenburg remains a mystery. I heard different stories, but it sounded like the same sniper that almost killed Hebert and me in the street got him. Apparently, the sniper had built a hide atop a mosque down the street and could see most of the neighborhood around the house.

Hebert saw the Muj up close and a lot better than I did. He told me they were nicely dressed and wore expensive watches. We later found out that most of them were Saudi Arabian foreign fighters.

Hours pass; I think only of Fallujah and my men. I wonder about their families, and how everyone's getting along. I should call the ones who survived, but I don't know what to say. Merry Christmas just doesn't cut it anymore, you know?

Jess returns home from her shopping trip. "Still not off the couch?" she asks.

I stand up and retreat to my war room. It is our extra bedroom, actually. I've filled it with photos of my time in Iraq, the certificates and diplomas of the schools I've graduated from since joining the Corps, and the coins I've been given. All these things are tangible reminders of the successes I've had in my life. They remind me that jump school is just the first step on my way back from rock bottom.

I will continue to achieve, and I will pick myself up again. But for now, I'll take comfort in this room, surrounded by these symbols of achievement, and I will remember my brothers. I owe them that on this blood-soaked anniversary.

Long into the night, I stare at the ceiling and work through my grief.

Chapter Thirty-Three

NO HIGHER HONOR

December 2006
Quantico, Virginia

THE MUSEUM BECOMES harder and harder work for me. Word has spread that a modern-day Navy Cross recipient works there now, and all sorts of people have started coming out of the woodwork to see me. Total strangers ask me how many people I killed. God, how I hate that question. Every combat veteran does.

Others want my autograph. One man comes to visit several times a week. He follows me around the museum, snapping hundreds of photographs of me. It gets to the point where I have to start avoiding him. One afternoon, he waits for three hours by my car as I hide inside the museum from him.

The attention's adding a lot of strain to my ability to recover. I fight through it, but Jess suffers as I grow tense and stressed. I finally give in and go see the shrinks again. I refuse to take any Clonopin, but allow them to put me back on Zoloft. Jess notices a difference almost right away.

At the museum, every day becomes a test. I never know what's going to happen or who will walk through the doors. Some of the folks are touchingly sincere. They press small gifts into my hands and thank me for everything I've done.

One afternoon, a man in a wheelchair pushes his way through the front entrance. I expect to see another aged World War II veteran. Instead, I see somebody my own age. He's missing both his legs.

He rolls his chair to me and introduces himself. He served in Ra-

madi, little Fallujah, where so many of my friends have gone to serve during their second and third tours. He'd been a wrestler at the University of Indiana before he joined the Corps. He's been recovering from his wounds at Walter Reed, where he recently was visited by President Bush.

He lost his legs to an IED, the ubiquitous roadside bomb.

"I came today because I wanted to meet you, Sergeant Workman," he says earnestly.

"Me? Why?" I ask, confused.

"It is an honor to know a Navy Cross recipient. You are a true hero." His eyes are full of emotion as he stretches an arm up to me. "I came to shake your hand."

I feel like a complete fraud.

The hero in this room is this wheelchair-bound Marine who has survived horrors I could never endure. He's the one who should have this Navy Cross on his chest, not me.

The world tilts. The edges of my vision grow fuzzy. I pull away and flee to the safety of a back room. I've made a spectacle of myself again, but I can't control how I feel.

Gunfire. I hear gunfire in the distance. Shell casings *tink . . . tink . . . tink . . .* off concrete steps.

My vision narrows, like I'm seeing the world through a tube.

"NO!" I shout fiercely. I will not let this happen to me again. I shake my head and suck air furiously, leaning against a wall for support. I fight this with all the will I have.

Workman, give me a pistol!

Not today. I'm not in Fallujah. I'm at the museum. I'm at the museum.

More deep breaths. My heart rate slows. When I open my eyes, my vision's clear. I feel suddenly exhausted, though, like all the energy I had stored up for the day just got burned in this effort.

I know what I have to do next.

You are not fit to stand in front of this Marine.

No. We need each other. We need that bond.

He'll see through the mask you've created for yourself.

Mask? What will he see underneath?

He'll see a Marine still struggling to find his way.

But I'm no longer lost. I know the path, it's just anything but easy.

True. But come on, who is the real hero here?

There's no argument there.

I straighten my dress blues and square my shoulders. The righteous path is the most difficult to travel.

I return to the front of the museum. My visitor waits patiently. I see a look of understanding in his eyes. We share the same pain, we know the same effects of trauma.

"Thank you for what you said earlier," I tell him.

"You are my hero, Sergeant Workman," he says as he extends his arm again. I clasp his hand with mine. We don't know each other, but we know enough. We share an experience that most will never understand. And that makes us brothers.

Long into the night, I ponder this encounter. I fought and won today. Six months ago, this meeting would have sent me into a spiral of guilt, shame, and grief. Instead, it has left me shaken and depressed. I won the fight today and First Sergeant Lewis would be proud. Nevertheless, it came at a heavy price. I'm left weakened, exposed, and vulnerable. Tomorrow, the fight will be exponentially harder.

Chapter Thirty-Four

FEBRUARY 21, 2007

Quantico, Virginia

"LISTEN," I WHISPER, "I'm not going to shine you on, or blow smoke. I have problems. I'd love to tell you that everything will work out just fine, that there'll be a happy ending, but I can't do that. I can't make that promise to you."

The hospital room is dark now. Jess is asleep in her bed. I cradle our newborn son in my arms and hold him close to my chest. Devon Workman. Our boy.

He's awake and looking at me with big dark baby eyes. I scratch his nose, and I swear the little guy looks perplexed. He's been floating around inside Jess, and all this stuff out here is new to him.

Every time I look in his eyes, we make a connection. I know he's curious, unsure of his new and strange surroundings, so I try to give him as much comfort and love as I can.

He starts to chortle a little, like he's winding up to cry again. I rock him and press him closer against me. That seems to soothe him for the moment and he falls silent again.

He was born a few hours ago after almost a day's labor. My mom arrived the night Jess went into labor. Actually, I think the stress of her arrival triggered her water to break.

The delivery was a miracle. Jess was amazing. I saw a wellspring of strength in her that I've never even glimpsed before. Between contractions, I fed her ice shavings and told her I loved her. She threw up several times, and seemed mortified to have done so in front of my mom. They don't get along very well. I washed her clean, and gave her more ice whenever she asked.

When Devon arrived, the umbilical cord was wrapped around his neck. The doctor cut it and took my boy away to examine him. Tears flowed. We cried together as only a new mother and father can do.

Right then, as the doc brought him back to us, I knew joy again. At the same time, I felt despairing sadness; Raleigh and Eric and James watched us as sure as I was there. I want to say they were happy for my new family, but the truth is I kept thinking how they will never experience this life-altering, wonderful event. My tears of happiness mingled with tears of loss. The moment became agonizingly bittersweet.

The nurses brought me part of the umbilical cord and asked me if I wanted to cut it. I demurred.

"Oh no you don't!" Jess roared at me from the bed. "I didn't just go through twenty hours of labor to have you not cut the cord!"

"Yes, ma'am," I told her and took the pair of scissors offered to me. I cut the cord symbolically, and turned to see Jessica's reaction. She was smiling. Still a rare thing these days, but we're working on that.

I hold my son and dream of summer softball and family barbeques. If he's anything like his old man, he'll be a holy terror. I can't wait to give him his first mitt and baseball. We'll go to the park and I'll teach him how to throw. In winter, we'll shoot hoops. I'll show him how to dodge and juke a linebacker right out of his jock. I know he has the genes of an athlete with Jess and me as his parents.

Oh yeah, and we'll teach him how to golf, too.

I hold my index finger under one tiny hand. His fingers wrap around mine with surprising strength.

Jess's family has this strange genetic trait. They all have crooked pinkies. When Devon was first handed to me earlier tonight, I counted to make sure he had all ten fingers and toes.

I turned to Jess and started laughing.

"What's so funny?" she said with an exhausted grin.

"He's got your pinkies," I said as I held up one hand. We both burst out laughing. My mother was not amused, which only made Jess laugh harder.

Now he holds on to his dad with all his newborn might.

There will be so much to teach him, not just the basics of all the sports I'm sure he'll play. I've got to teach him how to be a man.

That's a challenge, especially given the fact that at twenty-three, I'm still learning the ropes myself.

But I have many role models now to draw upon. Major D., for one. Phillip Levine, the Marine with the lion's heart, for another. When I am confronted with a challenge, I will turn to their examples and see what I can learn. I'll pass those lessons on to my son. And someday, when he's ready, I'll tell him of Raleigh and Eric and James.

"They'll always be with me, you know," I whisper to my son. "They're here right now. I blink, and I see them. That's what PTSD does. The record of my life has a scratch right on December 23rd. I see them over and over and over."

Jessica stirs, but doesn't wake. The monitor she's attached to blips softly in one corner. A nurse pops her head in the room and asks if everything is okay.

I give her a thumbs-up. "We're great."

As she leaves, I look down at my son again. His eyes are half-lidded. He's starting to drift in the comfort of my arms.

"I'll see them every day, Devon. You'll have to know this, and understand that there will be rocky days ahead for me. For Jess. For you. Decembers will be the worst."

His grip on my finger wanes. His crooked pinkie slips and slides off. His arm sinks into the warmth of his bundled blanket.

"It won't be Disneyland. I don't even know if Jess and I will make it. We still have so much to work on. But know that we love each other, and we will always love you. I will always love you."

Tears fall again. I'm not ashamed. These past two years I've cried more than the rest of my life combined. It is one of the effects of PTSD and the trauma that gave birth to it. I'm hyperemotional and live on the bleeding edge of my feelings now that I'm not zombied by a prescription drug cocktail. I still take antidepressants, but I am no longer a walking lobotomy patient. I hurt. I feel rage. I feel joy, like tonight. There is pleasure again in my life, as well as bouts of profound sadness. I'll take the bad with the good and try to be the man Jess knows lurks inside me.

"There will be times you'll hate me. I know that. You won't understand what I'm going through, and I'll take it out on you. I know my-self too well. But I will try to have the courage to admit when I'm wrong. I'll do my best to set everything right when I've messed up."

I look up at Jess and see that her eyes are open. She's watching her boys with such love on her face that I feel a spike of pure emotion.

"How's he doing?"

"He's just great, Jess."

"Having your first father-son talk?"

"I guess. Do you need anything?" I ask.

"You."

"I need you, too."

"Does that leave you conflicted?"

"Not anymore."

"Good." Jess sighs and starts to drift back off. I watch her in silence.

"Jessica? Do you still regret having the dream?"

"You mean our prophecy?"

"Yeah. That one."

"How can I when it led us here?"

We both smile. A teenage dream, adult realities—they make for an uncertain future I guess. I can't make any guarantees about it.

Then don't. Empty promises just lead to heartache.

"I want you to be proud of me someday," I tell my son. "I need that more than anything."

Every day is a new battle in this long campaign. There will be no decisive victory. There's no finish line with chronic PTSD. It all comes down to managing it and learning to live with its effects.

"It conquers you, or you conquer it. That's really what it comes down to, isn't it? And some days, I'll lose the fight. But that doesn't mean I'll give up on the campaign. It just means I'll have to come back harder and more determined the next day. And the next. To do any-thing else disgraces the men who died that day."

My son's eyes close. His fingers grow still and his breathing be-comes soft and rhythmic.

"I swear to you, no matter how many setbacks, no matter how many days I lose the battle, I will never stop fighting . . . because I'm fight-ing now for you."

My own eyes grow weary. It's been an emotional day. I have one last thing to say before it ends.

My lips touch Devon's forehead, and I kiss him with all the love a father can know. He smells fresh and clean, a pure soul with his tale yet to be written.

"I will never give up the fight, Devon. That's my promise to you."

I follow my son into a deep and comforting sleep.

THE SHADOW WAR

2008

I'D JUST FINISHED a speech in front of an audience of health-care professionals at a hotel in Crystal City, when the fifty-something woman approached me, looking grim and teary-eyed. Before I could extend my hand and greet her, she wrapped her arms around me and gave me a huge bear hug.

Marines don't do emotional. We don't like to admit that when a stranger embraces us with such desperate passion that it makes us feel worthy of the life we've chosen. This woman clung to me, and in my ear I heard her whisper, "I can see in your eyes you have PTSD, Staff Sergeant Workman. Just like my husband. My ex-husband, actually."

She broke the embrace and I regarded her. She'd had many hard years, and life had not been kind. Still, she possessed a spark to her that obviously refused to be snuffed out by whatever had been thrown her way.

"Where did your husband serve?" I asked her.

Direct eye contact. No wavering. I could sense I was standing with a powerful woman of much substance.

"My ex-husband is a Marine. Beruit, eighty-three. He survived the barracks bombing. He pulled the bodies of his men out of the wreckage for days after."

Behind her, others jostled to get a chance to talk to me. She looked over her shoulder and realized the brevity of this moment. Still, she wanted me to know she understood.

She embraced me again. This time, I held on to her fiercely and wondered if Jessica would be like this in twenty years. Worn by her fight to remain by my side, the years of stress and tension associated with my PTSD etched on her face, would she be able to survive it as this woman had?

"Staff Sergeant Workman, dear, just remember a few things," the woman said to me as we held each other again.

"What's that, ma'am?"

"Keep your head up. Always. Never let it get the best of you."

"I'm trying, ma'am."

Her grip became fierce, almost urgent. "Stay away from alcohol. That'll only make you spiral."

"Well, I already learned that lesson."

"Yes, but never be tempted again. No matter what happens, or how bad things get."

This woman understood. She has lived our nightmare.

When she let go of me, I felt suddenly alone in a room crowded with people wanting to speak to me.

The crowd moved in. I shook hands, and absorbed hugs. A woman thanked me for my service. Another took my hand in hers and with tears streaming down her face, explained she never had any idea how it was for us returning combat veterans.

A moment later, a man in a three-piece suit started to shake my hand, then suddenly changed his mind and enfolded me in another massive bear hug.

For twenty minutes, total strangers poured their hearts and feelings out to me. This day at Crystal City and the reaction my speech generated in my audience will always be close to my heart.

I never was a very good public speaker. I loved the limelight football afforded because I could be on the field, a barrier of space between me and the screaming fans in the bleachers. I wore a uniform and helmet, and I could keep my distance. Plus I didn't have to speak to anyone other than my teammates.

It is different now. After all I've been through, I've learned that winning my daily battle with PTSD requires me to get out there and find lost souls and show them the way home. We veterans of the War on Terror need not suffer in the shadows, feeling shunned by society and our families. And part of what makes me whole again is to fight this new war at home for all the broken warriors I've met over the past year.

It started at the museum. At first, I wanted to deny that these encounters with fellow vets had any positive effect on me. I would come home feeling drained, and I'd sometimes take it out on Jessica. When the *Washington Post* wrote an article about me, people from all over the country sent me gifts and notes of support. I couldn't believe it. Here I thought that most people would think us PTSD-afflicted veterans were crazies, better locked up than allowed to roam the streets.

Hollywood thinks so. Every time I see *Rambo: First Blood* while channel flipping, I want to vomit. *The Park Is Mine*, episodes of *Numb3rs* and *Bones, Lethal Weapon*, and countless other TV dramas and movies paint us combat vets as psychopathic criminals.

But despite the media portrayal, the heart of America still gets us. That's what all those gifts meant to me. People understood, they sympathized, and they wanted to do something for us.

The war didn't end on the Kuwaiti border, it just changed form. I realized that as I started to win the war within myself, I needed to get into the larger campaign.

In early 2008, I joined the Vets for Freedom Heroes tour. Veterans of Afghanistan and Iraq came together to travel across the country on buses, stopping to give speeches, meet folks, and show our support for the war effort. Every stop we made, we spoke of our experiences and what support here at home means to America's fighting men and women. We spoke of the men we lost; we spoke of heroism and selflessness, and the love that brothers-in-arms will always share.

I spoke of the men I saw rise to their greatest heights in Fallujah. Kraft and Levine and Gardiola and Snell—they were the subject of my talks. Each time I spoke, it drained me so thoroughly I came perilously close to the edge of despair.

But the company I shared propelled me forward. David Bellavia, Pete Hegseth, Marcus Luttrell, and all the other vets on the tour with me—these Americans are my kind of men. We bonded on the bus, and once again I felt that void within me seal shut. That void had existed inside me ever since I returned home and my brothers from 3/5 all went their separate ways. Though we didn't fight side by side during our time in combat, David and Marcus and Pete and I all understood each other. It felt comfortable and right.

One day, I sat down in the back of the bus, and one of my fellow brothers-in-arms suddenly spoke up. "You know, bro, I don't sleep at night."

I could relate. "Yeah, me neither. Not since I came home."

"Me, too," said another one of us.

That's when I realized I was not alone. Heroism, valor, and courage in combat do not mean the decorated warrior returns undimmed by his crucible of fire. It is the exact opposite.

I learned on that tour that we all had our scars. We all fought demons, and PTSD played a prominent role in our everyday life. Far from making us immune, the medals on our chests come with a deeply painful price.

All of us would pay it again, especially if it meant we could bring our brothers home alive this time.

One night, we stopped in San Antonio. I went to check on one of my brothers. I found him in his room, opening up a big bag of prescription medication. The vials spilled onto a table, and I recognized the names on every label. I'd been taking the same things for two years.

We looked at each other, and I think he felt a little bit of shame. I was not supposed to see this moment of weakness. Guiltily, he explained, "I stay up all night, Jeremiah. I stay awake until the sun comes up, then I finally can get some sleep."

In the darkness, dreams come and trauma endured boils within us once again. Blessed daylight is our lifeline, and at times no amount of drugs doctors and scientists can create or prescribe can fight these demons for us.

"I take the same things, bro. And I know what it is like to not want to go to sleep."

Yes, he and I shared more than medications. We shared the same wounds to our brains. I think he realized right then that this revelation was not worthy of shame. This was our bond.

The shame on his face fell away, replaced by relief. His public persona vanished, and for an instant, we shared an utterly naked moment. We knew each other's suffering, and the bond between us became sacred.

That connection, perhaps more than anything other than the birth of my son, helped get me to the point where I could stand toe-to-toe with my PTSD and win more rounds than I lost.

It also sent me down a different path with my public speaking. I knew I had to reach out. I had to stop feeling afraid to tell my story the way it needed to be told.

I threw myself into the fight. Every stop our buses went, I saw PTSD. It was stamped on the faces of Vietnam veterans who came out to greet us. It lingered in the vets of my generation who stepped forward after our speeches to share a little of themselves with me.

I saw the pain the War on Terror has wrought at home as Gold Star mothers shook my hand and thanked me for my service.

I saw a divided nation. Half appear to be clueless that a war rages across the globe. The other half is either fighting it, or has suffered from it. It was an odd dichotomy of complete ignorance and complete understanding.

Sometimes, in the waiting crowds, I saw warning signs. At one stop, I encountered a Vietnam vet. Face lined, skin turned to leather by drugs, alcohol, and exposure to the elements, he came to me and shook my hand with almost manic intensity. His eyes burned with pain. He never said which battle traumatized him and sent him into his spiral. He told me he'd been fighting PTSD since the Johnson Era. "I'm living the same book, I'm just a few chapters ahead of you."

After getting on the bus that night, I swore I'd fight the battle differently. In forty years, I don't want to be a man whose life has been defined by his PTSD-induced failures. I don't want to be broke, alone, and spiritually destroyed as I enter my Social Security years.

And I had things to fix in my life if I wanted to avoid that fate.

Part of the tour for me had been an escape. Jess and I had been fighting worse than ever. While I was gone with the boys from Vets for Freedom, she left me. I came home for a few days, and found the house empty—not even a dish remained.

I couldn't blame her, and I tried to feel good about it. Maybe we'd suffered too much, put each other through so much pain that we both just needed a fresh start.

I ached for her, and for the comfort of my son's embrace. No matter what we've done to each other, Jess and I have a connection that binds us together. No matter how hard we try, it can't be broken. Perhaps somewhere before we are born, a soul is severed and placed in two nascent lives. Once old enough, it is our job to search and find that other half. Jess and I—we're that match. We share different ends of the same soul.

I went back on tour feeling like a part of me had been amputated. The ache only worsened. Another yawning void opened up inside me, and this time I knew that nothing would fill it—except her. Her and Devon.

One night, the bus carried us through the darkened Minnesota countryside. As I gazed out the window, I came to the central truth of my life.

The bond I shared with the men around me? This is where I drew my energy. This is where I felt most at home.

I had no balance in my life. I couldn't let my connections to my fellow veterans replace that which I needed to have with my own family.

At the same time, I couldn't fight my PTSD battle just for them. It wasn't enough. I had to find the footing inside me to stand up and face it alone and for myself.

Through our stops all across the country, I found the strength to do this. Others may depend on me, others may look to me as a cautionary tale, or for inspiration, but ultimately, I go to sleep every night and wake up every morning with myself. If I was to survive, I had to honor that. At first, it seemed selfish. Then I realized I couldn't help others and I couldn't sustain a marriage and a son without first winning this fight for my sake as well as theirs.

Jess and I began to talk again. A phone call here, then another there, nothing planned or scheduled. Sometimes, we went days without talking. Other times, we had some hair-raising and brutal moments thanks to the modern convenience of cell phones. But when we stripped away our pride and shared honestly with each other, we discovered we felt the same pain. When we are apart, we feel severed inside.

The tour ended, and I returned to Quantico a different man. I had found the inner strength to carry this fight alone. While Jess was gone, I spoke to different groups about PTSD, and it became second nature. I met with veterans, and traveled to different Marine bases all over the country with the Corps' top enlisted man, Sergeant Major Kent. We inspected units, met with Marines, spoke to men fresh from battle and ones who were strapping on their gear in preparation for their first deployment.

We even went back to Iraq, and I saw the progress we had made since I had been there in 2004. Instead of battling house-to-house, the Iraqi Police were passing out speeding tickets while Marines looked on. The streets in Anbar province were peaceful at last. We had won, and the Stateside media either didn't even know it or didn't want to report it.

Back home, I saw the faces of the men who secured that victory. I met enlisted men and officers who shared the same gaunt and hollow expression I had when I first came back. The Corps doesn't realize just how widespread PTSD is within the ranks. But I saw it, and I realized my brothers-in-arms needed help.

One day, I spoke to an old friend who had seen a lot of combat. The now-too-familiar shame I once felt passed across his face as he revealed the depths of his own despair. In a hushed voice, he confessed that he slept every night in the back of his closet, armed and nursing a bottle of whiskey. It was the only way he felt safe enough to sleep.

Everywhere I went, I saw men and women hurting. Some were too proud to admit it, others didn't want to be stigmatized as crazy. Though we've come a long way since Shell Shock and the Great War, the fact is our society and military still view PTSD as a huge stigma.

The truth is, our system failed us at the start of the war. Planning for only 8,000 PTSD cases was the first mistake. The VA and the services were totally overwhelmed by the surge in cases. What programs and treatment options were available then were quickly taxed to the limits. Within the Corps, there was a feeling among PTSD sufferers that the navy doctors they saw kept them pumped up with drugs to keep them from getting violent. In some cases, the perception stretched to the point that some of us believed the Corps was keeping us zombified on drugs in order to prevent a media eruption. IRAQ VET KILLS FAMILY, SELF.

Fortunately, as the scope of the PTSD problem became understood, the VA and the military responded. The Corps now handles PTSD vastly different than it did in 2003. This started at the top with the Commandant and Sergeant Major Kent. They made it clear that no Marine will ever be denied a promotion or positions over a PTSD diagnosis. Through countless trips to bases all over the world, the Commandant and Sergeant Major Kent instilled this new philosophy and injected a fresh and constructive approach to dealing with PTSD within the active-duty ranks.

Screening for PTSD is now very different as well. When we came home in 2005, our platoon was hustled into a room where a doctor asked in a bored tone, "Are any of you planning to commit suicide?" That was about the extent of our screening. None of us took it seriously, or really understood what we would be facing after we got home. We just wanted to get to our families.

Those primitive days are a thing of the past, thank God. Now, every Marine coming back from an overseas combat deployment gets thoroughly screened and receives mental health checks along with physical exams. Marines coming home aren't released to their families directly anymore, either. Instead, the Corps eases the transition by keeping the units together a little longer once they're home and on base. During that decompression period, the officers and men attend classes on PTSD that teach them what symptoms and behaviors to watch for, and what to do if they should develop any of them. The classes show these returning veterans where to go to get help and support.

There is a lot more of both available now than there was in 2005. In '05, the psychiatric services within the Corps had been stretched way too thin. Now, it is a whole different ballgame. Many, if not most of the navy's psychiatrists who handle PTSD cases have deployed to Iraq and Afghanistan. Many are combat veterans now as a result. There is a level of understanding between doctor and patient now that simply didn't exist four years ago.

On bases all over the country, PTSD support groups have been stood up. They are running far more smoothly than the awkward one I participated in back in Beaufort. There are clinics and programs and new technologies and treatments that are being tried, some with great degrees of success.

One is called the Warrior Strengthening Program. For ten days, the Marines who go through it are introduced to a new treatment technique called Eye Movement Desensitization Reprocessing, or EMDR. This involves rapid eye movements during therapy designed to mirror what happens during REM sleep. These eye movements are connected to the way the human brain processes emotion and trauma while at rest. With PTSD, the veteran cannot get that same natural process while sleeping. This new treatment solves that problem, and results have been highly encouraging.

There are other facilities and programs all over the country now. In

Seattle, veterans can check into a thirty-day PTSD clinic where they live among their brothers and sisters from every service. The VA hospital in Roseburg, Oregon, has an outstanding and nationally recognized PTSD program. Other facilities exist in Palo Alto, California, and Barstow, California. More and more are starting up every day to address our needs.

Once out of the service, the veteran today has far more options than the veterans of 2003 and 2004. National Guard units have had a particularly high rate of PTSD, and individual states have taken steps to help their local sons and daughters. In Oregon in 2005, three wounded veterans of OIF II—Vince Jacques, Shane Ward, and Andrew Hellman—started what ultimately became one of the best and most successful reintegration programs in the country. The team found treatment options for suffering veterans, located housing for them, legal aid when necessary, and hosted job fairs at the armories around the state. The program grew from three wounded vets doing their best to support their brothers while recovering from their wounds, to a fully funded, state-sponsored program that works closely with the Oregon legislature, the VA, and a wealth of other partners. It proved so successful that other states have studied Oregon's program and have created their own reintegration units.

In the meantime, the VA has worked hard to catch up and reshape itself in the midst of the crisis. There were some nasty, well-publicized failures. And sometimes, gaffs are made over political correctness. In one case, the VA in Tacoma, Washington, subcontracted out therapy and counseling treatment to a psychiatrist of Middle Eastern decent who barely spoke English. When a female combat veteran of Iraq showed up for her appointment, his presence sparked a panic attack that sent her fleeing for her automobile.

These errors aside, the VA has generally done a remarkable job of recasting how it approaches the influx of PTSD-related care it now needs to provide.

The Corps has also started a new program designed to help wounded Marines who have separated from the service to get the support and help they need. Called the Wounded Warrior Regiment, its members reach out to a variety of agencies—including the VA—to ensure that these courageous men and women do not fall through the bureaucratic cracks. In the summer of 2008, I joined the Wounded

Warrior Regiment and began working closely to educate our partner agencies. I talk with social workers and VA officials and explain how PTSD affects Marines and their families.

The Wounded Warrior Regiment is headquartered at Quantico, but there are units at Pendleton, Lejeune, and Hawaii. Feeding into them are what we call "district cells." These are composed of reservists and are located in every state. The district cells give us a truly national reach to ensure that every Marine wounded in action or suffering from PTSD or other conditions isn't overlooked by the system.

The district cells locate and contact each wounded warrior. They then sit down with that person once they've left the Corps and build a treatment game plan for him or her. The cells help locate therapists and caregivers, and will battle any bureaucracy and cut through any red tape in order to get the veteran hooked up. The cells can find housing and get the veterans jobs.

At Quantico, we have what we call the "300 List." On it are the names of the most severely wounded or afflicted Marines whose lives have been forever reshaped by their combat trauma. These are men and women who cannot live unassisted. We call them once a week and make sure they have all the help and support these heroes need. Every day is a struggle for them, and the Corps is determined to make sure they don't fight on alone.

We still have our problems, however. The stigma of PTSD remains, both in our society at large and within the ranks. In truth, while the Corps has changed and the VA has evolved, we Marines and soldiers have yet to fully embrace the new, accepting atmosphere. We're still afraid PTSD will be our personal scarlet letter. The media barrage that derides us and portrays us as crazies propels too many into the shadows, where they suffer alone as their families disintegrate. All too often, those who do not seek help ultimately end up on the streets.

This has to change. Ultimately, that's why I chose to write this book. Perhaps if we can reframe the PTSD discussion in this country, those who fight for our freedom can return knowing they won't be ostracized for suffering its lingering effects. More important, we combat veterans have a responsibility to ourselves and to our families. We must find the courage to reach out to all the support and treatment options that are at last available to us. We cannot live in the shadows. To do so will only inflict more casualties, each one a victory for the enemy. Our service and our government has gone a long way to correcting its mistakes. Now it is up to us to shoulder the load and get the help we must have to survive here at home.

In all the speeches, in all the discussions and traveling, I found myself. The cause sustained me, but at the same time I discovered I could be a person I respected.

Jess and I started talking every day. The conversations grew more passionate and intense. The connection between us still existed. One night, across the miles that separated us, I told her I loved her. I sensed her silent tears, and through the crackling cell phone connection, I heard her say the same to me.

She moved back to Quantico, and that near-crippling ache vanished. The fights came less frequently, and the love we have shared for most of our lives shined through again. Our families thought we were nuts to try again, but the truth is Jess and I were born for each other. Our connection reminds us of that every day.

One day in the summer of 2008, Jess, Devon, and I piled into the car for a drive through the Virginia countryside. On the freeway, we ran across a female driver who decided we'd wronged her somehow. She sped up until she pulled alongside us. I glanced over and saw her giving me the finger and mouthing the words, "Eat shit, motherfucker!" at me.

My first reaction came swift and with tsunami-like intensity. I wanted to run her off the road and beat her face for this. Flushed with indignation, I flipped her off and started to goose the accelerator.

Then a voice inside my head said, *Jeremiah, you're better than this.*

Instantly, all the rage melted away. I slowed down and the woman sped up, cut us off, and gave me one more thorough flipping off as she sped down the highway.

I watched her go, finger still in the air, visible through her rear window. Two years before, the rage would have overwhelmed me. If I hadn't have taken it out on her, I would have taken it out on anyone around me, including my wife.

Not this time. This time, I had passed an important test. No, it was bigger than that. I had won. The pissed-off woman never knew the gift she gave me. But Jess knew.

We looked at each other and both started laughing.

Fall 2008

THE CAMPAIGN CONTINUES. We've had our ups and downs—wild swings at times, but Jess and I are still making it work. Devon's running around on his tiny legs like a sprinter on crack these days. He babbles and says a few words here and there. The best part of my day comes when I get to sit down with him. I've set goals for myself, and I am working hard to achieve them. In December, I will graduate from college with an associate's degree. Nobody in my family's ever accomplished that. In two more years, I'll have my bachelor's.

I have my good days and bad ones. Sometimes it looks like I've made a lot of progress. Other days, I slip and fall. That's the nature of the game now, and the point is to keep playing to win for yourself and family.

I've met so many Marines with PTSD over the past three years that I know now that almost all of us were changed by what we experienced, just like my grandpa. It affects us in different ways, but ultimately some of us develop the worst symptoms of PTSD: rage, overheated emotions, flashbacks, and overwhelming guilt. Our brains have been chemically altered by the trauma the war inflicted.

We're proud men and women who don't like to admit we're hurting. To do so is a sign of weakness that in our warrior profession we normally revile. Your pain is my pain. We share that as a bond, as do our families who have endured so much.

The truth is cold and harsh. Every one of us combat veterans who attempts suicide, every one of us who wakes up one day running empty on hope is a casualty of war just as sure as the men who died over there around us. If you are at that point, like I once was, all I can say is this: Don't give the Muj the satisfaction. You pull that trigger, you swallow those pills, and they win. I can't think of anything worse after seeing what total barbarians they are.

The fight didn't end at the Kuwaiti border. It just changed form into something far more subtle and insidious. It is up to us to soldier on. We carry that burden at home or abroad because we are America's protectors, her warrior class.

Do not be afraid to reach out for help. This is a war nobody can wage alone. There is no shame in PTSD, it is a human response to trauma that is a natural part of our composition. The shame lies in submission. Giving in, disgracing those we left behind, and dying here at home after all we've gone through is simply not acceptable.

That is why I wrote my story. Don't let the enemy who tore our brothers from us triumph after we've returned safely home. That is our challenge. That is our generation's new mission: Keep fighting, always, so there is not one more Ira Hayes.

Not one.

Acknowledgments

Jeremiah Workman:

David Bellavia, a fellow veteran of Fallujah, convinced me my story could help a lot of families who have fought the same battles Jess and I have since I came home in 2005. David, you are an outstanding friend, a true patriot, and I am in your debt. This book would have been stillborn but for your encouragement and guidance.

To Jim Hornfischer, my agent, you took me under your wing and guided me through this entire process. Being a neophyte in the publishing world can be frightening. Jim, you made it exciting and memorable. Your help, your counsel, and your friendship made this book happen.

Ryan—your team at Random House never wavered in its support for this project. Your editorial guidance has made this book stronger and more accessible. Thank you for your efforts. I knew right away that this was more than just another book for you, it was a mission. That sort of passion is all too rare these days.

Jim Hornfischer introduced me to John Bruning over the phone. Instant chemistry was the result, and I knew John and I would make a great team. Over the next fifteen months, though we never met face-to-face, John came to feel like a lifelong friend, not a writing partner. John, thank you for everything, and I can't wait to come out to Oregon and hang with you and Sergeant Jacques and the rest of your crazy 2-162 brothers!

To my mother, who has stood by my side through thick and thin. Though I know I've let you down plenty of times, you know I will always love you and will never stop appreciating all the little things—and big ones, too—that you've done for me throughout my life.

I would not be the man I am today without my circle of friends. Cory Hixson, Eric, Heather, Lauren Pitzen, Lance Hoffman, Angela French, Neil Kenney, David Kneiss, Phil and Marilyn Napoli, David Yates, Tony and Rena—I love you guys. Always.

Last, but certainly far from least, I must thank my wife Jessica for finding the courage to stay with me. Throughout our lives, we've had a tempestuous relationship, but I know we will always be connected on a level most people will never experience in their lifetime. With you, I find peace. With you, I feel the power of our love every time you enter a room. It surges through me with such strength that I know I will never stop adoring you. Thank you for finding the grace to forgive, the love to share with me and our son, the passion that fuels our life together, and the devotion to see us through the bad times as well as the good. I love you.

John Bruning:

David Bellavia called me one night and told me I needed to write a book with Jeremiah Workman. I'd never heard of Jeremiah, but I trust David like I trust my own family. When Jeremiah and I talked a few days later, I realized that this collaboration was a once-in-a-lifetime chance.

I have seen the effects PTSD has had on my friends in the 2nd Battalion, 162nd Infantry since they returned home from Baghdad, Najaf, and Fallujah about the same time Jeremiah and the 3/5 did in 2005. My first experience came when I met Bill Stout, an NCO whose courage under fire helped save two men's lives. Bill returned home and endured many of the things Jeremiah and I wrote about in this book.

The deeper my association grew with Iraq vets, the more I saw PTSD firsthand. Broken families, men struggling to break the circle their minds trapped them in—these were daily facts of life for soldiers I came to love while I lived side by side with them in New Orleans in the wake of Hurricane Katrina.

When I came home from New Orleans, I spent a year in counseling dealing with my own anger and pain from what I'd seen happen to that American city. I was not diagnosed with PTSD, but I sure had some of its features. I missed the adrenaline rush, the sense of brotherhood, and the sense of purpose I had out there with the 2-162. All of that, plus seeing dead Americans lying rotting in the streets of one of our most beloved places, left me reeling for months.

So when Jeremiah decided he wanted to work with me, I knew I had to give him everything I had. His story serves as a clarion call for veterans across the country who are still hurting, still struggling to hold their families together and figure out how they can find their way back from the darkness, guilt, and rage PTSD injects in them.

Thank you, Jeremiah, for taking a chance on me. Words cannot express how much it has meant to be working with you. Not only do I count you as a valued and dear friend, but you stand tall as an example to everyone who's ever been so far down there seems to be no redemption. You proved there is hope. In doing so, I pray that others in desperate straits read this book and see their own path to redemption in it. If that happens, I know we've done something truly meaningful here.

Shadow of the Sword never would have made it to print without enormous help from many friends. Jim Hornfischer is the best agent in the business, period. A true friend, a shoulder, and a man whose priorities are always in the right place, thank you for everything you've done for my family.

Ryan, you've set the new standard for editors everywhere. Your passion, your critical eye and sense of timing, plot, and tone took the raw manuscripts to levels we would otherwise never have reached. This is very much your book as well as ours. What a partnership; I mourn its passing.

David Bellavia, without you, I wouldn't have had the chance to help write this book. You don't call enough, you don't write enough, but you are one of the closest friends I've ever had.

To Jenn, Ed, and Renee: I have spent many, many nights away from the warmth of your love to finish this book with Jeremiah. I've laid awake nights missing you all with an intensity that underscores just how much I love you. Your support made this happen, pure and simple. Renee, we're going to go critter-hunting soon. Ed, I'm taking time off and we'll throw a football all day long for a week if you want. Thank you for understanding that the only way I can help tell Jeremiah's story is to closet myself away and live it until it's finished.

Sherry Bruning, my sis, who endured, and conquered, her own battle with addiction consulted on parts of this book. Your steadfast courage continues to be an inspiration to me. Thank you.

I would not be half the writer I am without Donna Henderson. Donna, your inspired epiphanies have opened my eyes and have led to solutions, insight, and ultimately, understanding. Thank you for everything you've done for my family.

Pam Erland served as our consulting psychologist. Not only is Pam a gifted and empathetic human being, she is also one of the most intelligent human beings I've ever met. Her insight, knowledge, and blunt honesty made this book far better than it would have been without her. Thank you, Pam, you are the best.

Shawna Akin: You've kept me organized for eleven years. Without you, I'd be unable to function and totally at a loss to find anything. You deserve the best out of life, and I'll stand with you and do everything I can to make sure that happens.

When I write, I focus on nothing else and live in my office. Human contact becomes something of a luxury. Amanda, Kali, Samantha, Chrystal, Sarah, John, Kiki, Jesse, Emily, Jake, Alex, Art, Pat, Denice, Andy, and Brenda: Your friendships, your food, and our many conversations sustained me through lonely mornings and nights. Thank you for taking care of me.

Chrystal: You asked me recently if writing with Iraq veterans affects me emotionally. I hope now as you read this book you'll see that I throw every ounce of passion I have into these words Jeremiah and I have crafted together. That is the only way to do justice to this generation of American warriors. And by the way, the dude from Gwen Stefani's band was an utter fool.

My friends—hell, friends is too weak of a word here—who wear the uniform of the Oregon National Guard, I would not be here writing if not for you. Every day I see you all in action, I marvel that we have such remarkable human beings ready and willing to stand tall for their principles. Vinni Jacques, Easy, Pete, Kris P., Bill Edwards, Dan Hendrickson, Cory Jones, Brian Hambright, Aaron Cochran, Travis Allen, Adrian Wilson (even if you did chip my tooth!), Chris Johnson, Tommy Houston, Tim Bloom, Eric Riley, Wyatt Welch, Mike Warrington, Mike Kirkpatrick, Chris Reese, Demian San Miguel, Scott Hildebrandt, Shannon Compton, Ed Tanguey, Bill Stout, Kyle Akers, Ken Leisten, Sr., Scott and Terry McCrae—and every one else from 2-162: Y'all are my extended family. I love you like brothers. And Specialist Moore: If they gave awards for pure heart and honest, transparent patriotism, you'd receive the Medal of Honor.

Lastly, I need to thank a very special group of Americans, whose love of our country goes far beyond just planting a *Support Our Troops* magnet on the backs of their SUV's. The 973rd Civilians on the Battlefield have not only been a sounding board for me and this book, but they have thrown their heart and soul into helping our local infantrymen prepare for close-quarters combat in their coming deployment. Mark Farley, Bethany Jones, Aaron Allen, John Walch, Spencer, Taylor, Gaelen, Andrew Bowder, Joe Mikkleson, Kyle Taylor, Shaun Phillips, Spencer Holman, David Akin, Kevin Keirwin, Joey Fugate, and Ben, and everyone else: You guys are the best and the pride I have for all you've accomplished will last a lifetime. Thank you for everything you've done for me and my writing, but most of all, thank you for all that you've done for our troops and our country. Please visit http://.973cob.org for details on these extraordinary Americans.

ABOUT THE AUTHORS

Staff Sergeant JEREMIAH WORKMAN is a seven-year combat veteran of the United States Marine Corps. After returning from combat, he was awarded the Navy Cross, the second highest medal for valor. Twenty-four years old and born and raised in Ohio, where he was inducted into the Ohio Military Hall of Fame, Sergeant Workman has been featured in national articles and television newscasts. He was profiled in the *Washington Post* and *USA Today,* has been a guest on Fox News and CNN, and recently spent a month touring the country as a featured speaker with Vets for Freedom's National Heroes Tour. He is currently assigned to the Corps' Wounded Warrior program, helping injured veterans receive the care they need. He lives in Virginia with his wife and young son, Devon.

JOHN BRUNING is the author, or coauthor, of ten books, including *Ghost, The Devil's Sandbox, House to House,* and *How to Break a Terrorist.* As part of his research for *Shadow of the Sword,* John took part in several infantry training exercises where he himself performed as an insurgent lying in wait for American soldiers. He fought room to room with the Oregon National Guard's 2nd Battalion, 162nd Infantry, and learned firsthand the deadly challenges close-quarters fighting presents for our Marines and soldiers. He lives in Oregon with his wife and children.

ABOUT THE TYPE

This book was set in Caledonia, a typeface designed in 1939 by William Addison Dwiggins for the Merganthaler Linotype Company. Its name is the ancient Roman term for Scotland, because the face was intended to have a Scotch-Roman flavor. Caledonia is considered to be a well-proportioned, businesslike face with little contrast between its thick and thin lines.